Winning at Internet Poker
FOR
DUMMIES

by Mark "The Red" Harlan
and Chris Derossi

WILEY

Wiley Publishing, Inc.

Winning at Internet Poker For Dummies®

Published by
Wiley Publishing, Inc.
111 River St.
Hoboken, NJ 07030-5774
www.wiley.com

WILEY

About the Authors

Mark "The Red" Harlan: Mark "The Red" Harlan was born in Rawlins, Wyoming and has lived exactly the life you would expect as a result. Armed with a degree in Applied Mathematics (from a school he never utters the name of), he began a 20-year stint in the computer industry. Red has worked with several cutting-edge Silicon Valley companies ranging from Apple Computer (where, among other positions, he was Human Interface Evangelist — making applications easier to use and openly berating those who didn't) to Danger (makers of the T-Mobile Sidekick). Alarmingly, Red has probably already touched your life, since he designed the bidding schema that is in use by eBay today. Red has a heavy writing background (some of it actually readable) having authored *Notes from the Fringe*, InfoWorld's most popular computer column in the heyday of the Internet; and the *DevEdge News* for Netscape's developer community. Red now sports the hefty title of Chief Marketing Officer at CyberArts Licensing, a company providing software for the next generation of poker rooms on the Internet (such as www.gamesgrid.com). CyberArts is the place where Red mixes his love of poker with his deep understanding of graphical user interfaces to make online poker easier to use, better looking, and considerably more fun. Today Red lives a glamorous lifestyle, roughly akin to a well-to-do college student, in Santa Clara, California. Red welcomes non-spam email at mharlan@cyberarts.com.

Chris Derossi: Chris Derossi is a 20-year computer veteran and serial entrepreneur. Having started his first company at the age of 14 he has worked at a myriad of corporations since (creating several along the way). Among other positions, Chris has been: the Chief Architect of the Macintosh Operating System at Apple Computer, the founder of ePeople, and the CEO of Trading Technologies. Chris was a founder of *MacTech* magazine and has written extensively for the computer industry, in publications such as *Byte* and *Dr. Dobb's Journal*. Today, Chris is the CEO of CyberArts Licensing, a software company working feverishly to take Internet skill games (including poker, naturally) to the next level. Aside from running day-to-day business matters, Chris is responsible for the entire architecture of CyberArt's poker offering (seen at www.gamesgrid.com), ensuring that the technology is stable, robust, and hugely scalable. For the last 15 years Chris has been an avid poker player and is often found clutching the first place trophy in the tournaments he enters. Chris was born in Laramie, Wyoming and today lives in Henderson, Nevada (a stone's throw from Las Vegas) with his wife and two children. Chris can be reached at cderossi@cyberarts.com. Red and Chris both man a *Winning at Internet Poker for Dummies* discussion board at http://pokerbook.gamesgrid.com.

Dedication

From Mark "The Red" Harlan: I dedicate this book to Jacqueline because I always said I would, to members of the Math Alliance just because, and to my Uncle Poison because legends should live on.

From Chris Derossi: I dedicate this book to my wife, Jennifer, and my children, Grayson and Miranda, who are always there with love and support.

Authors' Acknowledgments

From Red: My Mom, Marijane "Quarter Slots" Harlan, worked back-breaking hospital nights for 20 years, simply to assure I was educated and would turn out "okay." There are debts I owe to the world and then there is this. All moms *wish* they were as good as you.

Super-thanks to those Lakewood High School teachers from all those years ago: Luanne "Thesis" Rohovec (Pendorf), for teaching me how to write; Derald "Liver Green" Dunagan and Gary "Jag" Hurst for teaching me how to think; and Nic "Shorts" Ament for the bad ass poker nickname. You'd be amazed at the difference you've made in my life. Books can't be done without basic sustenance, which is to say music, food, and caffeine. So thanks to Isaac "Shaft" Hayes, Curtis "Superfly" Mayfield, Sly "Stand!" Stone, James "Mr. Dynamite" Brown, Donna at the Hick'ry Pit, Hanan at the Original Pancake House, Rahim at 7-11, and Clarus at the Bitmap Café. Dig it.

My Project Editor, Sherri "The Spine" Pfouts at Wiley was not only forced to endure my incessant sassiness, taunting, and flexing of deadlines; but she then went well above the call of duty by doing a bunch of stuff (I still don't even know what) to make my life easier when my eye exploded in the midst of writing this book.

Then there is Chris "No Nickname" Derossi. A true force of a human being, he's the smartest and most ethical person I've ever done business with. Chris has been and is *always* the calm in the eye of the storm that is my life. His continual unquestioning support, deep understanding of my psyche, and sharp attention to detail has made this book not only happen crisply, but also be twice as good as it would otherwise have been. And although I'm a considerably better person just by knowing him, I still have no idea what he did to deserve me. Thank you, sir.

And my sincere thanks to you, the reader. Nothing here is possible without you. It sounds trite, but that doesn't make it less true; you have helped fulfill a lifelong dream of mine. I sincerely hope something in these pages makes you think, learn, or at least laugh. In the Western world, time is the most precious of all commodities; I truly appreciate you spending it with us.

From Chris: My name would not be on this book at all if it weren't for the monumental talent, effort, and graciousness of my coauthor, partner, and friend, Mark Harlan. Writing a book takes an enormous amount of work and creates a mountain of pressure. Mark not only handled both with ease, he did it while keeping his sense of humor and unique, thought-provoking outlook on life. Mark deserves most of the credit for what's on these pages, and he has my thanks and respect for all of the sleep he gave up to get it done.

I must acknowledge Konstantin Othmer for introducing me to serious poker. Instead of keeping his friends in the dark to bolster his poker profits, he helped us learn. I owe thanks to Kon for many years of recreation and extra income.

Thanks also to Margot Maley Hutchison, who asked me if I wanted to write a book when I first met her a decade ago. She waited patiently until I said yes, and was very helpful throughout the entire process.

Finally, thanks to the many, many people who have helped and encouraged me while I've spent countless hours in entrepreneurial pursuits, of which this book is just a small part. I consider myself to be fortunate enough to follow my dreams thanks to my family, friends, and associates.

Publisher's Acknowledgments

We're proud of this book; please send us your comments through our Dummies online registration form located at www.dummies.com/register/.

Some of the people who helped bring this book to market include the following:

Acquisitions, Editorial, and Media Development

Project Editor: Sherri Cullison-Pfouts

Acquisitions Editor: Mikal Belicove

Copy Editor: Josh Dials

Technical Editor: Jay Greenspan

Editorial Managers: Michelle Hacker, Christine Meloy Beck

Editorial Assistant: Melissa S. Bennett

Cover Photos: © Getty Images/ Photodisc Green

Cartoons: Rich Tennant (www.the5thwave.com)

Composition Services

Project Coordinator: Adrienne L. Martinez

Layout and Graphics: Lauren Goddard, Stephanie D. Jumper, Barry Offringa, Julie Trippetti

Proofreaders: Laura Albert, Leeann Harney, Jessica Kramer, TECHBOOKS Production Services

Indexer: TECHBOOKS Production Services

Publishing and Editorial for Consumer Dummies

Diane Graves Steele, Vice President and Publisher, Consumer Dummies

Joyce Pepple, Acquisitions Director, Consumer Dummies

Kristin A. Cocks, Product Development Director, Consumer Dummies

Michael Spring, Vice President and Publisher, Travel

Brice Gosnell, Associate Publisher, Travel

Kelly Regan, Editorial Director, Travel

Publishing for Technology Dummies

Andy Cummings, Vice President and Publisher, Dummies Technology/General User

Composition Services

Gerry Fahey, Vice President of Production Services

Debbie Stailey, Director of Composition Services

Contents at a Glance

Table of Contents

Introduction

*F*or something like 150 years, people have been playing poker on shady riverboats, in smokey backrooms of otherwise legitimate businesses, in booze-laden college dorms, on cramped tent floors, and at family kitchen tables. Although the games are often social events, the underlying purpose is always the same: play, play, play, and try to take as much of whatever you possibly can from the steely-eyed person sitting across from you. Be it pretzels, lingerie, or cold hard cash, what your opponents have is what you want. Victors get the spoils; losers get large servings of crow (usually served cold with no garnish).

A few years ago, the Internet came along, and along with it, the first "Big Change." Now you can play against people anywhere in the world, at any time of the day, and for varying sums of money. And the card house where it all goes down is exactly as far away as your computer.

Early concerns of cheating and the inability to see the faces of your competitors, crossed with the uncertainty of passing electronic cash to an unknown foreign entity, gave many would-be online players reason to pause, but the efforts and technology aimed at making the game safe have prevailed. Internet poker has truly exploded in the past couple of years, no doubt due in large part to the numerous televised poker events and Internet sponsorship of some of the top players in the world.

The Internet traffic statistics are staggering, with the busiest poker sites dwarfing the clientele at brick-and-mortar casinos: At any given moment, tens of thousands of players duke it out on a multitude of tables. Internet poker was nothing 10 years ago, and today it's a billion-dollar industry with no signs of subsiding.

In some ways, the online world is identical to the real one. You can play Texas Hold 'Em, Omaha, and Seven-Card Stud. You can play less popular competitive games, such as Pineapple, Five-Card Stud or Draw, or wild card games, depending on the site. You can compete for play chips or hard currency. You can play in ring games or tournaments.

But in some ways, the online world is very different. You have to be able to judge a site for quality. You have to download and master the software. You have to make electronic transactions over-the-wire to move your cash. And don't forget that you have to choose between table sizes and game types.

At first it can all be a little much. But don't despair. You have a clear path through this wilderness. Come along, and we'll take you there.

About This Book

This book specifically covers the nuances of Internet poker as compared to everything in the brick-and-mortar world. You should think of *Winning at Internet Poker For Dummies* as an augmentation to any and all poker knowledge you already have; you definitely shouldn't think of this book as the stand-alone, end-all, be-all poker reference. We've written this text to dovetail cleanly with *Poker For Dummies* (Wiley), but it can just as easily walk hand-in-hand with any other beginning or intermediate poker text.

Thinking Internet poker is identical to brick-and-mortar poker can be a costly mistake. The two are similar, but they have key differences. Our main goal is to point out the differences and help you avoid the myriad of pitfalls lying in wait for the unsuspecting.

We help you discover the nuances of an Internet poker table, pick a site to your liking, and transfer your electronic funds. From there, we take a peek at online poker psychology and delve into some of the unusual table sizes and games that, for the most part, only exist online. After we get you playing, we give you handy tips and tricks on how to stay ahead of the game — and hopefully even win.

Conventions Used in This Book

Some of the special terminology we use in this book includes:

- **Brick and mortar:** We use this phrase to describe real, physical cardrooms where you sit across a table from live human beings. It doesn't necessarily have to mean casinos; in most cases, you can just as easily think about any home game you play in.

✔ **Godzilla:** Large radioactive monster that mostly hangs out in Tokyo bay. Aggressive player with a good poker face — bad temper when losing. Known as *Gojira* in Japan ("go" from the English gorilla and "jira," the Japanese world for whale). We talk about Godzilla a little in Chapter 13.

✔ **Hard currency:** When we use this phrase, we mean the money that you have on deposit with a poker site — the actual money that you gamble with. When you place a $1 bet online, you put hard currency on the line. We use this phrase to minimize confusion with money as a general concept. Chapter 4 is where we talk about transferring your money online.

✔ **Ring game:** A single poker table, with anything from two to ten players, where everyone competes for hard currency. You can come and go as you please in these games. Some brick-and-mortar players call this game form *money play*.

✔ **Tournament:** A special form of poker where you pay a set entry fee, plus a smaller registration fee, to receive a set amount of tournament chips. Players compete, busting out one by one, until only one person remains. Chapter 10 is where we start to get down with tourneys.

For a slightly longer glossary, head to the Appendix in the back of this book.

What You're Not to Read

Well, maybe you shouldn't take it to the "I boycott this" extreme, but we should let you in on a couple of things to know about this book:

✔ *Sidebars* contain information that you don't have to read to understand Internet poker. They serve as asides, anecdotes, or extended forms of examples. Only reading the sidebars in this book is the mental equivalent of sitting on the back porch and hearing your favorite poker stories from your uncle.

✔ Order doesn't matter. That being said, you can read anything you want without hurting our feelings. Read any chapter at any point. Feel free to skip around. We use copious cross-references to help you understand anything you may have skipped over during your reading journey.

Foolish Assumptions

In order to begin, we've made several assumptions about *you,* our dear reader. We assume that

✔ You're already familiar with the basic forms of poker, and that you have a cursory understanding of poker strategy. If you don't, turn around right now and buy yourself a copy of *Poker For Dummies* (Wiley) or some other introductory-to-intermediate text on the game.

✔ You can use a computer and have the ability to connect to the Internet. We also assume that you have downloaded and installed software onto your computer before. If these concepts are foreign to you, pick up a copy of *Internet For Dummies* (Wiley) and/or *PCs For Dummies* (Wiley).

✔ You've used the Internet to the extent that you're familiar with using search engines and making elementary transactions (for instance, you've bought something online).

✔ You think winning is better than losing. If you don't, we honestly can't tell you where to go for help, but we'd love to sit with you the next time you play.

✔ You're a noble human being. You must be if you're willing to spend this much time with us, and hey, we *truly* appreciate it.

How This Book Is Organized

We've intentionally written this book in such a way that you can jump into it at *any* point and just go. We haven't created complete word chaos, however; here's the method to our madness:

Part 1: Internet Poker Basics

This section talks about the hardware and software you need to play, includes a tour of an Internet poker table, tells you how to pick a quality poker site, and coaches you through the transfer of your precious money. By the time you reach the end of this section, you should be able to play a simple game of poker online.

Part II: Taking Your Poker to a New Level — The Cyber Level

Here we explore the variety of games available to you on the Internet, and we let you in on a few secrets about what's different in the online poker world, including a bit on the nuances of Internet poker psychology.

Part III: Taking Over Tournaments

Here you find the down and dirty on the strategic differences between the Internet and the brick-and-mortar world for tournaments. We also drill into unusual table sizes and those crazy single-table tournaments.

Part IV: The Part of Tens

Lists, lists, lists. This part is the dessert after your tasty meal. Here we give you ways to not screw up your Internet poker game, how to keep your head on straight in the heat of the battle, where to go to find more great Internet poker info, and tips on how to behave in the brick-and-mortar world after you leave cyberspace (should you ever venture out of your cave, that is).

Icons Used in This Book

Throughout this book, we guide you toward important points by using the following icons:

Next to this icon, you find information that you should keep in the back, front, and sides of your poker noggin as you play. We think this stuff is important to remember.

The information next to this icon tells you to do something that can potentially save you time, money, and poker frustration. It helps you in the end, so read it.

Make sure to read the text next to this icon. It can save you a lot of blood, sweat, tears, gut-wrenching pain . . . and money.

"Exactly!" is what you'll think when you read this icon's info — it should perfectly illustrate what we're trying to explain.

Where to Go from Here

Pretty much anywhere you want. Find something you think is interesting and go for it.

Can't make up your mind? Just pick a page . . . any page.

Part I

Internet Poker Basics

"I like Internet poker. What's annoying are those Word messages that keep coming up saying, 'It looks like you're trying to raise on the flop with a garbage hand. Would you like some help?'."

In this part . . .

*H*ere we cover all the basics: the hardware and software you need, criteria for choosing a site of quality, and the nitty-gritty of moving your money online. We even give a tour of an online poker table.

Chapter 1

Creating a Winning Combination: Poker, the Internet, and You

In This Chapter

▶ Winning cold, hard cash (or maybe soft, electronic cash)

▶ Understanding the differences between the real and cyber worlds

▶ Assembling the necessary hardware, software, and poker knowledge

*T*he online poker boom has been astounding. At the end of 2004, at any given moment, more than 10,000 players were competing on over 150 poker sites. On any given day, combined bets totaled more than $130 million. And the numbers keep going up.

And not surprisingly, not all the new attendees play poker well. Sure, you have to watch out for some sharks, hustlers, and poker savants; but the misfits, slackers, and the terminally distracted greatly outnumber the dangerous players. In online play in general, and especially at the lower-limit tables, you have the potential to make *a lot* of money.

In this chapter, we talk about the basics of Internet poker, as well as the raw materials you need to play a truly fascinating form of America's favorite card game (and recently, America's favorite game, period).

And the rest of the book? Well, we talk about everything else there.

Me, Winning on the Internet? You Bet!

In case you're confused by the title of the book, we should get one thing clear from the start: Yes, you *can* win money playing poker on the Internet. Recognizing that, however, doesn't make it easy. Even if you've "mastered" brick-and-mortar play, you can't simply walk in and take the candy from all the Net brats. You come screen to screen with some pretty tough players. Heck, Net dwellers have won the past two World Series of Poker Main Events in Las Vegas. But coming out on top of your favorite game is certainly possible, and to do that you need to know your poker theory and have money to put on the virtual table.

The most important thing to understand about Internet poker is that you're still playing poker.

Knowing your poker theory

With very few exceptions, nearly all the poker theory you already know and have gleaned over your life applies in the Internet world. You must deal with nuances and fine points, yes (and you can bet that we cover those in detail, such as in Chapter 3), but poker is poker, no matter the form or forum.

If you're looking for general poker theory, you can't find much of it here (with the exception of single-table tournaments on demand, which we cover in Chapters 12 and 13), but you can find the info in books like *Poker For Dummies* (Wiley). If you aren't familiar with the nuances of poker itself, you should read and study up on general theory first before you play with any hard currency online.

In any betting situation, the basis to making money is being more informed than your opponent. If you ignore reading up on poker theory, the players who aren't so cavalier *will* beat you in the long run.

If you're not completely up on poker theory, don't let it stop you from getting started. You can always play for free chips, which we talk about in Chapter 8. In fact, you can also play in *free-roll* tournaments, where you pay nothing and still have a chance to win hard currency (check out Chapter 10).

Just like real money, but faster

Yes, the money you play for online is the real deal. That's the good news, of course. The bad news is you can lose real money as well.

Because of the speed of computer play, a full Internet table goes through more than twice as many hands per hour than the brick-and-mortar equivalent. That means you can expect your money swings to be twice as big on the Net: If you play a winning strategy, you win twice as fast; if you play a losing strategy, you watch your money walk away at double the speed.

Chapter 8 goes into detail about easing into money play online with *micro-limit* (small-limit) games. We talk more about the ramifications of speed in Chapters 3 and 5.

Dealing with the dough

In order to win money, you have to throw in a few bucks yourself. Such is the law of the land when it comes to poker (except for those extra-special free-roll tournaments). So before you can play for hard currency online, you have to get money to your poker site — which can scare some people silly. We first want to tell you: You have safe outlets to get your money online . . . and safe ways get it out again. The most common mechanism for money transfer is through electronic payment services that you connect directly to your bank account. You can write an electronic check as well. For more information about all things green, see Chapter 4.

If you don't want to lose a lot of cash while you learn, we recommend free-chip games and free-roll tournaments as tools to get you up to speed. (See Chapters 8 and 10.) But only play these forms of "poker" to get used to the Internet and to get familiar with a particular game. When you're comfortable playing at these levels, make sure you move on.

If you play too long with no potential for loss, you're bound to develop some bad poker habits, which we also cover in Chapter 10.

Stepping Out of the Casino Mentality

Although they both offer run-of-the-mill poker, the online poker environment is far different from the brick-and-mortar world surroundings. You need to give up what you know and love about playing in the casino and hunker down by yourself, in the corner, with your computer. Besides your physical surroundings, you experience other differences too . . . like when you want to actually play, you have to first download a poker site's software. Next you have to realize that looking for tells is a bit different, because your opponent may be sitting somewhere across the planet rather than across the table in front of you. And if you're still desiring a bigger challenge, don't worry: You also have to deal with bigger bets online.

Playing poker on the download

To get up and running in the online world, you need a poker *client* (a program that runs on your computer) that you download from the poker Web site of your choice. When you play, your client talks to a poker *server* on your site. The server acts partially as a communication mechanism between you and the other players. When you make any action (call, raise, bet, fold, sit down at the table, and so on), your client passes that information to the server, which relays the action to all your opponents. When your opponents make an action, your site's server relays the information back to you.

We talk about how to pick a quality site in Chapter 2. Downloading software is super easy, and we also cover installation and use in Chapters 2 and 3.

Looking for tells online

The most obvious difference between the physical and the online world is that you don't have another player glaring at you from across the table. The lack of player presence directs your focus to the game, whereas before you may have split your time between looking at your opponent and the cards in play.

But being alone doesn't mean that you play in a world devoid of tells and clues about another player's bluff (or worse, when he tries to sucker you in with a killer hand). It just means that the clues you want to keep track of and watch for are different. We cover the psychological aspect of "reading" online players in more detail in Chapter 6.

Experiencing poker in the pure

Experience shows that, in many ways, Internet poker is a purer form of the game. The decisions you make tend to be more positional than in the brick-and-mortar world. Where you sit in relation

---

Your pal, the rake

We do know of one way that the online world is identical to brick-and-mortar casinos: the way they make money, namely through the rake. The *rake* is a small percentage of every pot that the poker sites take (usually 5 percent, but sometimes as high as 10 percent). They typically cap the rake at $3.

The rake is a good moneymaking mechanism for the house, because losers don't care where their money goes, and a winner doesn't mind scooping a $97 pot rather than one worth $100. But the erosion is real and unavoidable.

For tournaments, sites charge a registration fee, usually 10 percent of the tourney buy-in, that goes directly to the site. A $10 single-table tournament costs you $11 ($10 plus a $1 entry fee).

A few sites have a *no-flop, no-drop* policy. If the site's Hold 'Em or Omaha players never see a flop, it doesn't take a rake. Other sites don't rake any pot less than one dollar, which is nice for micro-limit games (for more on micro-limits, see Chapter 8). To find out about a site's rake rules, look at the *help* or *about* section of its Web site.

You don't have a way to reduce the rakes directly, but by taking advantage of sign-up bonuses and "bonus bonuses" (see Chapter 2 for all bonus info), you can certainly help reduce their sting.

Turbo tournaments sometimes cut the registration fee slightly. A $25 tourney may only have a $2 fee, rather than $2.50, and over the long run you can use every penny of your savings. For more on turbo tourneys, see Chapter 7.

---

to betting around the table and the number of chips you have relative to the other players (especially in tournament play) hold bigger roles.

In the online world, you see bigger betting (pushing all-in in no-limit games for example), largely because you come across more novice players and the stakes can be lower (so players don't have as much to lose). You also see a little less folding (especially in low buy-in, no-limit games) than in the brick-and-mortar world. We delve into these nuances, and more, in Chapter 3.

Gathering the Basics

Before you can play poker on your computer, you need three things: money, the right hardware and software combo, and a hungry poker brain.

Meeting the minimum requirements

If you want to play for money online, you have to have money. For the most part you need electronically-transferable cash (a few sites accept bank checks through the mail — the slowest and clunkiest way to transfer money — but many no longer accept checks directly). Credit cards usually don't work, but debit cards often do, along with electronic checks (*ACH* in bankspeak) and some forms of phone cards. We dedicate Chapter 4 to all money matters.

Sites also have an age restriction. You always have to be at least 18, and some require you to be 21. See the site's rules and regulations for the requirements.

Getting the computer goods

You need three things computer-wise to get going: the proper hardware, a good connection, and a site's poker software.

Hardware

For hardware, you need nothing more than a reliable PC that can run a fairly modern version of Windows (the later the better — nothing earlier than the 1998 version). As tempting as it may sound, you don't want to play on some flake-box machine that, say, automatically shuts off on odd-numbered days or tends to eat a hard drive about once a week.

Unlike when you're playing video games, the speed of your computer, as well as the speed of its connection, doesn't matter. But you do have to worry about the reliability of your connection. Poker isn't a game of millisecond reaction speed. Sites give their players plenty of time to act, so what matters most is that your connection is *reliable*. By reliable, we mean you don't get dropped after you connect to the Internet.

Although a newer version of Windows works best, if you have an old Windows '98 system parked in the garage, you may want to resurrect it for use as a dedicated online poker machine after you catch the online fever. It saves you some familial embarrassment caused by pacing back and forth behind 8-year-old Timmy while you anxiously wait for him to finish his homework on your home's main PC. We're not suggesting you buy a machine *just* to play poker, but if you have an old one lying around, you can put it to good use.

An Internet connection

A dial-up modem that never drops you is much better than a DSL connection that goes belly up every 20 minutes. If you have the luxury of choosing different connection means, pick the one that won't drop you mid-hand. See Chapter 2 for a little more on connection basics and Chapter 5 for information on detecting, and coping with, disconnection.

Poker software

Poker software itself is always free of charge from the site of your choosing. (Don't even *think* about playing a site that tries to charge you just to download its stuff.) Expect downloading to take just a couple minutes if you have a high-speed connection and possibly more than 20 if you have dial-up. We talk more about downloading and the fine art of choosing a good site in Chapter 2.

Bulking up your poker know-how

This book concentrates on the specific nuances of Internet poker. If you're not generally familiar with poker as a game, have never played for hard currency, or don't have a good handle on crazy poker lingo, you need to get a good primer and brush-up. *Poker For Dummies* (Wiley) is an excellent choice (we designed our book to dovetail with that one), as are any number of other poker texts. Chapter 16 gives some good resources you can check out for recommendations on general poker theory, as well as places where you can buy, buy, buy to your little chip-pushing heart's content.

Choosing Your Poker Path

You have many more paths you can take in the online world compared to brick-and-mortar casinos. You can play in tournaments or ring games. You can play fixed-limit or no-limit. You can play Hold 'Em, Omaha, or Stud (and even wild card games). You can play at tables with as many as nine other players or head's up against a sole contender. What separates the Internet world is that you play all these types of games at any time, not just when management gives you the go-ahead in a brick-and-mortar casino.

And you can skip around this book, depending on what you want to do:

✔ If you've never played poker before and you want to try it out for free right now, choose a site we list in Chapter 2. Download the software, go to Chapter 3 and figure out the button controls, and then start gambling with play money. All poker sites also have game basics in their help sections — you can definitely learn enough there to play.

✔ If you're an experienced hard currency player in the real world, take a quick skim of Chapter 3 to find out about your online controls. Make a hard study of Chapter 2 to choose a great site, and then follow the directions in Chapter 4 to make a financial deposit.

✔ If you're already a denizen of the online poker world, but you've just now decided to shift over to play seriously for hard currency, head to Chapter 5. Get our take on the psychology of online poker.

Chapter 2

Getting Online and Choosing a Site

*A*cquiring and installing Internet poker software ranks right up there with some of the most painless "new" computer experiences you can ever have. The hardware and Net connectivity required are minimal, and the whole software operation essentially boils down to clicking a download button on a poker site to get a poker client that runs your game. A single click of the icon after you download and you're off and running.

Your biggest concern should be picking a good site. With our checklist throughout this chapter, you can confidently put any potential host under the microscope of quality. But before you get too far along and jump straight into the downloading and playing process, you should tweak the real-world room where your computer sits just a tad.

In this chapter, we give you some tips on getting yourself comfortable — both physically and with your new poker site — getting your software situated, and crafting your identity for play.

Creating Your Virtual Poker Environment

The fight between online gaming sites for your business is fierce, and because of this competition, poker providers make sure that the hardware, software, and connection environment you need is fairly minimal and user-friendly. Such service allows you to focus on setting up your poker environment to maximize your gaming experience.

Figuring out hardware and software requirements

As it stands right now, online poker isn't computationally (nor display) intensive. Essentially, your computer acts as a glorified accountant and rule keeper; it really doesn't have any heavy work to do. If you're still trying to get by with that wind-up 286 box from the '80s, this could quite possibly be the best news you've heard all day.

Hardware

If you have a machine capable of running a fairly modern version of Windows — Windows 98 or later, for example — you have all the hardware firepower you need. The audio and video involved with an online poker game are extremely simple sounds and animations (cards flipped over on a table, a beep reminding you to bet or fold, chips pushed from one area to another, and so on). No site currently offers more sophisticated options, such as streaming audio and video from other players, although such perks seem fairly inevitable. (Start setting your computer camera up — strip poker can't be far behind!)

It doesn't matter if you want to play on a laptop or a desktop. If you have a choice of machines, pick the one you feel most comfortable using for long periods of time.

 If your screen is kind of fuzzy, and you don't normally stare at it for excessive periods of time, you may want to consider upgrading to a new monitor. Gawking at fuzzy images for hours at a time is draining, and when you play online poker, you have enough happening in the fatigue department without adding any grief.

The problem with Macintosh

As of press time, no hard currency poker sites that cater to the Macintosh are of high enough quality to discuss in this book. This doesn't mean that you Apple users are without options. You can:

✔ **Wait.** With the online casinos competing so heavily, the various sites can't afford to keep ignoring a base of potential customers. Keep an eye on the sites we list in the section "Sifting through the sites" later in this chapter. You can also occasionally look at a version site, such as www.versiontracker.com, or a software review site, like www.mygamblingdirectory.com, to check out various listings.

✔ **Play for free.** Find a site where it doesn't matter what computer you use. Many sites offer free poker online. For example, the games section of Yahoo! (games.yahoo.com) has Hold 'Em. The problem is that free play isn't a good reflection of money play. It doesn't make your level of play any better, and it may well make it worse. But hey, you do get to play poker against other humans.

✔ **Find a money site with a Java client.** We should emphasize that we don't recommend playing with Java clients because the user experience is so abysmal (very slow and uneven). But it does give you an option in a world where your choices are few.

✔ **Get a cheap Windows machine.** Heresy, you say? Maybe, but you should consider this: We both worked for Apple, but we play online on Windows boxes. (And when we do, Chris wears his super-nerdy-yet-sexy Apple belt buckle, and Red wears his ultra-cool Mac project T-shirts. It *is* true, however, that those items burn our bodies as we play.)

System software

As far as Operating System (OS) versions go — as with everything else in the computer world — the more recent the version, the better. You shouldn't start up anything older than Windows 98 if you can avoid it, although you can always try anything (especially if your threshold for frustration is fairly high).

If you have multiple Windows possibilities to choose from, we recommend Windows XP. Not only is XP a recent, currently supported version, but it also was most likely the version of choice by the programmers who created your poker site software. If you run into problems with your site's software, the support people are more likely to be able to help you on XP than with other versions of the Windows OS.

Poker in the palm of your hand

You can't, as of now, find any hard currency-based handheld environments (such as Windows CE, Palm OS, or custom cell phone environments), but we keep hearing a ton of rumors about them. It seems that their existence in the not-too-distant future is a near certainty.

The big problem the handheld world has is unreliable connectivity; so when poker finally does fall into your palm, expect the interaction to be a bit different. It may be something like head's-up play only, where you're allowed five minutes per betting decision. This is pure guesswork on our part, just to give you a feeling of where the future may lead.

If you try an OS older than Windows 98, be certain to extensively test the site you're interested in with free chips first. You don't want any nasty surprises when the hard currency hits the table.

Connecting your Internet necessities

One of the most attractive features of online poker is your ability to play with the barest of Internet connections. The only disadvantage of using a slower dial-up modem is the amount of time it takes to download the *client* (the poker program running on your computer) from the poker Web site; it takes about 20 minutes over a modem versus just a couple shakes of a mouse pad with a broadband connection (such as DSL). After you download the poker program from the site of your choice (see the section "Sifting through the sites" later in this chapter for the most popular), you're set to go. If you have to play from a world where your Internet connection is slow, don't fret: Your opponents have no strategic advantage, of any kind, in having faster network connections.

In short, if you can reliably connect to the Internet, easily see Web pages on your computer, and you use an Operating System version no older than Windows 98, you can play poker online.

Although a slow network connection is perfectly fine for online poker, a flaky connection that goes down often isn't (regardless of connection speed). If you lose your network connection in the middle of a hand, you may be able to reconnect in time before the site folds your hand, but not always. And when you play for hard currency, losing your hand to a bad connection can be costly if you've already invested money in the pot. See Chapter 5 for more on disconnection.

Getting comfortable at the computer

Playing poker online isn't only about computers and software; after all, you don't play *inside* your computer. Give some thought to the physical space you play in; the more comfortable and focused you can make your playing environment, the more focused you can become at game time.

Go through the following steps to ensure a comfortable and focused poker experience:

✔ **Set up your screen in as glare-free a position as possible.** You don't want to misread your hands — especially important in Seven-Card Stud (see Chapter 7), where you have to view a greater number of cards in various positions around the table.

✔ **Find a good spot for your drinks and food.** You have to sit for long periods of time, so you need to plan ahead of time for your sustenance. Remember: Bad beats are made about 10 times worse if you spill a soda on your keyboard as they happen.

✔ **Put a trash basket within arm's reach.** Respect the final resting spot for your waste and you greatly reduce the chance that you'll fling an empty bottle when you get outdrawn on the river. (Mathematical note: Having a trash basket at arm's reach doesn't reduce your chances of being outdrawn on the river.)

✔ **Minimize your distractions.** Sure, every brick-and-mortar cardroom has a television showing such superlative tidbits as the Saharan Dune Bobsled Racing Championships, but watching TV doesn't help you win; it can only hurt.

✔ **Play sober.** Yes, it may be tempting to knock down a few icy cold ones as you play, but it doesn't help you keep a positive balance in your poker site's account. Being drunk only lessens the pain as you hit yourself in the financial head, but it doesn't make the lump any smaller the next day.

Choosing a Site

You may be nervous when you first set up to play online, and you may have a ton of questions running through your mind. Is sharing my bank account information safe? Am I getting a fair deal? Or more generally, how can I trust these people?

Always remember: You're the customer

Above all, any time you're playing on a poker site for hard currency, never forget that you're a customer. If you don't like something about a particular poker site — be it the site's management, the response you get from the support staff, downtime on the poker site, or the way the poker interface works — feel free (if not obligated) to move along to a site more deserving of your hard-earned cash.

When you play for hard currency, the site reduces every pot you win with a *rake* that it keeps for profit. (See Chapter 1 for more on rakes.) Even though it may seem like a token amount (because you receive the lion's share of those pots), you *do* pay to play, and in the long run, you pay dearly (assuming you win a lot of pots . . . if not, you pay your opponents dearly). If you feel that you don't get your money's worth, quickly go and try another site.

And don't forget to extract your money when you leave a site for good. (See Chapter 4 for details on getting your money when you leave.) You don't have to feel good about the money you give to your poker host, but you should never feel like you're giving money to a lame organization, especially when you have a myriad of choices available to you. Make sure you're comfortable giving money to a respectable service that allows you to make money.

The site you pick is where the magic happens. The joys and tears. The fretting and calculating. The cursing and jubilation. The lucky draws and the bad beats. So how do you find a place worthy of all this emotion?

It turns out that finding a site isn't very difficult, and the process is surprisingly risk-free. Sure, you face a little uncertainty in any financial transaction, but this section shows you how to minimize your risks and helps you feel comfortable with where you finally end up. Hundreds of thousands of people in the world now play poker safely online; you can easily become one of them if you know what to look for.

Judging sites for quality

We want to stress that we're not recommending the individual companies or groups we mention in this chapter; we just want to give you guidelines with a little bit of logic so that you can make better decisions for yourself in the future. Consider the following factors when choosing a poker site, in no particular order:

✔ **The country the site is based in and its licenses.** Due to the way gaming restrictions work in the United States, all servers must be located outside America's borders. Until a few years ago, nearly all quality sites were based in Costa Rica. Subsequently, the Kanawake Indian Reservation in Canada has made site hosting attractive enough that most companies have moved there (those sites almost always boast a "Kanawake Gaming Commission" seal). Even more recently, the full-member EU nation of Malta established laws for Internet gaming licenses. Expect many of the best sites to be licensed in Malta until the UK enacts its online gaming laws, at which point Britain may become the jurisdiction of choice. In general, gaming licenses awarded by countries require operators to be held to higher standards. So if the site doesn't have a license, think twice. We expect fake poker sites to eventually start popping up with the sole intent to take people's money. Keep your eyes peeled and choose intelligently.

✔ **Badges of approval.** Given by organizations that provide secure transactions and/or auditing. One example would be Price Waterhouse Coopers (www.pwc.com — a well-respected consulting firm that has audited shuffling algorithms). It doesn't mean the site is great, but it does mean that a respected third party has looked at its software. Some of the same software scrutiny is involved when an operator applies for a gaming license, especially from governmental agencies such as those in Malta and Alderney.

✔ **Action.** The more regularly a site has active games going, the more legitimate you can assume it to be. A good way to see the top sites in raw number of players is to go to PokerPulse (www.pokerpulse.com) and look at the data it has on the number of players at a site. Be wary of any site that falls quiet due to periodic inactivity.

✔ **Use of third parties for money deposit.** If a poker site uses third parties for its money transactions (for example, NETeller or Western Union), that site has to be in compliance with the third party's regulations. Even if you don't transfer money through a third party, knowing your available options gives credibility to the site. (See Chapter 4 for much more on the subject of money.)

✔ **Free play.** All quality sites grant you free chips if you want to try the site for literally nothing. Even if you never play a single free hand, you should stay away from sites that don't offer free play.

✔ **The smoothness of play.** Quality also means how the site feels to you. Even if you have the most trusted poker site on the planet and all your friends dig it two times, if something really bugs you while you play there, you should go somewhere else. Follow these tips to get a feel for your site:

- Play for free on a site you're interested in for a long period before you switch over to hard currency.

- Get used to the action buttons and look for idiosyncrasies in the way the site works (like the bad overlapping action buttons we mention in Chapter 3).

If something rubs you the wrong way, keep looking.

✔ **Bugs in the software.** You can't find a piece of sizeable software in the world that doesn't have bugs in it, but if you find something glaring during free play (like the poker client causes your computer to freeze and become unresponsive), keep looking until you find something better.

✔ **Connectivity problems.** If you keep getting dropped from a site, the site may be having connectivity problems. You should also check to make sure you aren't having ISP (Internet Service Provider) problems by browsing around a couple of non-related Web sites. If you're still connected to the Internet but you're not getting poker from your site, your poker host may be causing the problem. Consider looking elsewhere. See Chapter 5 for more on disconnection.

✔ **Identical sites.** If you run across a site that looks and acts absolutely identical to another site, you may have found one site that licensed its software from another. Poke around a little to see who the copycat is. All else being equal, a site that licenses software has far less ability to fix bugs or implement new features because it doesn't have any software engineers working on staff. Also, a site that licenses software often has far less cash to use for marketing and promos. A site with its own software not only offers new features at a quicker rate, but it also stands a greater chance of staying in business two years from now. Even if the risk of any given site going under is small, if it does go under, your money may go with it.

✔ **User feedback.** When you play for free to get a feel for a site, ask other people at the table what they think of the site and what they like or don't like. Ask them if they play anywhere else. The answers you get may be the most telling of all.

Knowing you're getting a fair deal

If you pick a quality site, you're practically assured of getting a fair deal. Resting easy with your site choice is more a matter of psychology than it is of cyber world practice. A favorite rant of online poker players (always after another hand outdraws them on the river) is "that *never* happens in the real world." Well, we have bad news for you: It happens everywhere, and the site isn't out to get you.

Bad beat situations in the online world are no different than in the brick-and-mortar world, and the online poker world is no less fair. The one thing you do see more of in the online world is hands per hour, which means you also see more bad beats per hour. But the relative percentage of bad beats is no higher. Stop and think about it for a second: What advantage would a site have in dealing you an unfair game?

For starters, poker sites don't have a vested interest in your game; all they care about is the raw amount of action at the table — the more the better, because they make money off each game. So if you feel like the site cheats you, and you leave, it does the site no good. No site can afford bad word of mouth.

Sites on collusion control

Collusion happens when multiple players pool knowledge and use it against another player. It can be something as simple as two players at the same table telling each other their cards (by an instant messenger service or by telephone) so the weakest player drops his hand. Or it can be more brutal and aggressive, such as two players raising and re-raising each other until the unsuspecting third party simply folds his hand.

As a player at a table, collusion is extremely difficult, if not impossible, to spot.

Poker sites, however, have an easier time. They can see everyone's hole cards, so they can tell how often players make runs at pots with garbage. They also keep detailed records of players who consistently play together at the same table, as well each player's originating Internet address (sites can sometimes tell if people play in the same room).

By combining all this information, as well as a few other metrics, sites can have a pretty good idea of who tries to cheat the system.

And at high-stakes tables, such as $30/$60 Texas Hold 'Em, sites add human beings to monitor the activity — providing yet another level of surveillance.

Poker sites make plenty of money by doing their normal business without the need to cheat you. All any quality poker site wants to do is make its game run smoothly and keep you playing. No site offering regular hard currency games wants to risk having its business shut down permanently because of illicit activity. So not only do the good sites deal an honest game, but they also take active measures on your behalf to make sure it stays honest, like keeping an eye out for *collusion* (players ganging up to make money — see the sidebar "Sites on collusion control" for more).

In the early days of online poker, we came across some weird anomalies. We know of a site where you could predict the random number generator (the computer algorithm that "shuffles" cards by picking random numbers). On another, you could peek at the hole cards of your opponents. Fortunately, those bad old days are now long gone. Random number generators have become extremely sophisticated (including features like combining mouse movements across all computers on the site). Sites now send hole cards, in encrypted form, to only one player's computer and nowhere else.

If you choose a quality site, the cards you get are random. You get a fair game. It may be hard to believe when you get eliminated from your third straight tournament by your third straight bad beat on the river, but it doesn't make the game any less honest. (Check out the section "Sifting through the sites" later in this chapter for info on picking a quality site.)

Picking up your perks for signing up

The easiest way to make money is to have someone hand it to you, right? Well, that basically happens when you sign up as a new poker player on many, if not all, of today's online poker sites. It may seem like a throwback to the old crazy days of the Internet when companies gave away a free yacht when you bought a pound of dog food (and told investors they'd figure out how to make money off those customers later).

But it all makes sense to the online sites, because poker is incredibly "sticky." If you start playing at a certain site's place, it knows that you'll probably keep coming back. In these heady days of the Jetsons, where one or two clicks to download software from some other site just seems like way too much "work," poker sites figure (rightly) that you'll stay put after you start playing. So they assume that the money they give you now will end up back in their pockets in the form of rake sooner or later.

Don't judge a bonus by its cover

Say you're considering a site that gives you a 20 percent bonus on your first deposit of up to $500. You could conceivably get $100 added to your account if you don't mind ponying up the full $500. Close examination of the fine print shows that you have to play at tables taking an equivalent amount of rake ($100 in this case) before the site gives you your bonus, but the site has no time limit on how long it can take you to earn your bonus.

If you've played the site for free and decided you like it, it may be worth your while to go ahead and sink $500 and play until you hit your magic number. The site cashier keeps you informed of where you stand relative to earning your bonus.

Now say you're in the same bonus situation, but in this instance you have a time limit as to how long you can take to earn the perk (the site must get the $100 in rake in the first 30 days, for example). Now the situation gets more difficult. To get a rough feel for how much rake you may generate, go watch a full hard currency table at the dollar limit you're interested in. Keep track of the rake the house takes over several minutes, and then do the necessary math to figure out how many minutes you have to play to earn your bonus. This observation should give you a pretty good idea as to whether you can reach the amount of play you need within your bonus time limit.

Sites typically offer you a percentage of your initial deposit as a bonus — something like 20 percent. That means if you open an account with $100, your site gives you an extra $20. Sites always have a cap set at a maximum dollar amount, however. Something like $100 from the site's side.

Now before you go running off, depositing and withdrawing like a crazed bank clerk, you need to be aware of a mild catch that comes with getting (what our friend Mark "Solid" Goldstein refers to as) free money: You have to play a minimum number of hands to get your bonus. The hand restriction varies, but you typically have to play something along the lines of five times as many hands as you have dollars in bonus due to you, or you have to play at tables where the total rake the site takes while you play is equal to your bonus.

Before you transfer money for the first time into an online poker site's vault, be sure to read the fine print of its bonus offering closely.

Try to deposit in a way that allows you to maximize the bonus the house is willing to give you and still achieve your goal of actually receiving the bonus (such as the way we give you in the sidebar "Don't judge a bonus by its cover" in this chapter).

Bonus bonuses

To entice players to continue giving action, large sites occasionally offer existing players a chance to get bonuses if they transfer fresh money to their accounts. The terms tend to mirror initial sign-ups (20 percent with a cap), and the offers are definitely worth watching for. These bonuses nearly always correspond with promotional events (winning a seat at the World Series of Poker Main Event, poker site anniversaries, playing against super-models, and so on). You can always find the offers in the regular site news that you receive for being a member.

If you play a site that tends to offer bonuses, you should *never* transfer funds until you can get a matching amount of money (in the form of your bonus) from the site. It may mean lying dormant for a week or two while you lie in wait for an offer, but the cash reward is worth it.

Also (and *especially* if you have the money to spare), you should seriously consider transferring bucks even if you have padded your account and you're winning regularly. Keep an eye on your bonus standing, and after you receive your money, transfer it all right back out so you can repeat the procedure for the next promotion.

Bonuses are an all-or-nothing affair with online cardrooms. If you want to earn a $100 bonus and you get 80 percent of the way there, you don't get as much as a penny until you earn that last 20 percent. So if you deposit $500 and manage to lose it all before your deposit comes, you have to deposit more to earn your original bonus.

When making a decision on how much bonus money you want to earn, if you're unsure you can meet the criteria for receiving the bonus, always err on the side of playing less. Receiving a smaller bonus for less play is better than receiving no bonus for not playing enough.

When you first start playing online, a reasonable strategy you can try is to play on one site until you earn its new player bonus and then move on to the next, playing until you earn again. Lather, rinse, repeat as often as you like. Jumping sites for bonuses not only maximizes the amount of money you can earn from poker sites, but it also gives you a nice survey of the joint you may ultimately want to frequent.

Sifting through the sites

Situations can and do change in the online poker world, so you should think of the following list of sites as a cursory snapshot, circa late 2004, rather than recommendations, endorsements, or criticisms. Anything and everything can change, so you should do your own exploration and research to determine the current state of online poker, using this list as a good starting point. (You can always look at www.pokerpulse.com to determine the most popular sites at any given time.)

Without exception, every site provides Hold 'Em, Omaha, and Seven-Card Stud as standard poker offerings. We note those with more esoteric games.

PartyPoker.com (www.partypoker.com)

By sheer numbers, PartyPoker is the most popular Internet poker site in the world. The site is always jumpin', and the action in all games (including Stud and Omaha) is lively. The bad news is that PartyPoker struggles somewhat with its own success. In the past, it wasn't unusual to have the game servers go down, and players had to deal with an annoying lag in the interface that made it hard to get a seat at a table (by the time you clicked to sit, the table had already filled). PartyPoker has worked to correct these problems, and the situation today is better, although it still bears watching. We find it kind of weird that it uses images of avatars (essentially mannequin players) at its tables that never move; they look cool for 10 minutes and then kind of bug us, so we turn those off when we play. The interface hasn't had any major changes in a few years, and it now feels a bit tired. Right now PartyPoker seems to have the easiest games to beat, but you should assume player quality will increase (possibly dramatically) over time.

Ultimatebet.com (www.ultimatebet.com)

At one time Ultimatebet had the most advanced interface in online poker — mostly from a pure presentation point of view — with the ability to switch out backgrounds for a slightly different perspective on the playing table (looking out from a player's seat rather than gazing straight down from the eye-in-the-sky). Although the site is still interesting, others are beginning to narrow the cosmetic gap. Ulimatebet has a couple of new compelling features as well. One is a sophisticated buddy list that provides instant messaging — called *UltimateBuddy* — that lets you know when your friends (and presumably enemies) are online or playing. The other is an optional *mini-view,* which essentially reduces your table to a line of little codified lights. We find the mini-view hard to use and read, but the interesting concept may be improved upon over time. Phil Hellmuth is one of the pros associated with this site; in fact, you can sometimes play at a table with him (assuming you don't mind making a small donation, in the form of part of your stack, to his poker prowess). Omaha action on this site tends to be strong, and the site has recently started offering Pineapple, Double-Flop Hold 'Em, and Triple-Draw Lowball (the only online place to practice for Red's favorite obscure World Series of Poker event). You can find out more about offbeat games in Chapter 7. Overall, the play on this site tends to be very tough.

PokerStars.com (www.pokerstars.com)

PokerStars has an interesting claim to fame. The (James Bond creator) Ian Fleming-ly named Chris Moneymaker won the 2003 World Series of Poker Main Event title by qualifying for the championship via a PokerStars $40 buy-in tournament. The very next year, Greg Raymer qualified on PokerStars and went on to win the same WSOP championship. As a result, tournament players typically outnumber ring game players on the site 3-to-1. In our opinion, by caliber of opponent, PokerStars tournaments are the toughest currently on the Net. If you can win tourneys here, you can win anywhere. PokerStars also has the most Stud and Omaha action outside of PartyPoker.

ParadisePoker.com (www.paradisepoker.com)

ParadisePoker used to be the granddaddy of poker on the Net, but it was eclipsed when PartyPoker began advertising on the World Poker Tour (the WPT no longer accepts site ads). The presentation is slightly more interesting to look at (a paradise island theme) than on many of its competitors' sites, although we have had problems in the past with overlapping action buttons. You can almost always find a good Seven-Card Stud or Omaha game, and occasionally you can find Pineapple players. This may be the only site in the world where you can play Five-Card Stud and Five-Card Draw for hard currency. (See Chapter 7 for more on these games.) The higher the limits, the tougher the competition on Paradise. We suggest you stay away from the fixed-limit $10/$20 Hold 'Em games (described by one accomplished poker player as "nightmarishly difficult").

Pacific Poker (www.888.com)

This site is a step down in size from the big boys; it typically boasts about half as many players as the sites we previously list, but hey, all you really need is one seat at a table with action, right? Well, you can always find that here (unless you want to play Stud or Omaha at odd hours). We like the clean presentation of the interface, especially on the declaration of the winning hand. And maybe it's just us, but the players on this site seem a little friendlier than everywhere else.

GamesGrid (www.gamesgrid.com)

GamesGrid is the top skill-games-for-money site on the Net. It originally offered backgammon and gin rummy, and it recently added poker to its stable. GamesGrid places an emphasis on the casual player, including dealer's choice and wild card games. Think "Friday night poker, online." GamesGrid has a lively social community and hosts a discussion page for this book that we both participate in at `pokerbook.gamesgrid.com`.

Getting Your Game Going

You know how to choose a good site after reading the previous sections, so now the time has come to get down to the nitty-gritty of setting-up.

Downloading software

Downloading your poker program (the *client*) is very straightforward. You go to the Web site of the place you want to play and click on whatever super-obvious "DOWNLOAD NOW!" graphic it has. Follow the directions and in somewhere between 2 (if you have a broadband connection) and 20 (if you have a dial-up connection) minutes, you can install and run the software. (For the differences between the poker client, the poker server, and the poker Web site, see Chapter 1.)

Many installers for poker clients say something along the lines of "quit all applications before downloading." If you use a dial-up Internet connection (such as AOL), don't quit that application because you won't be able to download the client. You must have a connection to the Internet to be able to download. (This represents one of those rare situations where following instructions actually doesn't get you what you need.)

Logging in and starting up

After you install the client, click on the client icon to run it and get started. Don't be too surprised if the very first thing that happens, after you connect, is that the site offers an upgrade to your client. Sites upgrade their software often, sometimes more than once per week, so the downloaded version may be a tiny bit behind the latest and greatest offering. Although it may be annoying to go through another lengthy download and upgrade process, the offerings are the only way that some sites have of fixing problems and getting you improved software.

If you ever receive an offer to upgrade your poker software, *always* take it. Upgrades can contain bug fixes, feature enhancements, and new bonus possibilities. You want 'em. Always.

The bitter taste of Java

You may go to some poker Web sites that give you the option of playing poker immediately, without even downloading their (optional) client. On the surface, playing without using a poker client may seem like the thing to do, because you don't have to hassle with downloading and installing; unfortunately, the idea is only good in theory.

If you can play poker without installing a client, you're typically going to be using Java (or sometimes Flash) protocols to play poker inside a Web browser window. The first problem you may encounter is that you may not have the right version of Java installed. Upgrading can be a long, slow process, and it may require that you upgrade your Web browser.

Secondly, these programs come with a tremendous amount of overhead when compared to installed clients, which results in a horrendously slow user experience. If you do decide to play with a Java client, play will seem pokey slow (and if you're an Einsteinian physicist, you swear everything in your room is gaining mass). Even "immediate" betting decisions can take 5 to 10 seconds.

If you're playing on an installed client against someone else playing with a Java client, you have to wait an undue amount of time whenever Mr. Java has to make a betting decision. As if the situation wasn't bad enough already, the Java-based graphics are never as good as an installed client's. They tend to be noticeably lower resolution, making all the graphics look chunkier.

If you're offered a chance to play instantly, pass and bite the downloading bullet instead. You'll be very glad you did. If you do play on a site where some players use Java, and you find that waiting on their turns drives you crazy, pick up and move to another site.

You may be tempted to fill in bogus information when you create a new poker account — especially if you only want to play there for free chips. Don't do it. Sites allow users only one account per site, and the hassles of correcting some information can become monumental. Poker providers can also be hyper-vigilant when it comes to detecting unusual account behavior (they are, after all, trying to ensure that everything stays on the up-and-up to protect all players' accounts); you may get yourself banned from a site if you provide faulty info.

When playing a site for hard currency, you should give as much information to your poker host that you possibly can, including all optional fields (phone number, for example). If something goes wrong with your account, or your money in your account, you want your host to be able to contact you.

If you have the option of getting informational e-mails from your poker host, take it. Site newsletters tell you about upcoming events and tournaments, as well as frequent player and bonus promotions you may be interested in. And don't worry about poker sites selling your e-mail address so you receive tons of spam as a result: Subscriber lists for online casinos are some of the most carefully guarded in the computer world; sites never want to see you go somewhere even remotely competitive.

Crafting your identity

The last task you need to complete before you begin playing in the computer realm is to make a few decisions about your online persona.

What's your name?

The site asks you for a user identification name (*user ID*). This is the moniker (or if you're of the CB persuasion, your handle) that the site uses to identify you at the table. Unless you tell them, the other players at any table can never know your "for real" human name; nor can you know theirs.

After you pick a user ID, you're stuck with it for the life of that site; so make sure you pick something you like. Being called "Spice Girls" may have been cool in 1997, but it isn't so great now (although, personally, we'd *kill* to have that one).

Expect obscene and semi-obscene user IDs to provoke a reaction from your poker site's Thought Police; you can avoid the hassle by not goading them in the first place. Keep it clean cool guy.

What's your sign?

Some sites give you the opportunity to pick a small thumbnail-sized icon to represent your presence at the virtual table. Again, choose something you can be happy with for a l-o-n-g time, because some sites only let you change your icon once. Others never do.

Regardless of your sex, you may be tempted to choose a picture of some super-hunky dude or ultra-busty chick as your icon. We encourage you to think twice about this tactic, unless you really like the idea of talking about that image *every* time you sit down at a table.

Who *is* that old guy?

One time Red was playing at a table that was a real hoot; everyone was talking, joking, and living it up, without a single bad attitude in the batch. (And to show you how good it *really* was, everyone used the right version of the word "you're.")

One player's comments clearly didn't represent his septuagenarian icon; the big hint being that not many 70-year-olds say, "Bag it, dude."

Someone at the table asked, "Hey Leatherface, how old *are* you?"

"I'm 27."

"I thought so, you didn't sound old. Who is that old fellow in your pic? Your grandpa?"

"Nah. I just did a Web search for 'old man' and stuck the picture I liked best in there."

A unique approach if there ever was one.

People don't have a whole lot to focus on when they sit at an online table; you may find that some become obsessed with what little eye candy they do see. We've met several players from the virtual world who turned their chat off because they just couldn't take bantering about their picture any more.

You now have the tools to make an intelligent site choice, to get set up, and to log on. Have fun.

Chapter 3

Putting Internet Poker's Nuances to Work in Your Play

. . . .

In This Chapter

▶ Understanding your new poker world

▶ Looking over an Internet poker table

▶ Jumping into the poker fray

▶ Talking cyber-poker slang

. . . .

*T*he online poker world is truly its own environment, with a unique set of paradigms, customs, and standards. In this chapter, we talk about the fundamental differences between online and live players, take a tour of the cyber version of the table, and raise your hip poker vocab with some Internetese (spoken with a distinctive poker accent, of course).

Comparing the Real World Game to the Online Version

A few characteristics of the computer poker realm can be pretty jarring when you first run across them. The most obvious examples: the speed of play, the type of opponent you encounter, and the way your focus changes when you don't have a real-world poker-playing environment around you.

Considering the differences in speed

In a real-life cardroom, the physical manipulation of the cards (the dealing and folding of hands) and the general orchestration of the game (players placing blinds, taking seats, not paying attention to the game, flirting with cocktail waitresses, and so on) take more time than in the online world, which features automatic dealing, immediately placed blinds, and a lack of drinks spilling on the felt. Shuffling, dealing, and repeatedly asking slowpokes to hand in their cards at the end of a hand burn time on the clock. In the online world, these delays don't exist.

How fast is online play? A typical brick-and-mortar cardroom, with an efficient dealer and a full table, churns about 30 hands per hour (add two or three more hands per hour if the dealers use automatic shufflers); the online equivalent plays about 60 hands per hour, increasing to 65 or more at turbo tables (see the section "Going for super-speedy online play" later in this chapter for more). After you gain experience and make it to a head's-up match against only one other player, you can expect that number to jump to as high as a whopping 150 hands per hour! (For more on head's-up play, see Chapters 7 and 10.)

Because of the speed difference, you should play at limits about half the amount you normally play in the real world until you get used to it, even if you're a seasoned brick-and-mortar player. (See Chapter 8 for more on how to ease your way into the online world. And in Chapter 6, we talk about watching the amount of time your opponents take to play as a possible tell.)

Realizing the effects of faster play

The speed of the Internet impacts players in two ways. One is the different feel. The first time you play online, the action and the decisions can feel a little bit blurry. What's funny, though, is that in a short time you adjust to the new speed and you start to want to go faster.

The other factor is that the greater number of hands acts as a multiplier. If you play with a losing strategy, or you play at a table where better players outplay your strategy, you lose twice as much money per hour. But if you win, you win twice as much per hour.

The way card houses make money is through the *rake* (taking a very small percentage of every hand; see Chapter 1 for more on the rake), so the faster they can cycle through a hand, the more money they make. The house has no vested interest in the hand itself; it just wants to see action taking place and games running their course — as the players complete more games, the house gets more money.

Beating the online timer

In the online world, you're under a time clock for every betting decision you have to make, which is somewhat similar to the shot clock in basketball. The timing method varies from site to site, and it depends on whether you play in *ring games* (cash games where you can come and go) or tournaments. Some sites use a set number of seconds per betting decision (usually between 15 and 30); others have a set number of seconds of total delay you're allowed at that table during a single session (usually 60). Reading a site's documentation or experimenting on a play money table can familiarize you with an online site's timing custom.

Until you get used to it, beating the timer can be psychologically troubling. In fact, you may overreact by trying to decide too quickly. Don't be afraid to take all the time you need to act. Thirty seconds is longer than you think.

Play with your computer's volume turned on. All poker sites beep when your turn to act comes, especially if you start to run short on time. The alarm becomes especially useful when you want to work within other applications on your computer, play on another table simultaneously, or turn away from your machine for a few moments. (Don't get us wrong, we think playing distracted, especially by playing another table, is a bad, bad thing. See Chapter 5 for how shameful we think it all is.)

If your time limit expires and you haven't yet made a betting decision, nearly all sites fold your hand (scant few automatically check your hand if no previous betting action occurs in the seats before you, folding your hand otherwise).

Going for super-speedy online play

As if the online game doesn't move fast enough already, some sites provide even faster play. Like crazed mechanics in a pit crew, they shave the individual timing intervals down and use a few other tricks and gimmicks to jack up the need for speed. These tables always have augmented names like "Turbo," "Speed Play," or "Make That a Triple Espresso." If you're new to the online environment, we don't recommend playing on these tweaked tables. Wait until you're comfortable with online play first.

Adjusting to a Variety of opponents

In the real world, you know several things about your opponents immediately. Some traits are (usually) obvious, such as their sex and general age range. A few characteristics you may automatically take for granted without even thinking about them, like what time zone they play in. Others are subtle, like the ticks and tells some people exhibit while they play (we talk about the online version of tells in Chapter 6). But the online world is a different beast.

Analyzing your opponent

You play people not only in different time zones, but also very possibly in other countries. The Internet provides you, for the first time in your life, someone to play against in another place. He may be in the middle of his day, or it may be smack dab in the middle of his night. A tired player is always easier to beat than an alert player.

Any tidbit of information can be valuable to you as the game progresses. For example, someone playing from the city that hosts that day's Super Bowl team may be watching the game while they play on the laptop in front of the tube. Look for any edge you can find, based on even the smallest of information threads, because some edge is better than none; and in the online world, advantages are harder to glean than in the brick-and-mortar environment. You lose a lot by not having your opponent sitting at the table across from you.

Not everyone you run across in the virtual cardroom speaks English as a first language (you may also run into language barriers in brick-and-mortar casinos); a few may not speak English at all. Don't worry; their money is good (and never forget, so is yours), but you may not always get a snappy conversation.

On nearly all sites you can hover your cursor over an opponent's nameplate and find out his hometown, country of origin, or both. Do so.

Betting more aggressively

We find that online players bet more aggressively than their offline counterparts — especially in the smaller pot-limit and no-limit games where a player can risk her chip stack at any point to gain advantage in a hand. A generalization no doubt, but one that seems to hold true. For more on different game types offered online (limit versus no-limit, ring games versus tourneys), see Chapter 7.

Sticks and stones may break my bones, but Internet slurs can't hurt me

Unfortunately, because they feel empowered in the somewhat anonymous online environment, more rude opponents unleash their ugly behavior than in a brick-and-mortar establishment, especially in the emotional aftermath of losing a big hand.

You should shrug off their vile comments or turn off the chat feature of your table if their slings and arrows upset you. We suggest ignoring the behavior and looking closely for patterns and tells that your opponent may unintentionally display.

Watch for them to go on *tilt,* which means they may become more aggressive and stay in more pots because of their frustration.

A few sites offer a *bet the pot* button as one of their options in the betting round. In the real world, this action involves the player estimating the current pot, counting out chips to match that pot, placing that amount in front of her (possibly in multiple steps for large bets), and then making the verbal bet; an arduous process that often weeds out players trying to buy a pot (if for no other reason than the player's opponents can sit and watch her very closely for tells as she goes through the motions). The wonderful world of computers makes this process automatic, because it does the counting and places the bet in one step. And automatic means easy. And easy means more people use it more often than in the real world.

You may also find that your online competitors are more willing to push all-in compared to their felt-scraping equivalents. It becomes much easier on the mind when you don't have to physically see the stack of chips, feel the stares upon you, and wrestle with the enormity of the decision at the table environment. All it takes is a simple flick of the no-limit button control for betting, and whoomp, there it is.

Players betting all-in more often means that you see more variance in the game than you're probably used to in the real world. You're more likely to double your chip stack and more likely to go bust, because the frequency of big betting is higher. This doesn't mean that you should alter your play or strategy, but you do have to prepare yourself, or the frequency may shock you.

Keeping your focus on the game

What you experience when you play online differs profoundly from the environment during a real-world game. In the real world, your senses experience an overload: The sights of the people and events around you, the sounds of hundreds of clay poker chips clacking together, the inevitable flickers of 20 televisions broadcasting three different sports channels, the smells of a million cigars past, and the tactile nature of the cards and the table all add to your sensory perception of the game.

In the virtual world, your senses are strictly confined. The noises you hear from the computer are unnecessary artifacts, or mimics, of the real world. Noises like card shuffling, chips banging together, and sound effects for checking and folding. But the site adds them artificially; they don't have to be there for the game to run properly.

Motion and visual information is extremely limited. The deprivation of typical sights, sounds, and observations causes you to focus much more intently on the few things you do see: the size of a person's bet, the amount of time he takes to make this bet, and (to a much lesser extent) the conversation he has at the table through the chat system (more about this in the section "Speaking the Poker Dialect of Internetese" later in this chapter).

The more you force yourself to focus on these factors, the better you can exploit them to your advantage. We get into this more in Chapter 6. (Of course, we don't think that the online world is necessarily all focus — you are, after all, sitting in front of a computer. We talk about avoiding your in-home distractions in Chapter 5.)

Getting a Feel for the Virtual Game

Many Web sites model their online poker tables after real-world equivalents, and you may find them comfortably familiar if you've spent some hours in brick-and-mortar cardrooms. Still, you should pay attention to the details, particularly if home games, not casino play, make up your past experience.

Figure 3-1 shows a fairly typical representation of a classic Internet poker table. Most sites on the Net make their tables look something like this.

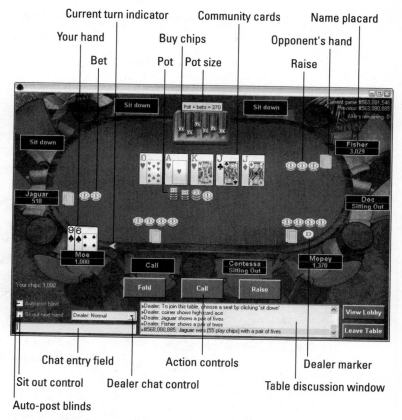

Figure 3-1: A typical fixed-limit Hold 'Em Internet poker table.

The classic table closely mimics the real-world equivalent, and first-time users shouldn't have much trouble navigating and understanding the setup.

Unfortunately, mimicking the real world isn't always the best way to design the layout of a graphical computer program, nor is it necessarily the easiest to quickly understand visually or use with a mouse. These limitations have brought about a newer, *modern* table (see Figure 3-2).

Laying it all on the table

Some features of the online table mirror the details of the brick-and-mortar poker world, and others are unique to the Net. We cover them all in this section to get you up to speed and ready to hit the virtual felt with confidence.

Chat entry field   Table discussion

Opponent's hand   Dealer chat control

Dealer marker   Community cards   Sit-out control

Pot size   Bet Pot   Raise   Buy chips

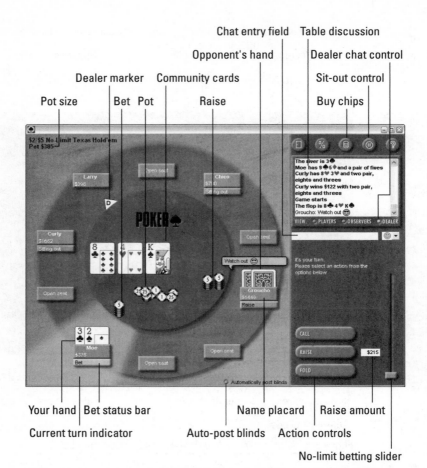

Your hand │ Bet status bar   Name placard │ Raise amount

Current turn indicator   Auto-post blinds   Action controls

No-limit betting slider

Figure 3-2: A modern no-limit Hold 'Em Internet poker table. Note the added space for user controls in the modern table over the classic (refer to Figure 3-1).

The following list highlights the important terms you need to know to get started (and you can check out Figures 3-1 and 3-2 for visual images of the following features):

✔ **Name placard:** Shows the screen name of each player, how much money the player has, and each player's current status (playing or sitting out). If no player occupies the seat, the site marks it as open, and you merely click on the name placard to sit down.

✔ **Individual bet:** Shown in front of a player's seating position. You can hover your cursor over the chip stack to see the amount of the bet.

✔ **Individual raise:** Shown as a separate stack from the original bet. You can hover over the raise with your cursor to see the total amount.

✔ **Pot:** Shown in the middle of the table. You can see the size of the pot by hovering your cursor over the chips in the middle.

✔ **Action controls:** You place a check, bet, raise, or fold by using the action buttons. The buttons display the action for fast and easy use.

✔ **Betting slider:** You can move this control to bet a variable amount during no-limit play (see Figure 3-3). You can also type the amount you want to raise in the corresponding text box.

✔ **Community cards:** Hold 'Em and Omaha flops, turns, and rivers are shown in the middle of the table.

✔ **Your hand:** The site always shows your hand face up in front of your name placard while you're still in the pot. After you fold, your hand disappears from the table.

✔ **Your opponent's hand:** Shown face down until the showdown, at which point the site turns the other player's cards face up if he beats you. If you beat your opponent's hand, he typically has the option of showing you what he had or mucking without a display.

✔ **Table discussion window:** Shows all the dealer chat (like what's happening in the hand) interspersed with all the player chat.

✔ **Dealer chat control:** Adjusts the chattiness of the dealer. You can typically set the chat on three levels:

- Succinct: Essentially, who wins and loses the hand

- Normal: Information about the cards shown on the table, along with the results of the hand

- Verbose: Tells you about everything you can see

On the classic table, you adjust verbosity with a pull-down menu; on the modern table, you adjust it by clicking on the little light menu and cycling through your choices (red for succinct, yellow for normal, and green for verbose).

✔ **Chat entry field:** Where you type comments to other players that show up in the table discussion window. The modern design allows you to add smiley faces (geeks like us call them *emoticons*).

✔ **Chip addition:** You click on the adding chips control button on the modern table. On the classic table, you click on the chip rack.

✔ **Dealer marker:** Shows the last person to act and moves clockwise around the table at the end of every hand to signify the dealer position.

In the online world, just as in a brick-and-mortar casino, the house doesn't participate in the game; it just provides a place for you to play and takes a piece of the action in the form of the rake.

✔ **Sit out control:** Any time you don't want to be dealt a hand, but you also don't want to leave your seat, you use this button. Sitting out is the polite thing to do if you need to take a break from the game, because it keeps players from waiting for you to act when you participate in other activities.

After you sit out (either by clicking the control or by timing out), you have to click the "I'm back" button that appears. If you sit out during a tournament, the site continues to post your blinds on your turn.

✔ **Current turn indicator:** Shows you who acts next. On the classic table, you may have trouble seeing this control, although you always get sound indicating your turn to act. On the modern table, the indicator is a light beam that sweeps from player to player.

Acing the action controls

Action controls are unique to the online world, with no brick-and-mortar equivalent. You click on these buttons to make your betting decisions (check, bet, raise, or fold) associated with a hand.

Present action buttons

When the betting action comes to you, the screen presents you with a set of *present action buttons* to choose from. Clicking one indicates your betting decision at that point in the hand. If no betting action has come in front of you, you can check, bet, or fold (nearly all sites remind you that you can check for free instead of folding here), just as in a brick-and-mortar game.

If a player bets in front of you, you can call, raise (if further raises are allowed, meaning that the betting limit hasn't been reached), or fold. You can see examples of present action buttons in Figures 3-1 and 3-2.

No-limit and pot-limit games also tend to have both a slider for easy betting use (see Figure 3-3) and a text entry box for manual betting for the particularly meticulous when you want to bet any amount over the minimum. You can see a no-limit slider on the modern table in Figure 3-2, and Figure 3-3 shows one from a classic table. (Due to table layout styles, the classic slider is horizontal, and the modern slider is vertical.)

Figure 3-3: A no-limit slider, which allows you to make a bet or raise above the minimum amount, from a classic Internet table.

After you make a present action choice, the site relays your decision to the other players at the table and the betting action passes to the next player clockwise from your position, just as in the real world.

Future action buttons

Before your turn to act arrives, if you already know what you want to do based on a strategic choice or an obvious decision (and assuming the betting situation doesn't change), you have the option of indicating your choice in advance. To do so, you use *future action buttons* (see Figure 3-4). Using these buttons may go against your instincts at first (because on a real-world table, the rules state that you can't act out of turn), but after a little experience they become second nature and certainly help to speed the game along.

When you make a decision with a future action button, nothing happens from the table's perspective until the action comes to you. The site automatically acts out your request, and you don't have a chance to interact with present action buttons. The betting action moves along to the next person clockwise.

If you choose a future action that isn't compatible with a subsequent play in front of you — say you choose to check but a bet comes in front of you — the site erases your future action and presents you with a set of present action buttons.

If you make a future action selection and someone increases the bet in front of you (by placing a bet when everyone else checks or by making a raise on a bet that a player previously made), the site resets your choice as though you never made a selection. Now you need to make another choice. This feature keeps you from making involuntary raises or calls if your eyes wander off the screen.

Unlike the present action buttons, you don't *have* to make a future action button selection. If you don't select a future action button, the present action buttons simply replace them when the action comes to you.

If no players have raised, your future action choices are check, call, raise, or fold. You also have the interesting option of "check/fold," which means you check if everyone else checks in front of you; but if someone bets, you fold. Check/fold keeps you from having to select the present folding action if you wanted to check a weak hand.

Figure 3-4: You use future action buttons to make your betting decisions instantaneous when your turn arrives.

Figure 3-4 shows future action choices that you find on the fixed-limit version of any online game (a dollar amount of the bet normally shows up on the bet button as well). Notice the gap in the future action bar — this feature prevents you from trying to hit the check button and accidentally raising if the betting status changes in front of you (and therefore changing your future action button choices).

If a bet gets placed in front of you, your future action choices change to call, raise, or fold. Checking goes away, of course, because you can't check when you face a bet (see Figure 3-5).

Figure 3-5: Your future action buttons change if another player places a bet, giving you the option to call, raise, or fold ahead of time.

The dreaded overlapping action buttons

Some sites have been a bit sloppy in the way they place their action buttons on the screen, and occasionally you find future action buttons that the site, on your turn, replaces with present action buttons that have a different intent in the same exact area of the screen. You can start to click on one item and then have the buttons switch out from under you, causing you to accidentally click on something else.

For example, before the action comes to you at the table, you may want to choose to check in turn with a future action button. Unfortunately, when your turn comes, clicking on that same exact screen location causes you to choose to call, thereby putting your money in the pot when you didn't intend to (and also possibly causing you to put your fist through your computer screen when you didn't intend to). A slow movement on your part to click that check button may cause you to bet.

For this reason, you should always play for several minutes with play money on any site you're not familiar with before you play with hard currency to check for overlapping issues. If they arise, get out of dodge and choose another saloon.

Another way to dodge this overlapping button problem is to never use future action buttons, if you can't get away from your trusted dive.

Again, the dollar amount typically shows up on both the call and the raise buttons. You can compare the future action buttons in Figure 3-5 to the ones in Figure 3-4 to see how the design avoids button overlap. (For more on button overlapping, read "The dreaded overlapping action buttons" sidebar in this chapter and check out Figures 3-6 and 3-7 for examples.)

Figure 3-6: If your site has overlapping action buttons, you may intend to click Check in Turn and instead click on Call when the site changes the buttons.

Figure 3-7: Here we see the new buttons that pop up after a site changes its action bar. This makes it quite easy to accidentally click on the wrong action button.

If you want to play no-limit, be very cautious about playing the *Check/Call Any* future action button. If a player bets a large amount in front of you, you may end up making a heftier call than you had originally planned.

Future action buttons can be a source of *tells* (possible indicators of the strength of a player's hand), both for you and your opponent. Read Chapter 6 for more on delving your opponents' hands as well as disguising your own.

Other action preferences

Some poker sites offer unique selections, usually in the form of preferences, to help speed up play.

Auto post

The most common selection is *Auto Post* if you play Hold 'Em or Omaha or *Auto Ante* if you play Seven-Card Stud. Choosing this feature automatically makes those pesky blind or ante housekeeping bets for you and moves the game along. Your opponents can get *very* cranky if you don't auto-post, because you slow the general action of the game, and for this reason alone you should check it. (In tournaments, the sites make this choice for you automatically.) If you choose to sit out and you enable the Auto Post feature, the action automatically skips you without posting your blinds (except in tournament situations, where you have to post).

If you're playing Hold 'Em and you want to leave the table before you're in the big blind, you should uncheck the Auto Post button. That way, when you need to post the big blind, the site prompts you to place the blind manually instead of automatically dealing you in the hand. At that point you can walk away cleanly without playing yet another lap of a dealer marker (an *orbit*) around the table.

Auto muck

You also have the option of choosing *Auto Muck.* Auto muck automatically throws away (or *mucks*) any hand that doesn't win a given pot, speeding up the play.

With auto muck on, you typically can't show any losing or winning hand that goes uncalled. If you want to show any of your hands at some point during your session, turn auto muck off. (See Chapter 6 for more on disguising yourself from your opponents.)

We both like to occasionally show our hands, especially when you can gain a psychological advantage by doing so, so we rarely select auto muck. Unfortunately, when you don't check auto muck on some sites, the site delays every hand to offer players the choice to show or muck. Watching paint dry can be more exciting, depending on the color.

When to show Dumbino he got lucky

Sometimes showing your cards can benefit you as your game progresses. Here's such a case from a fixed-limit Hold 'Em hand.

You're dealt Ah Kh, and you raise pre-flop. You get one caller: Dumbino in the big blind.

The flop comes Qd Jd 10s.

Dumbino checks, and you bet your nut straight. Dumbino mulls it over and calls.

The turn is the 4c.

Dumbino checks again and quickly calls your subsequent bet.

The river is the 4h.

Dumbino checks. You bet. Dumbino raises. You suspect something fishy, so you simply call.

The site flips over Dumbino's hand. He holds 10d 4d for a full house, 10s over 4s. You may want to voluntarily show your hand to let the table know you bet on both a good starting hand and the nut hand. Your display can be useful the next time you make bets and don't have a great hand. The other players have to respect your previous record of betting with great hands. Dumbino may not be so quick to call next time. But if you have auto muck turned on here, you never get a chance to show.

Playing Your First Hand

Enough with the gabbing already, start playing some cards! (See Chapter 2 for how to choose a great site if you haven't done so already.)

Selecting your table and seat

The entry point for all poker sites is the home screen (many call this the *lobby* — see Figure 3-8), which gives you a selection of tables, games, and limits.

You can observe any table, so poke around a bit and watch a few games being played at various stakes. When you take your first tour, refrain from conversation, especially with people at the money tables. Just observe. You only see the action buttons if you actually play, but everything else, like the chips, the cards, and all the player chat, you see in plain sight. Your objective here is to get a feel for the way the online world looks and how it behaves. Just take it all in.

Figure 3-8: The Internet poker home screen presents you with all your gaming options.

Even if you're an experienced online player, you should practice with free chips for a bit on an unfamiliar site. It doesn't cost anything to practice, and you get a chance to understand the idiosyncrasies of any given site's interface. Any site offering games for hard currency also offers games with free chips. To start your practice, head to the site's home screen.

Instead of standing and shivering on the diving board after you finally decide to jump in, make sure to select a table that has several players and an open seat for you. An open seat and willing enemies ensures you some playing action.

Click on the seat that looks coziest at the table of your choice and settle in. (This isn't a big decision; all poker seats in the online world are the same.) When you sit at the low-limit free tables, expect the play to be very loose (with nonsensical, overly aggressive, or atypical betting occurring with players who play every hand). Don't sweat it; you don't play these tables to make money, you play them to discover the online world.

Getting a feel for how everything works

Playing online is nearly automatic. Just sit back, relax (but pay attention), and play the deserving hands the best you can. Don't worry about getting a handle on everything all at once; let the game proceed at its own (what may at first appear to be frenetic) pace.

It sounds dumb, but the best thing you can do for yourself, especially at first, is to focus on the game with as few other distractions from the real world as possible. Turn off your television, put down that chainsaw, have your roommate put the muffler back on his low rider, and listen to the sounds of the game. Beeps, blats, and flashing icons remind you when you need to act.

Become familiar with the pacing. Keep an eye on the conversations and dealer chat in any text window giving you info, like when you have the option to bet and when another player makes a raise. These nuances can serve as the clues and hints to help you along in your game. The site can't tell you how to play better, but it does tell you what to do and when.

Take your time to explore the interface. Every site has small differences and features, such as the location of control buttons it uses, the way its chat mechanism works, and the controls you use to go to the site's home screen while you sit at a table. Play several orbits of the dealer marker (one lap is called an *orbit*). Poke, pry, and prod until you feel like you have a really good feel for what's going on. Play money tables really give you a good outlet for this kind of exploration.

If something bugs you about the interaction of your particular site, see if you can find a way to override it, and if you can't, play somewhere else. Testing a site is just like test-driving a new car. If something bothers you a little bit now, you may be insanely chewing on your keyboard in two months. Life's too short, and your computer is a bit too valuable, for that kind of aggravation.

Speaking the Poker Dialect of Internetese

If you use online instant messaging (*IM*), you're familiar with some of the shorthand abbreviations now prevalent in the Internet world (for example, LOL means "laughing out loud"). Internet poker has been around long enough to develop its own extensions to the messaging lingo. Although you certainly aren't required to speak this language, it does make the game more enjoyable and at the very least lets you know what people have to say about the poker prowess of the table (including what they say about you).

With the exception of referring to a card with capital letters (AKQJT), the custom with abbreviations leans toward using lower case because UPPER CASE MAKES IT SEEM LIKE YOU'RE YELLING. See Table 3-1 for a list of some of the common poker phrasing that shows up on the Internet.

Table 3-1 Common Internet Poker Chat Abbreviations

Abbreviation	Meaning
86	To remove or ban
Ac	Ace of clubs (or Ac)
Ad	Ace of diamonds (or Ad)
Ah	Ace of hearts
As	Ace of spades
bb	Big blind
bl	Better luck
brb	Be right back
C	Clubs
D	Diamonds
gc	Good call (rarely good catch)
gg	Good game
g1	Good one
gl	Good luck
H	Hearts
h/l	High-low
J	Jack
JK	Jack king
j/k	Just kidding
K	King or okay, depending on context
L8(r)	Late(r)
lol	Laughing out loud
M8	Mate

Abbreviation	Meaning
nl	Nice one
N	Nice or no, depending on context
nc	Nice catch (usually referring to a lucky turn or river draw)
Ne1	Anyone
nh	Nice hand
nhs	Nice hands (usually used when a great hand beats a good hand)
nl	No limit
o	Off-suit, written as 78o
ott	Over the top
pl	Pot limit
pls	Please
Q	Queen
qed	Math geek speak for so it is proven
rgp	Rec.gambling.poker (a Usenet group)
rofl	Rolling on the floor laughing
ru	Are you
S	Spades
sb	Small blind
sob	I think you're a particularly nice person, we should have dinner
str8	Straight
T	Thank you or 10, depending on context
tx	Thanks
ty	Thank you
u2	You too
X	Any non-specific card
Y	Yes

(continued)

Table 3-1 *(continued)*

Abbreviation	Meaning
y?	Why?
yw	You're welcome
:)	Smiley face (view sideways)
: (	Frowny face

From a general decorum and demeanor point of view, the online poker world is pretty similar to its brick-and-mortar equivalent. You play with good guys and loud mouths, goofs and silent mummies. Most people play online to kick back and unwind from their otherwise glamorous lives. The anonymity of the Net does produce a slight bit more aggression than you may otherwise find in the physical world, so when you sit down, don't wear your heart on your sleeve.

If you're playing at a table and an opponent takes an inordinately long time to make a betting decision, it does no good to comment on the fact. They have all the alerts and controls you do, and the triple beep of the site's "time's up!" alert does a better job than any nagging you can throw in a chat window. The vast majority of the time a delay like this happens, your opponent has connection trouble, so the last thing he needs or wants is aggravation from another player.

If a player's repeated delays bother you (even if he can't control it), pick up and move to another table. That lowers your blood pressure and keeps you on the karmic good side of the Internet poker world.

Your general rule of conduct is simple: be congenial, be polite, or be quiet. The guy who just beat your pocket aces with 2-9 off-suit may also drive a Gremlin and listen to *The Archie's Greatest Hits* 20 times a day, but you still shouldn't launch into a tirade. The percentages are on your side in situations such as this one, but percentages aren't certainties; play enough hands and the player with exactly one out (the only card that can help) will beat you eventually.

Chapter 4

Taking Your Cash to Cyberspace — Safely

. . . .

In This Chapter

▶ Touring the online money world

▶ Seeking a fair deal

▶ Moving your money

. . . .

*T*he scary (and sickly thrilling) truth about poker is that to win money, you gotta bet, and to bet, you gotta have cash. Playing online is no exception — if you want to win cash that is. The difference with playing online is you have to put your money out "there" . . . which is a spooky commitment. You may feel a bit queasy transferring money the first time; after all, you give your bank account information to a poker room or a third-party transferring site. Before you get too worked up, grab a glass of ice water and chill a bit; a couple of simple and prudent choices on your part make this process quick, easy, and extremely low risk.

Transferring money only seems hard (and possibly risky to your bank account) the first time you do it; after that, funding your fun is a snap.

In this chapter, we explain how the money transaction process works. We show you the various options you have and give you the raw information you need to make a good choice when you decide where to put your money.

Getting Familiar with Online Betting, Payouts, and Losses

Unless you choose to send a check to an Internet poker room via the old-fashioned post (see the next section for info on this and other methods), you use a third party to transfer money from your bank to the poker room. These third parties act as nothing more than a holding pen for your loose cash until you can herd it along to the online poker room of your choice. Online cardroom hosts don't want to be in the banking business, and they actually prefer not taking your money directly — they want to orchestrate your poker game and leave the funding business to someone else. It may seem like a hassle for you, but a nice side effect of the process is that online holding companies provide you with an extra level of security, because your online poker room never deals with your bank directly. One level of indirection between your real world funds and your potential Net poker palace is just another precaution that should make your poker experiences worry-free.

If you've ever used PayPal for an online transaction (like paying for a pair of fuzzy rabbit slippers you won in an online auction), you're familiar with the way third-party online holding companies work. The intermediaries you use for online poker operate the same way PayPal does for eBay. But PayPal made the decision a couple of years ago to drop support for online gambling (including poker), so you can't use the company specifically, but you can use other companies that perform the same service.

Looking at your money transfer options

You have several choices for getting your money to the Internet poker room of your choice.

Every online poker room supports a slightly different set of transaction methods and specific operators for each method of transfer you can use. The cashier on any given site always tells you the providers and methods the site supports.

Mailing a check

The postal system is the most old-fashioned and lowest-tech way you can move your money. Get a cashier's check or a money order (almost never a personal check) and send it via the real-human-carried postal service to the poker room of your choice. Live mail is also the slowest method due to the usual postal and check-clearing delays (slowest only because the Pony Express is no longer available as a delivery technique). Online casinos are growing weary of this method because of general real-world processing hassles, and this option may soon follow the ponies off into the sunset.

Sending an electronic check (ACH)

Many sites accept *ACH* (bank-speak for *electronic checks*). You provide all your checking account information with a firm that holds your money to play (Citadel, for example), provide the information on the online site where you want to play poker, and "write" your ACH. Basically what that means is you deposit a certain amount of money with the poker site cashier, which then sends you on to the firm holding your money, where you're asked to verify your password, confirm the dollar amount you want to deposit, and provide a blank check number. Your check goes through, and you're sent back to your poker site to start play. ACH transactions are typically instantaneous, but they may come with a small fee (usually a buck or two). All banks allow ACH transactions.

You have to give every ACH a number, just like the number you find on the upper right-hand corner of your paper checks. Make certain you don't write in a number that you may eventually use from your paper checks. Pick a number far beyond your check series (20,000 more than where you are now, for example) or use the very next number in your checkbook and then destroy the real-world check with the same number. Don't forget to record your transaction in your checkbook. If you do use the same number, your bank denies the second check, and you must pay all the hefty charges associated with a quick visit to Rubber Check Land.

Transferring money via an online holding company

You transfer money from your bank account to this trusted third party that makes it available for deposit to the Internet poker room of your choice. The most common technique is to transfer into the online holding company via electronic check, but some companies accept bank wires or a credit card.

To use this method, you have to set up an account with the online holding company in question. You typically give it your checking account information; the site deposits a few cents to your checking account (what we call the *tickle*); you verify that you receive it; and then you're set to go. Initial account set-up and verification can take as long as a week.

Always be aware of any fees these holding companies may charge you over and above the handling fees that your poker site charges.

Wiring money with Western Union

Yes, *that* Western Union. You give the company your credit card or debit card information, as well as information about the Internet poker room you want to engage, and you're set. The Five Americans may have liked Western Union in their song of the '60s, but we're not so keen on the company now because of the stiff fees it charges. As of late 2004, the company commonly charged $15 for a $100 transfer. Say *what?*

Charging with credit cards and debit cards

Most poker sites show that they accept payments from MasterCard and Visa, and because credit cards already have a certain amount of security built-in (not to mention no transaction fee), this seems like a natural way to go. Unfortunately, transferring your money via a credit card turns out to be difficult because credit card companies are finding ways to make it harder to play (and pay) with their money.

A few years ago, some credit card companies were sued because they refused to dole out money for cardholders who had run up online gambling debts. Naturally, the credit card companies have recoiled. But MasterCard is pressuring its member banks to drop support of transactions involving Internet gambling (including poker), and to the best of our knowledge, no one has been able to transfer money with this method in a long time. Visa is also clamping down by denying the vast majority of cardholders trying to deposit through the company.

We do have a few pals, however, who have had luck depositing with credit card-emblazoned debit cards — particularly those with the Visa logo. Not all (probably not the vast majority) work, but it may be worth a shot. If you try plastic, you have nothing to lose (this attempt is as safe as any other credit card transaction online, and you don't incur a penalty for denial). Just don't expect it to work.

If the card company does reject you, don't wig out if you get a confusing, complex, or flat-out wrong message back, such as "account denied" or "insufficient funds." The credit card side of the transaction (versus the poker room side) is denying you because it doesn't accept online gaming transactions. In turn, the site hands you some random error message to explain the denial. If this happens, check out another method in this chapter that actually works.

Paying with phone cards

You may want to explore versions of phone cards that you can "charge" with dollar credits online and then transfer the balance to an online poker room. Phone cards in name only, these money vessels actually behave almost precisely akin to pre-paid debit cards. You can usually find out if your poker site supports these cards through the cashier. From there, you can click through to set up an account that funds the card, using your credit or debit card to pay

---

Online poker: Where the dollar is king

In the online poker world, the U.S. dollar rules all. All deposits, all withdrawals, and all bonuses come in good old American greenbacks.

You may run across sites that allow you to play at a table with euros or pounds (the sites automatically convert from dollars for you), but the vast majority of your table stakes involve dollars. Such a nice convenience when you consider that the servers you play on are located outside of the United States. (American regulations require all gaming sites to be physically located outside the boundaries of the United States.)

If only you had a way to send a postcard back home . . .

---

for the transaction. Cards generally come in set amounts — $100, $200, and up — and you typically get a 7 percent (or so) transaction fee tacked on to your cost. This option seems to be gaining in popularity, mostly because of its convenience.

Considering transaction fees

Not all transactions are equal; at least not relative to the transaction fees the online cardroom of your choice charges you. The cashier section of all Internet poker rooms clearly marks the transaction fees associated with any given method of transferring money. Unless you have a good reason, pick a method with no, or very minimal, transaction fees.

Sites that charge a fee are almost always passing along the fees that third parties charge them (unless they want to offset other banking-related expenses). From your point of view, however, the charge comes from the site.

Many sites label transfer techniques with a gimmick along the lines of, "No fee — limited time promotion." Although some sites have tagged specific transaction methods this way for years, don't be lulled into complacency. When you transfer more cash to or from a site, check to see what fee the site associates with that particular transfer — the transaction fees associated with your money transactions can change at any time.

Because transferring money is usually a multi-step process, you should be aware that each step may have associated transaction fees. Make sure to examine the fee schedule your online poker site posts, as well as the fees it may charge for moving your money into the intermediate processing service.

Identifying Honest "Banks"

When you use an online holding company, you essentially establish a bank account online — a cyber version of real-world cash. Make no mistake; you play with hard currency. When you transfer $20 from your checking account to an online holding company, that money is gone, gone, gone from your account. Yes, you still have the funds under your name, but the actual dollars are now under the reign of your online holding company. For this reason, you need to pick a good one; fortunately, it's not hard to do.

Potential risks versus reality

On the surface, the online holding company business may feel pretty shaky. You use an unfamiliar company, it gets your banking information, and due to American gaming regulations, its head-quarters are outside the bounds of the United States. Sounds like a recipe for disaster.

The fact of the matter is that these companies simply fulfill a service. Putting aside all the whizzy new terminology, the underlying model is very familiar: You put up your money; you have an account; your account has a balance; and you can deposit and withdraw (24 hours a day) your money over the Internet.

Like any online banking activity, you must guard your password and account access information.

How online holding companies make their dough

When PayPal announced that it wouldn't continue to handle online gambling, a multi-million dollar industry was left in the breach, and multi-million dollar indus-tries don't lie in breaches for very long.

Companies quickly filled the gap to scoop up the oodles of money. Not only do they get transaction fees (if they charge them; right now most don't), but they also get what bankers call the *float.* You don't receive interest when your money sits with an online holding company, but *it* does on the float. And holding companies do charge transaction fees to your cyber poker rooms. So if you put enough transac-tion fees together and add in the float, you have the makings of some serious cash.

As with the online cardrooms, providing you with honest, straight-forward, and direct service is in the holding company's best interests.

With any financial transaction, you always take a certain amount of risk (consider when you send a credit card away with your server in a restaurant), but as long as you stick to known entities and use prudence, the risk you take is extremely small.

Managing your online money

You can take several steps with your online funds to shave any risk level to practically nil:

- ✔ Make as few transactions as possible. The fewer times you make a transaction, the less chance you take for something to go wrong. Move $200 once rather than $100 twice, which may be less expensive fee-wise, too.

- ✔ Along with your minimalist transaction policy, you should move as little money as possible. The less you bestow upon an online holding company, the less you have to worry about problems of some type suddenly cropping up. So in line with the info in the previous bullet, move $200 instead of $1,000.

- ✔ Use a known online holding company. By this we mean a company that multiple online poker sites utilize. (We recommend a few in the upcoming section "Methods and providers we like.") This route practically guarantees that you don't use a fly-by-night operation.

- ✔ Don't send a check directly to an online poker room; a lost check is much harder to track. Plus, when you involve a third party (like an online holding company) you get an extra set of transaction records. ("Look here, you poker room knotheads: Online Holding Company X transferred $50 to you on the first of the month. *Now* what do you have to say?")

- ✔ Password protect your computer. Remember, your PC is now the official home of some of your hard currency. You don't want anyone to be able to squander it. As always, squandering your money is a privilege that you should reserve for yourself.

Methods and providers we like

We must stress that we neither endorse nor recommend the following techniques and companies. We only know that the following options and providers have worked cleanly and smoothly for our online poker transfers, as well as for many of our pals.

Psst . . . what's the password?

With anything you access electronically, you want to choose a secure password that outsiders can't easily guess. In fact, many online banking services require that you meet certain formatting criteria, such as a minimum number of characters or having both letters and numbers in your password. Picking a tough password is good because it protects your cyber valuables.

The downside is that you have a harder time remembering them. Many people use the same password for every sensitive online site, or they write the passwords down, often in a text file on the computer. Both of these copouts are bad news. If you use the same password everywhere and someone discovers it, that person has access to all your accounts. If you store your passwords on your computer and a thief steals it (or it simply needs repairs), the crook has all your software and the passwords he needs, right in one convenient place.

How do you pick different, secure passwords that you can remember?

Our advice is to choose a process that you apply to a few memorable words, and then select words that only make sense together to you.

For example, Jennifer, a compulsive seamstress, needs a password. Remembering she once sewed some curtains for her aunt Liz in Auburn, she starts with the words "curtain" and "Auburn." For a process, she reverses the letters in one word and converts the other to digits based on the numbers on a telephone keypad. The resulting password, niatruc282876, is very hard to guess.

She can use a different project/city combination, but the same process works every time she needs a new password. And on the freak chance Johnny Hacker does figure out one of her passwords, it doesn't help him figure out any others she uses. If Jen needs a password reminder, she simply writes down her aunt's name.

Transferring via electronic check (ACH)

For ACH transactions, we have no problems with Citadel Commerce (www.citadelcommerce.com). It charges a small service fee, but the transaction is nearly instantaneous.

Using online holding companies

We use and like NETeller and FirePay. You should feel especially safe knowing that NETeller is a publicly traded company on the London Stock Exchange. Expect a delay, possibly as long as a week, when you first set up your account, but after you establish a veri-fied line to your bank account, money transfer becomes smoother. NETeller has a service charge on instantaneous transfers, but you can take the week-long route for free. As of late 2004, FirePay didn't have a service charge, but don't count on that lasting forever.

Transferring Money

The tables are waitin'. Time to take a big swallow and move some of your funds.

Walking through your deposit

The deposit process breaks into clumps with a few possible points where you have to just . . . wait. Be patient and begin the process with the following steps:

1. **Pick a quality online poker room.**

   See Chapter 2 for information on how to choose a site.

2. **Select your transfer method of choice from the online poker room's cashier.**

3. **If the transfer method involves a third party (meaning *any* method that doesn't send your online poker room a real-life paper check), go to the third party's Web site and register appropriately.**

   Make sure to follow the site's directions for account creation and verification to the letter. (If you send a check straight to the online poker site, skip to Step 9.)

   At this point you may encounter a time lag. If you use an online holding company, its tickle (the amount the company initially puts toward your account to make sure it has the correct bank info) and your verification of the account balance could take as long as a week.

4. **Check your online poker room for first-time bonuses. Weigh this figure against how much you're willing to use as a poker stake and determine the amount you want to deposit into your online poker account.**

   Many sites give you bonus money to play with for making their site your room of choice. For more details on sign-up bonuses, see Chapter 2.

5. **Transfer the necessary funds from your real-world account (checking account or debit card) to your online third party (the ACH provider or online holding company).**

   Don't forget to move enough money to account for any service fees that the poker site or holding company charges you along the way. You may experience a delay of a day or two as your funds seep from one account to the next.

6. **Verify that your online third party deposits the correct amount of money and that your real-world account reflects the withdrawal properly.**

   An error anywhere in this entire process is unlikely; but if one occurs, it may be something like a double withdrawal.

7. **Make the deposit to your online poker room from your third party.**

   This action is typically instantaneous, but you may experience a lag period of a day.

8. **Read the confirmation dialogs of your poker room carefully to see how soon you can expect the deposit to show up.**

9. **Verify that you receive the funds in your online poker room in the expected time frame.**

10. **Verify with your online third party that it has withdrawn the proper amount of cash relative to your poker room deposit.**

11. **Play online poker shrewdly.**

12. **Play in a promotional event that wins you a seat in the World Series of Poker. (Optional)**

13. **Win the World Series of Poker in the brick-and-mortar world. (Optional)**

14. **Buy us each a lobster dinner and let us fondle your World Series winner's bracelet. (Not optional if you made it this far.)**

The list may look daunting and vague, but the process is practically automatic, although it varies slightly depending on which site you head to. All it really takes is money and a little patience. After you complete your first transfer and become comfortable with a certain method and provider, the rest of your transactions go much faster.

If at any point your money transaction looks suspicious or just plain wrong, contact your transferring parties immediately. The best way to communicate is by e-mail (so you have a verifiable trail), and anytime you have a phone conversation, be sure to follow up with an e-mail recap.

As you make transactions (or dispute transaction errors), be sure to take notes — and save them. This helps you keep track of all details — dates, times, and the names of people you speak with as you go along.

Keep a separate record of all your online poker room deposits —
not only to follow your deposits and withdrawals in the real world,
but also to track whether you win or lose money over the long run.

Going the other way: Cashing out

Like you may expect, cashing out of your online poker room
is a tiny bit harder than cashing in. Different sites have different
rules — all plainly discussed in the withdrawal section of your
poker room's cashier — but here are a few universal snags to
lookout for:

- ✔ Withdrawals often have to take place at least 48 hours after
  the last deposit.

- ✔ If you want your online poker room to cut you a check, expect
  a $50 minimum withdrawal and a 15-day wait.

- ✔ Online poker rooms tend to prefer paying back via online
  holding companies. You may have to endure a delay of a day
  or two during this transfer. Online holding companies, in turn,
  may delay you a day or two as well before they process the
  funds and send them back to you.

- ✔ Read details of any bonus you want to receive. Typically
  you can't withdraw a chunk of cash and then immediately
  re-deposit it to score a bonus. (See Chapter 2 for more details
  on bonuses.)

In short, if you need money out of your poker account, anticipate a
delay. Don't turn to this account when you need money to buy a
fire extinguisher at the very moment your house is burning down.

Part II

Taking Your Poker to a New Level — The Cyber Level

The 5th Wave · By Rich Tennant

"I think if you're trying to bluff in Internet poker, it's probably not a good idea to follow your bets with a winking emoticon."

In this part . . .

*T*he Internet has the largest variety of poker games in the world, from the obvious (Hold 'Em, Omaha, and Stud) to the eclectic (Pineapple and wild card games). Here we discuss ring games and tournaments of all sizes and the strategic differences between playing ring games in the online world versus that clunky old brick-and-mortar place you used to hang out in. We also cover the basics of Internet poker psychology and the first steps to take in sharpening your game.

Chapter 5

Adapting to a New World: Internet Poker

*O*n your first pass, the online poker world may seem to be nothing more than a dim shadow of the real-world brick-and-mortar equivalent. If you can't see the face of your opponent sitting across the table from you, what's the point?

After you dig under the surface a bit, however, you discover that online poker is profoundly different in some very interesting ways. Psychologically, you experience a very different game: You see *far* more hands than in the brick-and-mortar world, you play with money that may seem fake (oh, but it won't for long), and because everything happens on a computer, you encounter a whole new set of ways for things to go wrong.

In this chapter, we cover some of the fundamental underpinnings of online poker — characteristics that make it truly different from the brick-and-mortar world — and we look at ways to understand and deal with them.

Grappling with the Psychological Basics

From a psychological point of view, the biggest differences between online play and the brick-and-mortar world include the radical increase in the speed of play and a heavy (mental) disassociation from the money you put in play.

Understanding the ramifications of speed

In the online world, you have a chance to play between two and three times as many hands per hour as you get in the normal brick-and-mortar environment. Online poker rooms do everything in their power to accelerate play, resulting in some interesting (and sometimes odd) ramifications in the way a player perceives the game.

Coming to grips with quick-hitting bad draws

Probably the biggest psychological hardship for any poker player is the *bad beat,* a situation where you have a better hand than another player during the first couple betting rounds, but your opponent draws a long-shot card and beats you toward the end of the hand. A lesser hand outdrawing you is a hard thing to take under any circumstance.

As you play online, it may seem like you see more bad beats than you do in the real world, and guess what? You do. Because you see two or three times as many hands, you also see two to three times as many bad beats. You see all types of hands more often. You need to keep a realistic perspective, because if you focus solely on the bad beats, you slowly drive yourself crazy. But if you can balance the bad-beat blues with the realization of how many more winning hands you see and have, you can hang on to your sanity.

If you play and discover that bad beats really stick with you, that you truly can't shrug them off for the statistical anomalies they are, you definitely shouldn't play no-limit. No-limit is the cardroom equivalent of performing circus acts without a safety net — the trick isn't any harder, the penalty is just more severe. An unfriendly card can cost you a significant amount of money or your chip position in a hard-fought tournament.

A long string of bad luck

Every player has a favorite bad beat story, especially from online play. Here's Red's . . .

Red's favorite form of online poker is a single-table no-limit Hold 'Em tournament (see Chapter 12). When Red plays online, you can find him there.

In 2004, he had a string of not one, not two, but 27 consecutive finishes out of the money (meaning he busted out early before the prize money kicked in). In 25 of these 27 tournaments, other players eliminated him with all-in plays where Red was the favorite. Red had the best hand going in; he just didn't have the best hand coming out.

Disheartening? Sure. Especially if, like him, you have an over-analyzing mind and a degree in mathematics.

Runs of this nature are a fluke, but not impossible. What you need to do if a streak like this ever takes hold (and if you play long enough, a similar streak *will* come) is to keep your wits about you and don't let the statistical weirdness of the past affect your play in the present. Take time off, because you need to adjust, re-coup, and re-finance. And make certain that you just ran into bad luck and didn't expose some fundamental flaw in your poker strategy. Think back to what you thought before your plays, the time you took betting, and your betting strategy to search for a pattern.

But what about Red's bank account? Well, his 28th tournament began a string of six tourney wins, completely reversing his debt. (Now he could call that a statistical anomaly, but he prefers to call it the consequence of his cunning skill.)

Of course, the torturous part of fixed-limit is that more opponents hold out (sometimes justifiably) for underdog draws because of the cheaper price, and as a result, you actually see more bad beats in the limit games. If taking a bad beat in no-limit is like taking a sword through your midsection, losing with bad beats in fixed-limit is like getting 1,000 papercuts. (For details on the bankrolls you need to withstand bad beats, head to Chapter 8.)

Celebrating the micro-second win

Along with moving past the increase in bad beats of the Net (see the previous section for advice), you have to psychologically adjust to the wins also coming far more quickly. If you catch a really big hand or have a very unusual sequence of cards hit the board, baddabing, baddaboom: The screen displays the hands still in play, the site pays out the pot, and the play continues with new cards. You may have played your entire life waiting for a royal flush

Dealing with bad beat whiners

You can't find an Internet poker room where players don't type a phrase like, "This never happens in the real world!" every second. The fact of the matter is, yes, bad beats *do* happen in the real world. When the randomness comes out of a computer rather than a dealer's ring-laden hand, the whole process just seems more suspicious.

And the online world seems to have a disproportionate number of people who complain, and then *keep* complaining, about their bad beats. Part of it, no doubt, is due to the anonymity of the Internet; people can whine without really losing face. Some of it probably has to do with the number of bad beats that any given person sees. And a few whiners may be people who don't have much raw playing experience, so they taste the bitter end of the bargain for the first time. For this reason, the whining seems to be the shrillest at the lower-limit tables and lowered to a soft murmur at the higher limits.

In any event, it pays to be psychologically braced for opponents who take a bad beat and suddenly lose it. They may even rattle on and on, after being eliminated from a tournament, as an observer.

As a player you have a couple of choices. One is to ignore your table's version of Mount Vesuvius and wait for the eruption to cease. Cover the fan vent of your computer to keep any ash from coming out. If you need help focusing, always remember that you can turn off player or observer chat.

If the whiners get threatening or abusive, you can also report them to your site's support personnel for corrective action. Nobody needs to hear that kind of stuff, so you do all players a favor.

The one thing you shouldn't do is engage the hothead in baiting conversation, no matter how tempting it may be. If the site does decide to levy ramifications on the jerk, you don't want to be associated as an instigator or accomplice.

and then, when it *finally* hits your Seven-Card Stud hand in the online world, the site treats it with exactly the same dignity and respect as a king-high hand full of junk. Be warned: Online poker is a place where you have to provide your own celebrations. Best get the party poppers out before you log on.

Getting used to money that doesn't feel real

One of the biggest dangers to your bankroll during online play is the fact that your money doesn't seem real. You may face this problem in the brick-and-mortar world when you look at a stack of

Play to win — and keep track when you do

When you begin playing online for the first time, you should work up to limits that measure about half the size of what you ultimately want to play and stay there until you get comfortable and can regularly beat the game. Keep close track of your wins and losses; advance no further until you have a certifiable winning record.

Remember, whatever you lose at your current level is doubled on the next. Never, ever, move up to a higher level with the idea that you can recover your losses faster. When losing, the best way to recover is to move down in limits, not up. The competition isn't as stiff and the decisions you make are purer because they don't have as much riding on them, leaving you less worried about your monetary risk.

chips, but the online world amplifies it by an order of magnitude when you stare at a number on the screen that represents your bank account. You can't see it, smell it, touch it, or listen to it crinkle between your fingertips, and if it didn't show up as a withdrawal on your checking account statement last month, you may not have even remembered it was yours.

As a result, you can easily become lax about money: lose 5 bucks here, 20 bucks there. Who cares? It doesn't really matter. But it does matter. A lot. You work hard for your money, even (maybe especially) if you win it at the poker table. If you ever find yourself playing nonchalantly or, worse, thinking you want to just lose money so you can close an account (sounds weird, we know, but we have friends who've done it), you need to stop and seriously consider your situation.

If you find yourself behaving like the money doesn't matter, check your pulse and back away from playing. In fact, you should seriously think about completely withdrawing the money from your account and then restarting in a week or so, if you feel up to it.

Closing your account is very simple. You go to the cashier and go through the equivalent of clicking the "I want all my money *now*" button. Some sites require a minimum withdrawal, but if you want to close your account for good, the sites nearly always waive that requirement. If you want to close an account that contains less than the minimum withdrawal amount, contact your site's customer support service.

Examining the Limit Differences Online

The games that truly set online play apart from brick-and-mortar play are micro-limit matches (games with $1/$2 limits and below) and no-limit (or pot-limit — we lump both together throughout the chapter) ring games.

When you play lower-limit games online — *especially* the micro-limits — you're still playing serious poker. In the real world, micro-limits are often taken lightly — friends and neighbors play for fun and use the same pennies that always go back in the community jar anyway. The skill level contrast is but one symptom of the difference between serious online money players and fun-loving home-gamers. And don't even ask about micro-limit games in cardroom establishments.

No-limit games are different primarily due to the frequency of large bets. More people are willing to click a mouse to risk it all on draws or good hands than you find willing to push clay chips across the felt while staring an enemy directly in the eye.

To understand the online mutations of the micro-limit and no-limit forms of poker, read on.

Looking closely at micro-limits

In brick-and-mortar cardrooms, the lowest fixed-limit games you can find are $1/$2 Hold 'Em, $2/$4 Omaha, and maybe $1/$2 Stud. In the online world, however, the limits go right on down to $0.02/$0.04 for Hold 'Em and Omaha and around $0.04/$0.08 for Stud.

The average player can take his lowest brick-and-mortar buy-in and get about 50 times as much action online, making the Internet a great place to learn and master any game — without the threat of losing much money.

Knowing your competition

Don't be misled by the low stakes. Yes, beginners do play at the low stakes tables (and if you're a beginner, we strongly encourage you to start on these limits), but you shouldn't mistake online micro-limit games for the carefree penny ante games you may have played in junior high school.

The competition on these tables is tougher and more advanced than in the games you grew up on. For starters, everyone you play against is, in theory, at least 18 (because you can't see your opponents it may be hard to remember that sometimes), and the maturity of players makes a difference.

Along with the beginners, you may encounter a few seasoned players who read new poker texts and want to try out ideas and theories. Some veteran players are just now reading their first books after having grinded for years in the school of hard knocks. Those seasoned card-slingers still know how to take you down, new theories or not. Other players go to the lower limits purely as a fundraising source for paying their entry fees at the higher-limit tables. And all these gamblers can be formidable opponents.

Your favorite opponents, of course, are the ones who don't really care what happens to their money. They log-on for the entertainment. But the fun-seekers make up the minority. Most online players are more serious about the game than other micro-limit players you take on in home games.

We don't mean that playing micro-limit poker is the equivalent of walking down a dark alley in the worst part of town with a dollar bill sticking out of your pocket. You're not going to get clubbed for it. But you should always remember that your money is someone else's potential prize. (See "Grappling with the Psychological Basics" earlier in this chapter for more about the psychology of playing with online money that doesn't feel real.)

Changing your strategy — or not

Strategically, you want to approach micro-limit games the same way you approach their larger-staked siblings. When you take a seat at one of these tables, be prepared to play a solid game of poker. Don't stay in with substandard cards or unlikely drawing hands "because it's cheap." You can develop bad habits that carry over to the more treacherous stakes.

Instead, take the time after you fold shoddy hands to observe your opponents, figure out who plays loose or tight, and adjust your play accordingly. Those pennies and dollars start to add up over time, and you should start moving up in limits after you regularly beat the micro-limit games, which shouldn't take too long. If you don't underestimate your opponents and play a solid game, these limits are definitely beatable.

Pondering the no-limit/ pot-limit differences

In the variable betting world, you often play Omaha as a pot-limit game and Hold 'Em as a no-limit game (rarely as pot-limit). (Seven-Card Stud is always played fixed-limit — for more on the different types and limits of games offered online, see Chapter 7.) The betting limits cross over both game-type sub-species: tournaments and ring games. You see pot-limit Omaha tournaments and no-limit Hold 'Em tournaments just as often as you see pot-limit Omaha ring games and no-limit Hold 'Em ring games. And both have distinct differences and flavors when compared to their brick-and-mortar counterparts.

Experiencing no-limit/pot-limit tourneys online

Unless you come from a very sophisticated home game, have participated in a neighborhood-organized tournament with friends, or have a fair amount of cardroom tournament experience, you'll likely get your first exposure to no-limit poker tournaments in the online world. The boom in poker popularity, driven by endless televised tournaments, has created legions of nearly frantic poker zombies wanting to risk it all in the same tournament settings they see on TV.

No-limit and pot-limit tournaments are the battlegrounds where these zombies feed. And no wonder. Tournaments are an easy and attractive choice for anyone, because for as little as $5, you can get a stack of around $1,000 in online chips. In exchange for cash, even the most meager and timid person gets a chance to become a fierce road gambler and join the ranks of the ruthless super-rich — betting thousands on a single hand and hammering away at everyone else in a winner-take-all format. (Chapter 10 has more on tournaments in general, and Chapters 12 and 13 drill deep into the single-table version.)

Rushing all-in

If you have experience in no-limit tournaments in the brick-and-mortar world, keep smelling salts by your computer and prepare to be shocked by the raw number of times you see people push all-in. The frequency of all-in pushing is *far* higher in the online world.

The lower the table entry fee, the worse the all-in frenzy gets. Free-roll tournaments (which we discuss in Chapter 10) are especially riddled with loose cannons, and these tourneys are unrealistic enough that they border on being nothing more than bad sitcoms

Loose cannons in Hold 'Em and Omaha

You're in the early stages of a no-limit Hold 'Em tournament, and everyone holds roughly the same chip stack size. You receive A-K as your hole cards for a hand. You bet and get raised from behind by Nice Ace, a player you've noticed makes a habit of playing any hand with an ace (hands like A-4 off-suit). How does she play them? She likes to bet strongly and isn't afraid to call. Her pre-flop raise is an indication that she probably holds some type of ace. The flop comes A K 8.

You now have the top two pair and almost certainly the best hand, barring trips from your happy-footed opponent. In the brick-and-mortar world, your opponent may call you on a bet equal to the big blind, and maybe double if you're lucky. But Nice has a tendency to show just a little too much pride in her aces. She may or may not call an all-in bet; a better play may be to bet half your stack. She may get greedy and raise you back all-in. If she merely calls, you can push her all-in on the turn, regardless of the card that comes. We don't know of a brick-and-mortar house in the world where you see this kind of brash calling behavior, but such hubris is a surprisingly common occurrence online, especially on the smaller buy-in no-limit tables.

After your Hold 'Em experience, you decide to test your broadening skill in a pot-limit Omaha tournament. Similar to the Hold 'Em tourney, most players are still evenly chip-stacked. You're dealt Ad Qh Qs 4d. All players at the table call the big-blind pre-flop. The flop comes Qd 10d 3h. This flop is nearly perfect for your hand: You now hold the top set of trips and the nut flush draw. Any board pair gives you the top full house. The freak Qc hitting on the turn or river gives you quads. Your odds of winning this hand, irrespective of the next cards hitting the board, are very high.

If you're in an early position in a small buy-in pot-limit Omaha tourney, we can nearly guarantee that if you make a pot-sized bet, someone at the table will call it. Another player (especially someone with a lower flush draw) may think that you want to buy the pot. A better play may be to check and then max raise any action that comes behind you. If you do check and the betting round checks all the way through, you should make a pot-sized bet on the turn card.

If you're in late position, especially on the dealer marker, consider making a bet equal to half the pot. To the other players, your bet is hard to interpret — are you betting a flush draw or just mildly betting your position, trying to force other players out? You may even entice someone to raise, which means you can make a pot-sized re-raise. If you do get a caller on a half-pot bet, make a maximum bet on the turn, regardless of the card.

for the first few rounds. Even at medium hard-currency limits (say, $30 buy-in tourneys), the all-in-push is probably one and a half times what you see in the brick-and-mortar world.

An aggressive no-limit Hold 'Em primer

Most players today have their first experience with a no-limit Hold 'Em tournament online for a low buy-in entry fee. The aggressive online style immediately becomes the norm for these players. If you've played in tournaments in the brick-and-mortar world, however, the far-more aggressive online style may catch you off guard. During the first few orbits of the dealer marker, when the blinds are still low, you need to brace yourself for a few all-in plays post-flop.

If you're up against a player you have no previous experience with, and you face an all-in (as a raise or as a bet in front of you), you have a couple of choices. If you're up against a player you know you can beat from your observations of his play to this point, your best move may be fold and wait for more advantageous circumstances.

If, however, you're feeling continually pushed around by the same player; you have strong reason to believe he is bluffing; or you just want to take a step up to a world with larger swings (where you can quickly double your stack or lose it all), here are some possible ways to react:

Call the all-in bet if you have

✔ Any trips or two pair

✔ Top pair with the highest possible kicker (only)

✔ Queen high or better flush draw, along with any pair

✔ Top pair and an open-ended straight draw

✔ The best flush draw, but *only* if you face more than one caller on the hand (you need good odds on your money)

✔ The best straight draw, but *only* if you face more than one caller and a flush draw isn't on the board

Fold all other hands. You can hold your ground by using this strategy in low buy-in tournaments, but you should be prepared to occasionally call an opponent's set of trips. Your best strategy is to stay patient and play a solid game. Don't get caught up in the action or take another player's looseness personally!

Taking down loose callers

The online all-in fad breeds an interesting side effect: Because players are so cavalier about pushing all-in, opponents in the online world are also more likely to call. You can use this behavior to your advantage. If you observe a loose-calling opponent, feel free to up your normal brick-and-mortar bet in any situation by at least 20 percent in the online world. If you can get called for more money (and assuming you want to be called), you should. If you don't mind taking occasional bad beats, go ahead and push all-in. Larger bets reap bigger rewards in the online world than in the brick-and-mortar world, simply because more people are willing to call large bets.

Although you may put yourself in a good position by taking down crazy callers, you don't want to fall in love with the action and become a loose caller yourself. Stick to your game and make the loose players pay. Don't be too proud to muck cards if someone comes at you hard and you don't have it. Your cards will get better, and other opportunities are just around the corner. And if your opponents adjust to your tight, aggressive play and tighten up themselves, you can loosen up and drive them nuts.

Going micro in no-limit/pot-limit ring games

Only fairly serious poker players have played no-limit ring games or pot-limit Omaha outside of the Internet, because the lowest limit you can find in the brick-and-mortar world is around $1/$2 Hold 'Em with a $200 maximum buy-in. You can only play Omaha ring games with pot-limits. On the Net, you can play both no-limit Hold 'Em and pot-limit Omaha for around $0.01/$0.02 blinds and a $2 maximum buy-in.

Your initial reaction may be that these games are a bargain. You can buy-in for almost nothing and play to your heart's content without risking a fortune. Yep, you're right: If you're looking for no-limit ring games, the micro limits are *the* place to start.

Winning . . . and losing, too

The low-stakes form of no-limit ring games are also the toughest games to beat in the micro-limit world. But they can also be some of the most enjoyable, and you can win consistently if you stick to a solid game plan.

The strategy and dynamic of no-limit ring games are strikingly different from no-limit tournaments. Think of micro no-limit ring games only as a stepping stone to other no-limit ring games with higher table stakes, *not* as a stepping stone to no-limit tournaments.

When you first sit down at a ring game table, especially as a beginner, you should expect to lose your entire stack. And then expect that to happen again. And again. Experienced players come to these games to tap bankrolls. It doesn't seem like you can make much money at the micro-limits, but many players make more than $10 per hour in games with a maximum buy-in of $2.

Play gets tougher as you move to the higher limits, so be sure to play within your bankroll. (We cover bankrolls and philosophical differences between ring games and tourney play in Chapter 8.)

Watching out for gorillas

No-limit ring games restrict you as to the amount of money you can bring to the table. If you sit down and another player has considerably more than the upper amount allowed (say, more than three times), you may want to consider another table.

What about HAL?

In the world of software, *robots* are computerized programs that automatically perform tasks. In the case of poker, a robot is a software program that humans develop to play Internet poker. Robots play with a certain pre-programmed amount of *artificial intelligence* (meaning strategy, in this case). If you come across a site that even mentions robots, you can be certain it has a flat out ban on them. The reasoning is robots could be an unfair advantage, and thanks in part to *2001: A Space Odyssey,* they just kind of creep people out.

So do poker robots still exist on some sites? Almost certainly. Although we've never actually seen any with a lot of strategic intelligence (sites use dumb ones for internal testing all the time to make sure their poker software is behaving properly), we've heard plenty of talk about them around Silicon Valley. In the software world, any time you hear a lot of talk, you can be certain someone is working on it somewhere.

The important question is: Are smart robots a threat to you? Poker is based on *incomplete data;* you don't know what your opponent holds, and you intentionally try to disguise the true strength of your hand. Along with not having the intuition that humans possess, having incomplete data creates some of the most difficult problems for computers to tackle.

Due to luck, robots certainly could beat anyone now (just like any player can beat anyone else through luck). In the distant future, robots may be able to beat the best human players consistently, out of sheer luck. But today the problem is too complex, and humans don't understand the computer models well enough to make a program that can beat the best players consistently.

You could set up a robot that dependably makes money on something like a $0.50/$1 Omaha table, because of the general level of play you find there (the stakes are so low that you mostly find beginners who may not be very good; you also find veterans players trying to make easy money, but as we said, even a robot can get lucky against these players despite their vulnerability). A program that applies a simple formula, such as which hands to play in which positions (and then just calls any bet), could be a moneymaker against a table full of low-limit players. But the predictability of robots, as they almost certainly stand today, makes them ultimately vulnerable to a sharper player.

If you suspect a robot is playing against you, pay attention to the opponent's playing style. You'll probably make the player out to be a human playing predictably. And anything predictable is beatable, robot or human.

When you sit across from someone with a tremendous stack over and above everyone else at the table, you see two things. A smart gorilla with plenty of chips, and a bunch of bananas who aren't smart enough to leave the table yet. The gorilla, after he or she becomes large enough, makes (or calls) bets of a crushing size at any time; and the best players win the hands most of the time. How do you think this player built such a stack in the first place?

However, if you observe a gorilla who you think plays poorly and has enjoyed a ridiculous run of luck, you can take him down to baboon status if you play well and become the alpha male.

Dodging (and Dealing with) Online Pitfalls

Problems unique to the online poker world have nothing to do with the game of poker itself and everything to do with the fact that you play on a computer. Here are a few steps you can take to avoid trouble, along with what to do when you find yourself stuck.

Staying sane in a world of distraction

In the brick-and-mortar world, your distractions consist of a few nattering players, televisions silently glaring long-past sporting events, and a cocktail waitress who's always elsewhere no matter how badly you need her.

Thanks to the wonders of modern computing, your online environment can be about 1,000 times worse. If you let your eyes and mind wander, you may realize that you're playing under an animated billboard with the computer stereo blasting and an Internet mailman knocking on your door every 10 seconds with new e-mail. And that only covers the happenings on your computer. (It gets more complicated if you've got kids, pets, or angry spouses who think you play too much Internet poker. We know, we know . . . too much? Not possible.)

Tie your hands to your sides or wear blinkers like a racehorse if you have to, but when you play, stay focused. Ask yourself the same question you should ask when contemplating whether to play multiple tables (as discussed in the following section): "If my opponent doesn't have the same distractions as me, does she have an edge?"

Steering clear of multiple-table play

You can't play multiple tables simultaneously in the brick-and-mortar world, due to both physical and rule restrictions. (We find it weird enough to play at a casino poker table with one of the seated players also betting on the ponies. Can you imagine the chaos of watching half the people on the floor running back and forth between different poker tables?)

In the online world, however, you can play at multiple tables (playing different game types and limits) simultaneously. Some sites restrict the number of tables you can play; others make the sky the limit.

When you first start playing online, especially on the Hold 'Em tables, you may find the speed a little disconcerting. Just the thought of playing two tables at once may seem a little overwhelming. It doesn't take long, however, to get into the swing of the action. After you play only one table for some time, you start to picture yourself playing on another table simultaneously. In fact, your inner action monkey may start to crave it.

Think of this situation exactly like you think of repeatedly hitting your hand with a hammer: Just because you can do something doesn't mean you should.

The problem with playing more than one table at a time, as if we even need to state it, is splitting your attention between multiple games. You have more opponents to keep track of and more hand and chip stack information to be aware of. You take on a lot of responsibility, and it gives your opponents (who may not be playing multiple tables; use the site's player-finding feature to get a report) an immediate advantage over you.

We absolutely don't recommend playing multiple tables, but if you're enough of an action monkey to insist on doing so, you should avoid one situation at all costs: Don't begin play in two tournaments of the same size and type at the same time. If you manage to do well in both, you can ultimately find yourself playing head's-up simultaneously on two different tables — a challenge that only *Star Trek's* cyber-human Data could successfully conquer (and even then, only with special effects).

Avoiding a wrong click

If you run multiple applications on your computer, you naturally click on a window in the background to bring it forward. But if you click on an actionable area and make a betting decision, the

Two-fisted Karpov

Our friend Karpov is an avid online player who nearly always plays on two tables at the same time. "After playing online for a while, I just found a single game to be a little too slow," he says.

Karpov's particular flavor of insanity is to play single-table tournaments only — pot-limit Hold 'Em with his left hand and pot-limit Omaha High/Low with his right. "I play pot-limit Hold 'Em because I think the competition is a little easier than no-limit, and you're less likely to lose it all on one hand, especially when the blinds are low," he says. "I play Omaha High/Low for the variety."

He always registers for both tournaments at the same time because he knows the Omaha High/Low tourney takes longer to finish (opponents need more time to evaluate the hands, and the split pots slow the elimination of players), so he never ends up playing head's up on two tables simultaneously.

A fanatical record keeper (he can tell you the results of every online tournament he's ever played in — well over 800), Karpov knows he makes more money from the Omaha side than the Hold 'Em side.

"I know I could do better if I only played at one table. I just prefer the action and variety of playing two-fisted," he says. All his opponents appreciate his attitude, we're sure.

program passes, processes, and acts on the click in the application window.

For example, you decide to work on a spreadsheet of your poker history in the foreground and play at a table in the background. You receive an alert from the game indicating your turn to act, and you click on the poker window to bring it forward. If you happen to accidentally click on the *Raise* button when you just want to bring the table to the front of the screen, guess what? Yep, you raise the hand accidentally.

To avoid mis-clicking, you should call the application forward by clicking on the icon on your tool bar or grab the poker window by the top of its windowpane. (If you accidentally click on the close box of your poker table, don't worry. All sites ask you if you're sure you want to leave the table.)

Be aware that some sites force your game table to the foreground when your turn arrives. If you want to work on a spreadsheet during your game (which you shouldn't, because you should focus on the game), you may easily make a click that gives you more than you bargained for if the table pops to the forefront when you're not expecting it.

Mis-clicking usually doesn't cost you much money, but it does feel like it trims years off the end of your life when it happens, and it does put a ding in your lifetime winnings if it happens a lot.

Preventing machine crashes

You want the computer you play on to be as "clean" as possible. Nothing spells more trouble for your online play than a crashing machine. Can you imagine trying to play in a casino when the roof keeps falling in? You essentially experience this when your computer crashes. Here are a few tips to help you avoid online poker catastrophe:

- **Do some silicon stretching.** Every time you prepare to start a new poker session, do some minor Web surfing and check your e-mail. Make sure you get the kind of connection you expect. You want to see a nice steady flow of data. If your system doesn't seem quite right (and you have the ability, like on a dial-up service for example), disconnect and reconnect to see if you can make it better. If you can't improve the situation, wait and play another day.

- **Stay cyber slim.** Keep the number of applications you have running on your poker computer to a minimum, being especially mindful of any that have given you fits in the past.

- **Get your digital flu shot.** Reduce your chances of having problems by regularly scrubbing for viruses (you can use Trend Micro's scan for free at www.antivirus.com).

- **Take your online vitamins.** Any time a poker site offers you a software upgrade, even an optional one, you should take it. Upgrades give you new features, important bug fixes, and in some cases may increase the security of your data.

- **Don't do double time.** You know we don't like playing two tables anyway. (If you don't know this, read the section "Steering clear of multiple-table play" earlier in this chapter.) But playing two different sites at the same time is a really bad idea. We've seen crashes in the past that were a direct result of different poker applications not playing nicely in the same digital sandbox.

Coping with disconnection

No matter how bulletproof your computer is or how reliable your Internet Service Provider may be, sooner or later you find yourself disconnected from an online poker game.

In the good old days (two years ago), sites provided a service called *all-in protection.* If you were suddenly disconnected, the site treated you as though you were all-in and protected your hand to the end. Unfortunately, too many people abused this service as a strategic edge, and all-in protection went away. Today, on nearly all sites, if you get disconnected, the site folds your hand. (Sites sometimes abbreviate their lack of all-in protection with the confusing *no all-in* moniker.)

Getting disconnected is only a big deal during tournaments because the site slowly but surely blinds your chips off. You have to get back on if you want to save your stack. In a ring game, the site simply changes your status to *sitting out,* and eventually you lose your seat. The site re-credits the chips you had at the table to your account.

Getting disconnected is a jarring experience, but after it happens, you need to put it behind you. Focus harder than you normally do on the game and calm down. You already had to deal with the inconvenience the disconnection handed you — you don't need to make it worse by playing it over and over in your head.

Resuscitating your game (and computer)

The first hint you get that you're disconnected is the normal flow of the game suddenly stops. No bets. No cards being dealt. No chat from players. Nothing.

Say goodbye to all-in protection

All poker sites used to have all-in protection, but abuse of this privilege caused it to go away.

For example: If a player was in, say, a Hold 'Em tournament with Ah Ad, and the flop came over 10s 9s 8s, her pocket rockets were now vulnerable to both a spade flush and a straight.

If a player pushed all-in in front of her, all she had to do was disconnect from the Internet. If the flush or the straight hit, she lost only her original pre-flop bet. But if the flush or the straight missed and her aces held up, she still won the pre-flop bet.

Poker sites caught on to this kind of behavior, and for the most part, all-in protection has been eliminated from sites.

Server outage? We don't need no stinking server outage!

Our old sidebar friend two-fisted Karpov was battling it out in a single-table pot-limit Hold 'Em tournament when the situation became dire. With three players left, he had already placed in the tournament money, but he had a measly 520 in chips compared to his gorilla opponents, each sporting more than 3,000 in chips.

Karpov posted the big blind at 400 and was dealt 2h 4d. The small blind raised to 800, and Karpov, figuring it was now or never, called with his last 120.

The site exposed each player's cards, and Karpov's opponent had Jc 10c.

Flop: Ah Ad Js

Turn: Qs

River: Qh

An extremely fortunate turn of events for Karpov, because each player had two pair, aces and queens, with a jack kicker. Karpov split the pot and lived to play again.

But his situation was about to get even better.

The site didn't reconcile the betting at the end of the hand, and everything froze. Karpov checked his computer, discovering that the problem happened on the site's side. He waited and waited. The table closed and then disappeared from the site's listing.

Still in a daze, he received a mail from the site's customer support:

"Due to server outages, we've decided to split the prize money evenly between all competitors in your tournament. We apologize for any inconvenience this may cause."

One of two things may be wrong: Your computer or the site dropped its Internet connection.

To find out which is the case, quickly launch a new Web browser window and do a search for something (anything) you've never searched for before (just look across your room and type in the name of the first object you see if you have trouble thinking of something). If you can bring up information from your search, the problem belongs with your poker site, in which case you should just sit tight and wait. If the poker application quits while you wait (sites often reset if they have a wide outage), re-launch it.

If your Web search doesn't go through, the connectivity problem is on your side. Perform the following tasks in order:

1. Close out your poker application.

2. If you have a dial-up Internet connection (such as AOL), close it out and restart.

3. After you re-connect, launch your poker application. If you can't, try to avoid chewing on your arm (which doesn't help you get your slowly-blinding chip stack back).

4. Log-in to your poker site.

5. Perform the *find a player* search on yourself and go to your table if the site doesn't immediately direct you there.

Practicing Poker Patience Online

You need to be patient when playing online, just as patient as you are when playing in a brick-and-mortar environment. Remember you're going to catch long streaks of dead cards. You take your share of bad beats. Rough spots happen to every player, so the better you can ride through them, the higher you can rise above the other guy in the long run. Here are some things you can do to remain calm and learn from each online experience.

Taking a break from play

Many players find it just a little too easy to play like a demon online.

Win or lose a tournament? Doesn't matter. Click, click, and you enter into a new one. Just lost your 50th hand in a row? You can shake it off. Keep playin'. Or don't.

You (for your bank account's sake) should take stock of what happens as you play. Are you winning or losing? Do certain opponents always beat you? Can you find a consistency in the way you lose or win? Are you beginning to show repeatable, predictable behavior?

We strongly suggest that if you experience some bad luck in play, stop for a moment, take a deep breath, and answer the previous questions. What you find may give you deeper insight into your game.

Poker is like life: It goes a little better when you think before you act.

Keeping a poker journal

An excellent way to stay on top of your game and analyze the happenings in your poker world is to keep a poker journal. Obviously you want to add information that makes the most sense to you, but we suggest tracking the following:

✔ The number of players in your session

✔ Unusual plays you make that work and those that don't

✔ Mistakes you make, and how you can try to avoid them in the future

✔ The time of day you play

✔ The stakes and game you play

✔ Your wins and losses

You can set your journal up in any format you like. Microsoft Excel is good for laying out spreadsheet information, of course. If you want something more free-form that you can read from any computer, you should consider setting up a journal on a site like www. livejournal.com. Or you can do it the easy way by using www. pokercharts.com or www.pokertracker.com.

The only bit of info we don't suggest putting in your journal is commentary on specific players. Reserve those details for the player notes feature on the site, which we describe in Chapter 6.

Chapter 6

Figuring Out Your Opponents (Without Them Figuring Out You)

*T*he biggest difference between brick-and-mortar play and online play, and certainly the aspect that immediately raises the eyebrow of an experienced casino player, is not having a warm-blooded body across from you at a table, staring you down. Just how in the heck are you supposed to read tells and recognize a bluff if you can't actually see the other players?

Picking up important information is harder, for sure, but the other players do provide hints and clues (and you may too). Time to slip on your trench coat, put on your sunglasses, and follow along as we point out some tips, tricks, and gimmicks for figuring out your opponents and masking your own intentions.

Evaluating Your Online Opponents

Your ability to evaluate your online opponents can be the difference between winning and losing. Do it well and you can rake in the bucks and marvel at the greatness of your poker prowess. Do it poorly and you augment the bank account of everyone else at your table.

Although you don't have the mug of your opponent to stare down during a crucial all-in decision, you do have some tools at your disposal. Take the basics, stir in a good dose of human psychology, and you have a good start on your Poker Counter-Intelligence Camp. (One of the interesting things online play teaches you is that the physical tells of your opponents in the brick-and-mortar world aren't nearly as important as you thought they were.)

Taking notes — the online way

The raw number of opponents you play against online can be overwhelming. A popular site may have more than 10,000 players at any one time. With so many players, why even try to keep track? And for that matter, *how?*

In the online world, you need every tiny hedge you can possibly come up with against your opponents. You need to track their actions to get into their mindsets, to understand how they tick, and, ultimately, to use your knowledge against them.

One big advantage the cyber poker world has over brick-and-mortar cardrooms is that sites give you the ability to take notes on your opponents. Note-taking is awesome (to use California

---

Note-taking: Brick and mortar versus online

Successful brick-and-mortar players keep notes on their play and their opponents', but they encounter problems: Notebooks are bulky; you have another thing to keep track of while you play; you have to update your records religiously to create value; and referring to notes mid-hand is nearly impossible.

Oh yeah, and one other problem . . .

Chris was playing fixed-limit Hold 'Em in a Las Vegas casino last year when he noticed a player at his table sporting extensive notes. The guy wrote down *every* hand he had, as well as the result ("4-7 off-suit, folded, no loss"). To stay on top of things, and to ensure he didn't miss a play, he wrote down his hand as soon as he received cards.

Unfortunately, Mr. Stenographer was so engrossed in the game and his note-taking that he didn't bother to hide what he wrote. Whenever Mr. Steno stayed in a hand, all Chris had to do was look down at the guy's scribbles to figure out his hole cards. (Not that Chris would do that . . . would he?)

You don't encounter these problems in the online world, of course . . . unless you're *really* sloppy with copy and paste.

Ways you can lose your notes

Although you keep your notes from poker session to poker session, you may encounter two situations on sub-par sites where you can lose the notes you so studiously prepare:

✔ **If your computer crashes, or your poker site freezes and forces you to restart the application.** When this happens, you lose all notes you have made for that particular session, but the rest of the notes you've made in earlier sessions are held intact. Losing your notes is especially irritating when you've been playing in an extremely long tournament.

✔ **If you have to re-install your poker software.** Lame sites hold the notes you take on your opponents local to your computer. That means if something happens to the poker application on your machine (say it becomes corrupt) and you re-install, you lose all your notes. Try to avoid latching on to this type of site at all costs. Your player notes are valuable, and they take a fair amount of time and work to establish and maintain. You don't want to hand away all that hard work to a sub-par site. (To check out a listing of popular sites, head to Chapter 2.)

surfer-speak) because you can easily log information on every online opponent you ever run across. By taking notes, you can track an opponent's play, and even if you don't run up against him for six months, the next time you do you can quickly call up exactly what you said about him.

Your opponents don't know you made notes about them, and you can refer to your insights at any time during play without disrupting the game. Super-great, right?

Be careful: Your opponents can track information about you as well. Always try to mix up your play and avoid creating patterns.

You normally get to the notes feature by right-clicking on an opponent and entering text. (If not, take some time to glean the site while you play with free chips until you can find the note-taking mechanism.) After you enter a note, most sites give some indication on the name placard, like a small I or N or something similar. Notes persist from one session to the next, and over time your notes accumulate.

Sites that allow you to see all the notes you take, in their entirety, are extremely rare. Typically, to view the notes on any given player, that person has to actually sit at your table.

Developing a shorthand notation

Due to Internet poker's speedy nature, note-taking almost always takes place under a fairly rigid time constraint. Sites quickly snap your hands away from your view, and on some sites you can only make a note on a player in a game — if he busts out and leaves the table, your chance to comment on him disappears as well. For this reason, you should develop your own shorthand notation — a few quick letters you can jot down to note a situation (*sb* for small blind, *ai* for all-in, and so on; see Chapter 3 for a table showing common abbreviations). Whatever notation you pick, be consistent.

Keep a note attached to your computer (or in an open window you can easily access) that holds a glossary of your note-taking abbreviations. This way you ensure consistency, and you don't accidentally mistake *B* for *bluff* when it actually means *blind*.

Scouring the details for great notes

As you take notes, you should be mindful of several specific details in your records of other players. We approach this problem in different ways.

Red likes to keep track of details from individual hands he finds interesting, such as the types of hands people play in certain positions and the types of hands his opponents tend to bet heavily.

As with everything in his life, Chris takes a slightly more analytical approach. He almost never takes notes on a specific hand, because it means having to go in and re-interpret individual hand actions. He instead comes to general conclusions about a player. His conclusions often include advice: "Against this player call on the flop and bet out if an ace hits the board," or "This player only plays three suited cards, three cards of a straight, or a pair as starting cards in Seven-Card Stud."

And don't forget, if you make an unusual play or a mistake against an opponent (a bluff that doesn't work, for example), you should make a note of that, too. Your short-term loss may turn into long-term gain, because your opponent thinks your level or style of play is different than it actually is and you can use that thought process to your advantage.

By their very definition, notes are highly individual and tailored specifically to your tastes. Have a look at the next section and start thinking about the kinds of details you want to track.

Gathering info about your opponents

Although you don't know several things about your online opponents, using the available information that you have can give you an edge.

Where are they playing?

Know the location of the other players. You can usually discover this information by hovering your cursor over their name placards. Doing this lets you determine, amongst other things, their time zones. Most likely you would rather face someone playing at 3:00 a.m. on a Thursday than someone playing at 4:00 on a Saturday afternoon. The sleepy and inattentive are always easier to beat than the sharp and focused.

What other games are they playing?

Many sites support a *find a player* feature from their home screen menus. With this feature, you can discover if your opponent plays multiple tables and use it to your advantage. If your opponent is playing you and is also at the final table of a multi-hour tournament, you can bet he isn't devoting his complete attention to your game.

Pinpointing personality types

It may seem hard to believe, but online poker players are actually just people, too. And, for the most part, non-elite players are creatures of habit; they repeat the same kinds of actions in the same positions. If you can figure out how people behave in any given situation, you can beat them. Consistently.

Check out the traits to keep track of:

- **Noticeable changes in personality.** If someone has been quiet and then starts talking at the table, think about the potential culprits. Is it because he's winning or losing? Or does it have something to do with the hand? If a player becomes a Chatty Cathy every time he has a great hand, or whenever he bluffs at a hand, you have your clue.

- **Reactions to winning and losing.** If losers go on-tilt and start spewing money, you may be able to help ease their chip burden. Likewise, if a winner gets tight-fisted and backs off on his betting with anything but the best of hands, you can make him drop a little of his spare change to your lesser-handed bluffs.

Whatever you do, after you figure out a player, don't tell him what you know. We've seen countless people say things like, "You know, Timmy, you always raise pre-flop with nothing." Or at least he did until somebody said something.

Keeping track of poker styles

You don't have to keep track of every single play at your table, so don't get carried away with your notes. You are, after all, a poker player first and a private detective second, so you should focus the vast majority of your efforts on playing the game. However, you do want to get in the habit of keeping your unblinking surveillance eye on unusual plays and unusual players.

Tracking playing and betting styles

As your tournament gets going or as you play a few orbits during a ring game, you should watch for patterns your opponents start to display. You can exploit patterns if you discover them. Here are a few areas to keep an eye on:

- **The tightness of their play.** A tight player only plays the absolute best cards in the absolute best positions. A loose player plays anything anywhere. Knowing this characteristic helps you plan your moves against opponents: Tight play against the loose players helps you take their foolishly cast bets; aggressive play against tight opponents can cause them to drop winning hands.

- **The aggressiveness of their betting.** Some people come at you with their chips like a rabid junkyard dog on nothing but junky hands, and others hang back and merely call when they hold the nuts. Aggression directed back at bold players often demands respect, causing the aggressor to back down. And knowing a passive player only stays in with the best of hands can save you a few bets.

- **The amount they bluff.** Heavy bluffers need to be called (and raised) more often. You should generally believe and carefully watch players who haven't been caught bluffing.

- **Their betting position style.** Some people *always* make an opening bet of the pot size (especially on sites that have a "bet the pot" button) in the first betting position. If you see this happening repeatedly, make a note of it and assume that the player's opening bet is nothing more than random noise. Obviously, you want to avoid folding good hands that have a good chance of winning. (In fact, you may want to sporadically raise these aggressors back when they launch those big first bets to see how they react. Make a note of their reaction.)

✔ **Their sneaky tendencies.** Players who get too caught up in the notion of fooling their opponents can become predictable by too frequently representing strong hands as weak and vice versa. You should avoid betting your marginal hands into someone slowplaying a great hand, and you can sometimes call an apparently strong bet when you think you have a sneaky player's weak hand beat.

✔ **Their reaction to raises.** If a player drops anything but the best hand every time he's raised, use this to your advantage by betting on weaker hands to take down a pot or by folding hands he stays in on. Likewise, if a player in early position bets, you raise, and then he does nothing more than check-and-call from that point on, take your cue to bet if you have a strong hand (to maximize your return), but check if you have something lesser.

Observing pauses

You can't catch the body language tells of your opponents over the Net, but your opponents may interact with your site's software in telling ways.

As you read the following samples about pauses, think about the underlying psychology of what they represent and start building a list of things to watch for.

Make sure when you observe these behaviors that you judge them against the player's recent activity. If someone pauses before most actions, he may be playing at multiple tables at the same time or just doing something else on his computer while he gets his poker fix. In fact, if a slow opponent starts acting quickly, it may be because he has picked up a real hand and put aside the spreadsheet for the moment. Dramatic changes in behavior make great online clues.

Pausing post-flop

Whenever you play Hold 'Em or Omaha against someone who always acts quickly (either checking or betting) in the first betting position post-flop, be very careful if you see her pause, especially if she pauses and then checks. When most players flop a big hand, their natural tendency is to stop, read it over to make sure they see it correctly (possibly with a little internal gloating as well), and then act. The reason you see this happen more often in first position is because you don't have ample time to react in the first position. In other spots people have time to evaluate or use advance action buttons.

Unless your nemesis has gone to get some ice cream out of the freezer, an unusual pause is highly suspect.

Pausing on large calls

A large-call pauser is even scarier for you than an opponent who pauses post-flop. If you have an opponent who pauses until his action timer is almost out, and then he does it *again* in the same hand, you can bet 99 times out of 100 that his hand can clobber any callers. What he wants to do is make it look like he has to make a difficult call, when, in fact, he has an extremely strong hand.

Players who pause and truly struggle with a betting decision nearly always fold.

Watching hand and position types

Some players only play certain hands, and they play them a certain way. Others develop positional patterns, only playing certain hands from certain positions.

If you combine all the hands together and compile enough raw data on your opponents, you can amass great power and wisdom, rivaling the greatest of wizards. After you gather plenty of data, you can (and should) draw conclusions about your opponents' play and then create counter-strategies that beat these players at their own game.

Watch for the following trends and watch your account balance start to rise:

✔ The types of starting hands they play:

- In Hold 'Em, especially on the lower-limit tables, keep an eye out for people who play any two suited cards and/or any two connectors. These players tend to chase hands, so you should heavily punish them for it in no-limit. You also don't want to fall victim to the chasers when their three suited cards or straight-makers do hit the board.

- In Omaha, keep an eye on players who become overly obsessed with starting pairs, being sure to note how they bet if they hit trips. In High/Low, watch for players who always raise holding A-2. Your notes may become reliable enough that after time, these raisers may as well show you their hands. And some people play, literally, any starting hand in Omaha — what you have to watch out with these action junkies is how they bet their cards post-flop.

- In Seven-Card Stud, you don't get to see other players' hands very often because of frequent folding, so keep a close eye on what they consider to be good starting hands and try to remember their betting patterns as hands mature. (For more info on these particular games, flip to Chapter 7.)

✔ **The likelihood of a player calling relative to the number of players in a pot (and regardless of the starting hand).** If someone always calls from last position, regardless of the hand quality, you may want to drop your junky hand in the next-to-last betting position, because you know you have a player calling behind you. If a player only plays strong cards from the last position and they call behind you, you know you have something to watch out for.

✔ **The types of hands people play relative to their betting position.** In general, you should only play better cards in earlier betting positions and let your guard down with weaker hands in later positions (because in earlier positions, you don't know how many callers you may have). If you see players bucking this trend — especially if they play weaker cards in earlier positions, note it and always consider raising behind them before any more cards are exposed. Weak hands should have to pay a premium to see cards.

If you play the same player, or players, for an extended period of time, you should take a look at your hand histories (you can usually find this function on your site's home screen). Hand histories show everything an observer sitting at the table would see (bets, chat, and cards shown), including the cards you had every hand. Going over these histories can give you subtle hints about the way your opponents play.

Keeping Your Opponents from Figuring You Out

As you try to figure out what your opponents have, how do you hide what you have? Very few people lose money by assuming their opponents are overly smart; that can't be said for players who think their enemies are remarkably dull. And even if you don't take every word in this chapter to heart, make sure that you still mix up your style so others consider you un-trackable in the poker jungle.

When you start to think about how your actions create an image in your opponents' minds, you can easily fall into the trap of always acting the opposite way. You know that people tend to pause before checking when the flop hits their hand, so you always check quickly in those situations.

Don't let yourself form habits. Your opponents can start identifying your pattern before too long, and then you're fixed to be cooked.

Smarter opponents can always figure out the predictable players at a table, so stay with any one behavior only long enough for your opponents to think they have you nailed and then move to another behavior.

Disguising your online hands

The key to disguising your hand online is to remember what the screen forces your opponents to watch. Because they can't see your face, other players focus almost exclusively on your bet sizes and your timing delays in making those bets. So to disguise your hand you have to not allow your bet sizes be indicative of the hand you hold.

Keeping them guessing

If anything, you want to be wrongly predictable. You want opponents to think you have a strong hand when you're weak and a weak hand when you're strong. You want your enemy to stay in and play when you have him beaten and fold when he has you beaten. The majority (but not all, for obvious bluffing reasons) of your betting needs to indicate strength, and you need to be sincere about it. If you show strength, it makes opponents take you more seriously and drop hands more often.

If you can't produce this scenario, you want the next best thing: being unpredictable. Your want your opponent to mutter, "I have no idea what that person has."

As a general rule, if you have a good starting hand, you shouldn't let the blinds see cards for free. Make sure to get a raise on the table as a "card tax." If you hold A-A pre-flop and don't raise, and the guy holding 5-7 off-suit gets to see the flop come 4 6 8, you can't blame anyone but yourself.

Leveling out your raises

We should also point out another form of hand camouflage in no-limit and pot-limit games: utilizing one raise-size amount (say four times the big blind) — especially pre-flop. No matter what you have, if you think you should raise, always raise the same amount. By taking away variation in your raise sizes, you give your opponent one less criterion to judge your hand by. Your opponents know your hand is good if you show them good hands a couple of times, but they don't know how good.

The alternative — randomly choosing how much to raise — creates too much possible variance in your chip stack. Crazy bet sizes are okay when you win, but if you lose a couple of disproportionally large hands, you can't play aggressively any more. Random raises may sound good in theory, but the practice is potentially damaging.

You may be tempted to conceal the strength of a hand in Omaha or Hold 'Em by never raising pre-flop or in Stud by checking after each card. On the surface, not raising seems like it may give you the kind of cover you want. Unfortunately, it also lets opponents (especially those in the blinds) play cards they should otherwise fold. The lucky flops they catch slowly (or quickly, depending on how ugly the hand becomes) can bake you to a delicate crunch.

Varying your speed of play

One way to throw your opponents off is to vary your speed of play. Sometimes play fast. Sometimes play slow. Sometimes use advance action buttons. Sometimes don't. Changing up your speed works if

---

Becoming Johnny Random

Random speed playing skills are sitting, literally, in front of your face. If you want to vary the pace of your play to disguise your hand strength and intentions, you can base it on the cards you're dealt. Consider wacky strategies along these lines:

- ✔ If the cards you're dealt are red, play slow; if black, play fast.

- ✔ If your first card is 8 or higher, play slow; if lower, play fast.

- ✔ Play fast until you see the seven of hearts and then switch to playing slow until you see it again.

You may want to bias toward faster play, because you face times when you want to consider your play, and you automatically need to play a bit slower. Just don't slow down every time you need to make a big decision, or continue your slow play for a while after you slow down once.

You get the idea. But don't get so caught up in being Johnny Random that you forget to keep track of the poker game.

The "pause fold"

An interesting device you can use to help mislead your opponents is pausing before you fold. Consider two cases:

- A player makes a bet in front of you, and you know you want to fold.

- You make a bet as a bluff or semi-bluff (if you have a decent hand with a chance to improve but not the nuts), and your opponent raises. You now want to fold.

In both scenarios, you may want to consider giving a long pause before you fold. In the first case, pausing makes your opponent think that you may call, and if he's bluffing, your pause may make him think twice about doing so in the future (he thinks he dodged a bullet the first time). In the second situation, pausing makes your hand look much better than it is, and it makes your opponent wonder why you're pausing.

Pausing before folding, surprisingly often, entices your opponent to show his cards to you, a case of "See? I really *did* have a hand." And his need to establish dominance gives you another nugget of gold for your intelligence bank: specifically knowing what your opponent played, in what specific game position, and how. The next time a similar situation comes along, you have a history to look back on for guidance.

you have opponents who try to track your style of play. Some players in the online world always use advance action buttons, unless they have a difficult decision to make. Don't be this type of player.

Acting quickly when you're the best

When you think you have the nut hand (one that can't be beat), particularly if you're playing at a table with aggressive players, try checking nearly immediately (especially if you're the first to act). A player's natural tendency is to pause and then check on a strong hand. If you can check quickly, you eliminate this clue. But, as always, don't make it a habit.

Using advance action buttons

If your poker goal is to be unpredictable, and it should be, you need to use the advance action buttons — but not religiously. You should use them regularly, however, because you don't want to look like a person who never uses advance action buttons (which constitutes a trend). By using them in different situations and at different times, you have yet another trick to keep your opponents guessing.

Establishing a table image online

No matter how humble or cocky you think you are, you always have a table image, whether you create one consciously or unintentionally. And you build your image differently online than you do offline. For one, your online table image is much harder to separate from your actual betting actions, because very little else about you comes across on your opponent's computer screen. Second, the sheer number and fluidity (how they come and go) of online players (at least until you get to the higher stakes, where not as many people play) means you have to reconstruct your table image from scratch every single session.

Your opponents use your image to evaluate you, and because of this, you should manipulate it on your behalf. The image you project often works best as a tall tale — loosely based on what you are as a player but somehow distorted to make it not so precisely (nor correctly) discernable.

If you can project a table image that doesn't reflect your style of play, other players ultimately make wrong assumptions about you, and you can capitalize on their errors.

Just like the guy who is seven feet tall but tries to act like he's a dwarf, you may have difficulty consistently acting the opposite of your natural character. Eventually you bump your head. If you're a conservative, serious player, you may find it hard to maintain a wild table image. If you're an adventurous player, you may not be able to represent a super-tight image for very long. You're better off choosing a table image that you can easily sustain.

Using advance action buttons to project your image

If you fold a series of times by using the advance action buttons, players get used to the timing of the fold as betting goes over your position at the table. For everyone at the table, your contribution becomes rote: When your turn to act comes in the rotation, the site gives the typical pause caused by the action button use, you fold, and then the game moves along.

If, at some point, you pause and then raise, everyone at the table thinks twice before calling you. The action is so different from what you've done in the previous several hands that the other players immediately notice it both consciously and subconsciously. You're likely to see many, if not most, opponents fold.

Hold on tight: Projecting a tight image

You're playing fixed-limit Hold 'Em from the big blind. The other players allow you to see the flop with no raise. Five of the ten players, including the small blind, are in the hand. You have 2c 6d.

The flop comes over 10s Jh 5s.

The small blind checks, and you immediately fold. Yes, you can check for free here, but the odds of you winning the hand are extremely low. You have to pair your hold cards (and hope your opponents don't hold a larger pair) or double-draw the straight, which probably won't happen.

Folding actually buys you much more in the eyes of your opponents, because the sharp-eyed take notice and become much more aware the next time you check or bet from the same position. By folding here now, you make other hands in this position appear stronger in the future. And the next time you get a garbage hand and flop in this position, you can bet or raise and possibly take the pot right there.

Micro-limit games (which we discuss in Chapter 5) are a good place to "try on" different table images. They provide a cheap way to explore a few different personas and parade them in front of a test audience. Does a serious image fit your style of play best, or are you more comfortable (and profitable) being the talkative buddy? You can use micro-limit games as a forum to fine-tune your image, even after (and maybe especially after) you move on to higher stakes.

Creating a tight table image

We enjoy the most success by establishing a tight table image (especially in tournaments, where you can't wait forever for perfect cards; you need to be able to bluff), because it makes your opponents more likely to fold when you bluff. And by tight, we mean that you should want people to think you squeak when you get up for a glass of water.

You can help foster this image in the online world with advance action buttons.

Ultimately, you create a tight table image with actions that show you to be a very conservative player, only willing to be aggressive with strong hands and ready to fold quickly when the odds are not in your favor. The more obvious the actions, the better. (Of course, you're just displaying your *image;* after you establish it, not all your subsequent play should conform to this facade, or else you become predictable.)

Playing with a loose image

If you're a bit of a loose player, you can play and win at the loose end of the spectrum, of course, by choosing to present an even looser and wilder image to your tablemates. It doesn't take too many hands to convince people that you're a maniac. After you do, the nervous players tend to stay out of your way (even with significant hands), and others tend to call you more often, frequently with very weak hands. If you can create a loose image and then shift gears to play more solidly than your image suggests, you can get more money out of your good hands because people (incorrectly) assume you're a lunatic.

How do you look like a maniac at the online poker table? It boils down to betting and calling when you really shouldn't and then letting your opponents know about it, which usually means exposing your cards. The best scenario is to make a bet with complete garbage and then catch a miracle card to win the hand, but it also works if you miss. When your opponents see your hand, they begin to think you're crazy (and may take one step closer to insanity themselves).

One side effect of giving people a loose table image of yourself is that you take bad beats more often (especially in a no-limit or pot-limit tournament setting, because one hand can cost you all your chips). The crazier opponents think you are, the more opponents you have to deal with every hand you stay in.

Duping opponents with loose play in Hold 'Em

You're the small blind in a fixed-limit Hold 'Em game. You receive 5s 7h as your hole cards. Eight people stay in the hand, and you make the half-bet needed to call pre-flop.

The flop comes Kd 9s 8s. You have an inside straight draw and decide to check. Everyone behind you checks as well.

The turn is the 4c. Everyone checks.

The river is the Ad. You check. A player makes a bet, and everyone folds to you. Calling here is insanity. All the opponent needs is one card larger than an 8 or a pocket pair of any size and you lose. However, for just one large bet, you can call and then show your hand. You don't make a play at the pot by raising or some other strategic move the table could understand. After the others see your hand, they automatically think "fool" (and maybe think it forever if they make a player note about you). You can easily get that bet back many times over in the future. Your opponents continue saying something like, "Oh that idiot is in. No problem."

Falling victim to your Omaha insanity

You're in the middle of a pot-limit Omaha tourney, in later stages with the blinds fairly high. You watch as the As Ac Jh 6h flash in front of you. Three opponents call your bet.

The flop comes Ad Kh 3c. Jackpot. You now have trip aces, and because you gave people the impression that you're crazy earlier in the game, you actually get a caller when you bet the pot (which amounts to an all-in bet).

Sure enough, Debbie Doubt with 9d Qd 10s 9c thinks you're bluffing and trying to buy the pot. She calls you with her pair of nines and a straight draw and is now all-in as well. Everyone else folded to watch the drama.

Debbie is kicking herself while you do a jig around your computer desk. The turn is the 9h. Debbie now has three nines but still trails you. She lightens up, and you stop to watch the screen.

The river is the Jc, and Debbie's straight beats your trips. All because she believed you had nothing before.

Keep in mind that a loose table image encourages more volatility, because people are more likely to bet heavily against you and call more often. Expect wild swings if you portray a loose image. If you can't deal with that, you may want to portray a tighter, less call-inducing image.

Even the loosest players tighten up as tournament limits increase. Be careful not to categorize someone as a loose or bad player if he continues to survive in the tourney, and especially if you see him start to slow down his wackiness.

Showing your cards to establish an image

We show our cards much more on the Net than we do in a brick-and-mortar establishment (which is to say a few times in one sitting as opposed to almost never in the physical world) — especially in tournaments — because it helps to cement a particular image we try to project at the table. Clicking over the cards is a good way to use your opponents' sensory depravation to your advantage.

If you want to establish a tight image, you should show your cards when you have a very strong hand, especially if you've only played a hand or two. You let the other players know that, yes, you do play hands of quality, and yes, you do bet them (or not).

You can also show your cards after a bluff to promote a loose image, of course. If people think you're a loose player, they call you more often in the future, even if they don't have great hands. If you do show a hand, you should expect to see more callers on any pot that you're part of in the future (especially if you lead the betting) — not necessarily a bad thing, because if you tighten your play after you show a bluff, you may notice the average pot size start to increase when you're in a pot, giving you all the more money to win in the future.

After you show a very strong hand, don't do it again. You want people to keep a tiny bit of doubt over exactly what you're playing.

Bolstering your image through chat

You shouldn't ignore that little chat box on your screen. You can use it to help your table image as well. Whatever you want to portray, a few lines of text can help drive home the point. The laughing, joking guy, the disinterested sports watcher, the whiney loser, the dumb student, or the lonely bachelorette. You can be any of these characters. (Chapter 3 has the details on how to use the chat feature.)

Strike up a conversation about any recent sporting event and make a comment about a famous player if someone rises to the bait. Even if you know nothing about the game or sport, you can always do a Web search for "best catcher 2005" and make some bone-headed comment, like "How about that Martinez?" It doesn't matter that you don't know anything; in fact, it may be good to blather on a bit about things you know nothing about. If the other players think you're an idiot, they may treat you that way and ignore you as any danger on the card table.

Card-revealing strategies

You're dealt A-A in the first betting position in a no-limit Hold 'Em tourney. You make a raise of three times the big blind, and all players fold. You show your hand to indicate you had the pocket rockets.

On the looser side of the coin, you can bet the same amount from the first position with a hand such as 2-6 off-suit. After all players fold, flip over your garbage for the whole table to smell. Now you can elect to play great hands while the rest of the table still has your garbage hangover and take down pots of greater size (assuming you avoid the bad beats).

Misdirecting opinions with chat

You're playing Seven-Card Stud, and your hole cards are the 5d and 5s with 5c 4c 6s 9h showing. You have two opponents left: one showing four clubs, and the other showing two-pair.

Your river card is the disappointing Jh, and you fold.

One opponent asks what you have. You can say that you missed your straight draw. The clubbed opponent likely has a flush already, which makes it look as though you were drawing to a dead hand when in reality you were drawing for the full house. This assertion may make your opponents think you're on a draw again the next time you hit a big hand.

You can also add a level of misdirection about your card play here. If someone asks what you had in a hand, you can answer in any way that seems fitting — truthful or otherwise. When you fold a hand, you can tell people what you laid down (because you don't have a way to show a hand you fold online) — again, truthful or otherwise.

Which way you go is entirely up to you, but keep in mind the table image you want to project. Loose or tight. Liar or truth-telling scout. Whatever you find fun and useful.

The one technique we don't recommend is aggravating your opponents. Although you can undoubtedly set someone on fire if you want to, it doesn't serve you well in the long run. Imagine yourself as a store clerk at a table where you're the best player. The others at the table are your customers. Only by treating them well will they come back time and time again and bring you more money. Besides, you don't ever want to get in a position where you show up on your site's support staff as a troublemaker — if you manage to get your chat privileges revoked, you have one less possible weapon in your arsenal.

Chapter 7

Exploring Your Online Game Options

In This Chapter

▶ Coming and going with ring games

▶ Spicing up your gaming experience

▶ Checking into tournaments

The online poker world is a wild and wooly place. Large sites can have more than 10,000 people playing at any one time. (Can you imagine walking into a brick-and-mortar room of that size? You could *never* find a cocktail waitress.) Because of the high-traffic of online play, you can find almost any kind of game you want at nearly any table or stake size: limit or no limit; Hold 'Em, Omaha, or Seven-Card Stud; and tournaments or ring games. We explore the staggering array of options in this chapter.

 Regardless of your skill level and game of choice, the first time you play a new site (and especially the first time you play on the Internet) you should play with free chips to get used to that site's interface nuances. (Check out Chapter 3 to become familiar with general Internet nuances and Chapter 8 for tips on where you can play to practice.) Graduate to playing at very low limits before you move to playing higher limits. If you're in for any nasty surprises, you don't want them arriving when the big money hits the virtual table. The sidebar "Deciding what to play" later in this chapter gives advice on how to move up in the limits you play.

Melding in Ring Games

Ring games (the fancy term for a poker game where you can buy in and cash out as you please) are the most popular games on the Internet. Betting typically comes in three forms: *no-limit,* where you can bet any amount at any time; *pot-limit,* where you can bet any amount up to the size of the current pot at any time; and *fixed-limit* (sometimes referred to solely as *limit*), where you bet in specific, pre-determined amounts.

With the no-limit and pot-limit games, if you're unclear about the buy-in and limits from looking at the home page, go to any table and try to sit in an open seat — the site gives you very explicit details of limits and buy-ins from the chip purchase dialog (and you can always cancel if the requirements are too rich for your blood).

If you frequent a particular site, regardless of the game you play, keep an eye on any regular who always seems to win — especially if she always wins and then leaves. What you've encountered here is a certain sub-species of Internet poker shark who plays at limits lower than her skill level dictates, merely to pad her account balance or to win the entry fee for higher-level games. You may feel a temptation to stay in the game and swim with the shark, but in the long run your bankroll is safer if you move to another table. (Flip back to Chapter 6 to get a head start on reading your opponents.)

Hankering for Hold 'Em

Texas Hold 'Em overtook Five-Card Draw as the serious poker player's game of choice in the middle of the 20th century. The takeover was so complete that the player who wins the $10,000 buy-in no-limit Hold 'Em event at the World Series of Poker in Las Vegas automatically attains "World Poker Champion" status. No questions asked.

An example Hold 'Em hand

You receive Ah 10h as your hole cards. The round of betting ensues.

The flop appears on the center of the table Ad 2d Jc. You go through the second round of betting. (You have a pair of aces and bet on it.)

The turn is the Kd. You bet with your pair of aces and straight draw.

The river is the Qd. You decide to keep betting your hand.

The good news is that you have an A-10 straight (known in poker slang as *Broadway*); the bad news is that any player still in who holds even one diamond beats you with a flush.

Hold 'Em has such a stranglehold on the brick-and-mortar world, you can barely tell other variations of poker even exist. And the online world is no different. Hold 'Em easily outstrips all other games that you can play online.

The game dynamic in any environment is simple. All players are dealt two hole cards and take a round of betting. Three community cards are dealt face up (the *flop*), followed by another round of betting. A fourth community card is dealt (the *turn;* more rarely called *fourth street*), and the remaining players bet again. A final community card is dealt (known as the *river, fifth street,* or when Lady Luck flips you the bird, your favorite string of expletives), and the final round of betting ensues. The player with the best five-card hand takes the pot — you can use zero, one, or both of your hole cards to make your hand.

Hold 'Em is extremely well suited for computer play, adding to its popularity and domination of the Internet. Dealing happens automatically with no delay for shuffling, and because your visual focus falls almost exclusively on the community section at the center of the table, even the little chicklet versions of the playing cards aren't too troubling.

In sheer number of players, Hold 'Em games outnumber all other forms of Internet poker combined roughly 6 to 1. That doesn't mean you can't play other games, but it does mean that you find the most competition, the largest spread of limits, the widest tournament variety, and the greatest selection in table size if you play Hold 'Em.

Hold 'Em games also stage the most promotional events. The vast majority of advertisements you see, ranging from "Win a seat in the World Series!" to (we swear we're not making this up) "Play poker with supermodels," involve Hold 'Em games. (For more on Internet promotions, have a gander at Chapter 2.)

The overall skill level of an Internet Hold 'Em player is widely variable, but roughly speaking the situation is exactly what you may expect: The higher the table limit, the better the competition.

Most Hold 'Em tournaments (especially large multi-table tourneys) are no-limit. Ring games tend to be roughly split between fixed-limit and no-limit. The biggest moneyed ring games are usually fixed-limit (say, $100/$200), although you can find a few monster no-limit games out there ($25/$50, with some player's stacks as big as $50,000).

Sampling Omaha

The playing mechanics of Omaha are identical to those of Texas Hold 'Em (see the previous section for Hold 'Em info), with two big exceptions: You receive four hole cards rather than two, and when determining your best five-card hand you must use exactly two of your hole cards combined with exactly three of the five community cards.

Until you warm up to this dynamic (especially if you've resided under the polluting influence of Hold 'Em for years on end), playing Omaha can be mind-bending. When you first start playing the game (or if you're tired), you can easily misread a hand. Some poker sites have coaching text that tells you the best value your hand can represent at any given moment ("You have two pair, aces and eights," for example). If you play on a site that evaluates your hand on the fly, keep an eye on what the computer knows you have versus what you think you have or have a chance of making.

Omaha just squeaks over Seven-Card Stud as being the second most popular card game on the Net, but Hold 'Em is so overwhelming in popularity that many sites may have only a table or two where you can play Omaha (especially in the wee hours of the morning when the poker crowd thins out).

You can play Omaha in two versions: standard Omaha (sometimes referred to as Omaha High) and Omaha High/Low, which is a split-pot game where both the high and low hands reap equal shares of the pot. You generally play Omaha, in all forms, with pot-limit or

What happened to no-limit Omaha?

Omaha is unusual in that the common "big betting" format is pot-limit rather than no-limit.

According to poker writer Bob Ciaffone, Omaha was introduced in Las Vegas as a no-limit game in the early 1980s. But a problem quickly arose with this type of play. During the course of a hand, anyone who hit the best hand (the *nuts*) automatically pushed all-in, thereby shutting out any future betting (and the myriad of draws Omaha lends itself to) from all but the truly crazed who didn't mind risking all their money on a draw. No-limit killed all the betting action — fast.

Partially at the behest of the players to help spice up the pots, casinos switched Omaha to a pot-limit game (just days after its introduction). Sure enough, the table action increased. Casinos, and now Web sites, have offered it as a pot-limit game ever since.

Decision time: Omaha high

You receive Ah Kd 10s 10h as your hole cards. You bet during the first round.

The flop comes 7s 7c Jd. At this point you have two pair: sevens and tens, with a jack kicker. (Remember, you must use exactly two of your hole cards.) You decide to check and call a bet.

The turn is the Jh. You still have two pair: tens and jacks with a seven kicker. You're worried about another player having trips or a J-7 making a full house. You call a moderate bet.

The river is the 10d. You now have a full house: tens full of jacks. Anyone who holds J-7, J-10, 7-7, or J-J as hole cards beats you, but you have a pretty good hand. Decision time! (Check out Chapter 6 for info on reading your opponents.)

---

fixed-limit betting. No-limit is an Omaha rarity. (Refer to the sidebar in this section for related info.)

Omaha High

In the standard version of Omaha, the best (highest) hand takes the entire pot. Sites offer Omaha almost exclusively as a pot-limit game, and to us it seems to be the hardest game to beat on the Internet.

As a gross generalization (but still an essentially true generalization), Omaha players tend to be very skilled and very dedicated. Compared to Hold 'Em, experts haven't written nearly as much about Omaha. As a result you tend to see more experienced players in the game, while the truly bad players stay away.

Pot-limit Omaha is the most popular game in Europe, and it also enjoys extreme popularity in the southern United States. The pot-limit version is a gambler's game in a big way — you see a huge variance in the hands compared to Hold 'Em, and it seems as though pretty much any hand has a shot pre-flop. The skill in this game, for sure, is knowing when to run away and knowing when to stand and fire.

If you decide to start playing Omaha online and you haven't played it before, you need to read some of the rare theory books to have a fighting chance. (As we discuss in Chapter 8, you can play for free, but the crazy play that occurs when you play for free makes this a bad way to learn.) Pick up *Poker For Dummies* (Wiley) and nail down basic strategy there. After you get a feel for the game, start on the lowest limit you can find. If you don't, expect your learning tuition to be pricey.

Omaha High/Low

Easy now Tex: You can't automatically count on your three Cowboys taking down this pot. In the High/Low version of Omaha, the high hand splits the pot with the low hand if, and only if, the low hand contains no pairs and no cards higher than an 8 (with aces counting as 1). Straights and flushes don't matter for the low hand. If no low hand is possible, the high hand scoops the entire pot. In High/Low, you can use different cards for your high hand and for your low hand. In both cases, you must use exactly two cards from your hand and three cards from the board to determine your high and low hands. You find roughly the same number of players in both the pot-limit and fixed-limit forms of this game, based on nothing more than personal preference.

Omaha High/Low, certainly at the low limits, is a great game to cut your teeth on, especially if you need a break from Hold 'Em. The split pots mean that you can enjoy the fun of seeing the site rake chips to your side of the table about twice as often. (The increased action can, however, be a little psychologically dangerous, because you can get used to the new scooping rhythm of Omaha and end up staying in too many pots when you go back to Hold 'Em.)

Pure Omaha players tend to look down their noses at High/Low players, because they consider it a less skillful game. Don't go

---

An Omaha High/Low winner — squared

You receive As 3c Js Jd for your hole cards, a good starting hand with both high and low possibilities.

The flop comes over 4s 7d Jc. You now have three jacks for the best high hand currently possible. Your A-3 gives you a shot at the second lowest possible hand if another card 8 or less that doesn't pair the A, 3, 4, or 7 shows up on the board.

The turn is the 2s. You now have the lowest possible hand at the moment (A 2 3 4 7), the highest possible hand, and a shot at the nut flush draw. Not a bad situation.

The river is the 3s. An odd draw. You no longer have the nut low hand (A-5 beats you with a *wheel,* ace through five). You now have an Ace-high flush, and only someone holding the 5s 6s can beat you with a straight-flush. If no player has a wheel or the straight-flush, you play your A-3 for your low hand and the A-J for the high hand, taking the whole pot.

Slow and steady Seven-Card Stud

In a brick-and-mortar environment, Seven-Card Stud is the slowest game in the house; the physical mechanics of pushing a ton of cards around on the table and the perpetual delay of slowpokes who wait to toss in their antes at the start of each hand can slow play to a snail's pace.

Online, however, the feeling is a bit more disconcerting and herky-jerky. With Stud, some of the action comes faster (like the general dealing mechanics), but other actions (like players evaluating their hands) are nearly the same. Because of this, to us at least, Stud never feels quite right.

Obviously this is a matter of personal preference. If you're a big fan of Stud in the brick-and-mortar world, you should give it a whirl in cyberspace and see what you think. People who play Stud exclusively in the brick-and-mortar world usually love it online, but players who simply want to play a variety of games on their computer may not be as thrilled.

---

bragging about playing High/Low to any of your high-end, super card-playing friends without expecting to get a little harassment.

If you see a game labeled solely as Omaha, always expect it to be Omaha High. Make sure before you evaluate betting on a possible low hand that you're playing at a High/Low table. If you don't and you're playing Omaha High, you end up betting on a losing hand.

Serving up Seven-Card Stud

Seven-Card Stud is probably the best-known poker game to people who have wandered no farther than their kitchen table to play cards. Every player is dealt two hole cards and an up card, which is followed by a round of betting. The remaining players get another up card (referred to as *fourth street*), followed by a round of betting. Another up card is dealt (*fifth street*), and everyone bets. Yet another up card is dealt (*sixth street*), and everyone bets again. Players who haven't folded by this point receive a final card face down (a third hole card — referred to as either *seventh street* or, as with the last card in Hold 'Em, the *river*), and the final betting round follows. To recap: All players still in on the river have three cards down and four cards up. The best five-card hand takes the pot.

Like Omaha (see the previous section), you can play Seven-Card Stud in two forms: standard and high/low. And, again as with Omaha, you can expect to find significantly fewer active games to join on the Internet compared to the number of Hold 'Em games because it simply isn't as popular with today's poker generation.

Aesthetically, Stud often doesn't translate as well to the computer screen as Omaha and Hold 'Em do, primarily because you have to look at many more cards spread around the screen instead of seeing them grouped in one community playing area. Sites that use smaller card images can really make you squint.

If you play online Stud, be sure to put your screen in a nice glare-free spot — you don't want to experience the aftertaste of not seeing an opponent's four aces showing because of a bad reflection.

You play online Stud almost exclusively with fixed-limit betting, in both tournament and ring-game situations. To be honest, we aren't sure exactly why, but it may have something to do with the game's history. Stud is an older, slower game, played before the new fan-gled "big betting" methods of pot-limit and no-limit.

Standard Seven-Card Stud

As with Omaha, if you ever see a listing that labels the game "Seven-Card Stud," the highest hand wins the entire pot.

In general, standard Stud games are very accessible, playable, and winnable — especially at the lower limits. The general level of play doesn't seem as good as it does in Hold 'Em and Omaha, possibly because not as many people play, or possibly because Stud scholars haven't written as much on the game, allowing for fewer Stud scholars to develop. For information on general strategies for playing this game, check out *Poker For Dummies* (Wiley).

As a general rule, if you can't beat what you see face up from the other players' hands, get out while you can. If you can't quickly improve your medium pair, and an opponent has two queens showing, you may be throwing money away trying to catch cards on a dead hand.

Seven-Card Stud High/Low

As you may have gathered from the name, in High/Low the high hand splits the pot with the low hand, if, and only if, the low hand doesn't include a card higher than an 8 (the *qualifier*). Straights and flushes don't count against the low. (You can have an ace through five straight for the high *and* the low, however.)

Seven-Card Stud High/Low is beatable, but it takes more time to master than its standard (high only) cousin. As with Omaha High, this game tends to breed specialists, and you have *very* little written theory at your disposal. You should play low limits until you get comfortable with the different pacing and have a good feel for the kind of behavior you see from better players.

Straight from a Stud's mouth

An example from a standard Seven-Card Stud game:

You receive 8h 8d as your hole cards and the 7s face up. (Online, your hole cards are shifted down in the card line-up slightly.) You go through a round of betting with your pair of eights.

Fourth street is the 6c. You bet.

Fifth street is the 10c. You bet. You still have a pair of eights with an inside straight draw.

Sixth street, your last up card, is the Kd. Your hand hasn't changed much with the King.

Seventh street, your third hole card, is the 6h. You bet with your two pair, sixes and eights.

Be careful when you play High/Low, because it can drain your bank account (especially if you're new to it). Because you play High/Low nearly always as a fixed-limit game, players with strong opening hands (vying for high or low) tend to raise and re-raise in an effort to get you to pay dearly for drawing cards. As a result, the betting limits of the game can become doubled (due to many players raising the original limit).

Playing Crazy Pineapple, Five-Card Stud, and more

Hold 'Em, Omaha, and Seven-Card Stud are the staples of online play. But other games come and go occasionally as sites experiment with what customers want to play. Each of the following games is, or has been, available online. Have a look on any given poker site in the lobby under something akin to the "Other Games" tab to find these little creatures.

You can't really find much written theory on any of the following games, but you always play them for low stakes, due to a general lack of popularity. You also don't swim into waters with many sharks, which is a nice break from the normal Hold 'Em, Stud, and Omaha minefield.

Getting quartered

Imagine this situation: You're playing a High/Low game with two other players, and you're dealt the best possible low hand, A 2 3 4 5 (the hand known as the *wheel*), so you know you're guaranteed at least half the pot. You should raise without abandon at every possible opportunity here, right?

Not necessarily.

You encounter a problem if one of your opponents also has a wheel and a third player has a better high hand than your five-high straight. Your opponent with the high hand takes half the pot. You split the other half between you and the other player holding a wheel. Although you contributed one third of the pot with your bets, you only get one-quarter of the pot back when you tie for the low; therefore, you lose the difference between the quarter of the pot you won and the third of the pot you contributed (namely $\frac{1}{12}$th of the total amount of the pot). Unfortunately, you've been *quartered*. (Of course, this scenario is exacerbated if you have to split with even more players.)

Getting quartered is rare in Stud High/Low, where everyone plays their own unique hand, but the situation is surprisingly common in Omaha, where players share community cards.

If you suspect you may be in a situation where you're donating money, even if you have a wheel, you should merely call all bets. Don't raise and don't make the first betting action (allowing for someone else to raise you). You may hear the expression "Don't raise a naked low" in Omaha High/Low, which is exactly the situation we're referring to: A case where you have a low hand that may be duplicated, giving you no shot at winning the high hand.

Pineapple and Crazy Pineapple

Crazy Pineapple is a variant of Hold 'Em with one big exception: You get three hole cards rather than the usual two. You bet and see the three community cards, bet again, and then discard your least-helpful hole card before you see the fourth community card. From there, play continues like regular Hold 'Em. In the less-common *Pineapple,* you receive three hole cards and discard one before the flop.

Winning in both forms of Pineapple takes experience, because you regularly face stronger hands compared to Hold 'Em. You may be amazed at how often you find yourself holding the second-best hand (the quickest way to go broke). The good news for a beginner, however, is that you don't come across many Pineapple players, and because of that, all the games you find are low stakes and fixed-limit ring play only.

Watch a bit of the action first instead of playing right away. And after you get started, always keep an eye out for specialists who lurk, waiting to pounce on your stack.

Five-Card Draw

Yep, we're talking the *Five-Card Draw* of the Old West. All players are dealt five cards and then bet. Players discard (you can throw out none, some, or all your cards) and receive replacements from the dealer, and then you make the final round of bets. Lay your cards on the table and become the toast of the saloon (or the target of a few 6-guns).

Five-Card Draw works surprisingly well online because you focus only on your cards until the showdown, and all you have to do is click on the cards you want to discard. The pacing online is near perfect, very close to any home game. Even if you haven't played before, it takes only an hour or so to warm up to the betting and game dynamics, as well as the caliber of hand you need to win any given pot.

Unlike the rest of the online poker world, every Five-Card Draw table we've played on has been congenial (if opponents chat between play), and most games have been outright fun. As with Pineapple, you can't find much Five-Card Draw action, and you can expect low fixed-limit ring games. Unless you get reckless, you shouldn't lose much money in a Five-Card game.

You Seven-Card Stud . . .

You receive Qh 2s as your hole cards and the 8s as your first up card. You go through the betting round with your queen high and two cards toward a low hand.

Fourth street is the 3s. You have a three-card flush draw and three cards toward a low hand.

Fifth street is the Qs, giving you a pair of queens with a flush draw for high hand and three cards toward a low hand. You stay in through the betting round.

Sixth street brings the 4s. You now have a queen-high spade flush for your high hand. You also have a pretty good low drawing hand — you need one more card under an 8 that doesn't pair up. You keep on through the betting round.

Your third hole card is the 5s. Your high hand is a Q 8 5 4 3 spade flush. You also qualify for a low hand with 2 3 4 5 8 (remembering that the flush doesn't matter). Unless another player has a monster hand, you should rake in at least half the pot. Well done!

If you need a break from the tedium of the larger Internet games, the Western movie's game of choice can be an excellent decision. If you want a poker game on the Internet that you can just dive right into, Five-Card Draw is it (because of the low limits, congenial atmosphere, and general pacing of the game).

Five-Card Stud

In *Five-Card Stud,* all players are dealt a hole card and an up card. After a betting round, you receive three more up cards with betting rounds following each. The remaining players have a total of five cards. Best hand wins.

Five-Card Stud has the same game-dynamic problems as Seven-Card Stud (see the "Serving up Seven-Card Stud" section earlier in this chapter), although we like it even less. Having images of cards (often small ones) spread about the screen just doesn't feel right. You can easily overlook someone else's hand, especially if a lot of players are in the pot. And overlooking another player's hand can be financially deadly.

In Five-Card Stud, you can't expect a whole lot of mystery to come with any hands, because 80 percent of what you have is face-up. No mystery and no betting action lead to no thrill and no money. We know there must be a reason why people want to play this game; we just don't know what it is.

Wild card games

You break out the kitchen table games, like *Baseball*, *Follow the Queen,* and *Spit in the Ocean,* when you play with your poker buddies. These games often require less skill and more luck, and because anyone can get lucky, these games allow more people to play more hands, and you tend to see more betting going on than in the Stud games online. Sitting down at the kitchen table and playing a game like Spit in the Ocean gives you a chance to have more fun playing and spend less time thinking about strategy.

Brick-and-mortar cardrooms have never provided wild card games, partially because players take too long evaluating the hands. You also run into discrepancies in the ways different players interpret the rules. You can, however, find online poker sites with these games offered. Online sites spell out the rules precisely and never mis-evaluate hands, making the Internet the best wild card game destination outside of your kitchen.

Keep in mind that wild card games are still poker games, and if you don't pay attention, you will donate some of your net worth to your opponents. Don't get so caught up in the fun that you disengage the strategic thinking portion of your brain completely.

Have some fun by resurrecting a table of your old poker buddies to play online wild card games. (Don't forget to invite that one guy from your old game who always lost.)

Player's choice (mixed games)

If playing only one type of game puts you in a funk, or if you want to get a feel for your overall poker prowess, player's choice may be for you. In this world the game changes, typically after every orbit of the dealer marker (after the deal makes its way around the table). You can play a round of Hold 'Em, followed by a round of Seven-Card Stud, a round of Omaha, and so on.

You get variety without changing tables, and you get to exercise different parts of your poker brain. And player's choice isn't some online whim: You can play a mixed game at the World Series of Poker. *H.O.R.S.E.,* which stands for Hold 'Em, Omaha, Razz (Seven-Card Stud, low hand wins), Seven-Card Stud, and Seven-Card Stud High/Low (E for eight-or-better), combines all the major poker games. Check out *Poker For Dummies* (Wiley) for more info on Razz and other games.

The shift in rhythm can get to you, particularly if you're tired, and you always have to avoid misreading your Omaha hand after you play rounds of Hold 'Em.

Taking On Tournaments

One way in which the online world truly trumps the brick-and-mortar world is through tournaments. The concept of a poker tournament is very simple. Everyone *buys in* to the tournament for a set amount and receives a fairly huge stack of chips ($5.50 can get you 1,500 in chips). Play commences, with players busting out one by one, until only the victor remains. A *payout* schedule determines who gets money, as well as how much, depending on where a player finishes in the tournament.

Whatever interpersonal elements you lose by not having the other players seated across from you like in a real-world tournament are replaced with other perks in virtual-world tourneys. You don't have to deal with prolonged seating delays, poorly organized tournament directors controlling the show, and the endless movement involved in setting up and tearing down tables as a tournament progresses.

Online tournaments give you a chance to play considerably more hands than what you get in ring games for the same amount of money, an opportunity to be king of the mountain, and quick-and

Deciding what to play

Now that you have a feel for all the different online poker opportunities available to you, the big question is: What do you want to play?

Your decision is obviously a matter of personal taste, but we recommend taking the following approach:

✔ Play several hands with free chips to get comfortable with the user interface of your poker site and the general playing dynamic.

✔ After you get a good feel for the game, switch over to hard currency in a low-limit ring game. Play a bit. Win a bit.

✔ Move up in stakes in your ring game play until you reach about half the limit size you want to eventually play.

✔ At this point you have a choice. You can continue to move up in your ring game stakes, or you can play in (or move entirely over to) tournaments. Again, start at a low entry fee tournament and work your way up.

easy-chances to hone your tournament skills. When you play online, you have the opportunity to play literally any time, in table sizes as small as head's up (against one other player) to huge affairs with several thousand players.

One downside of tournaments in any environment is your money tends to move more in blocks and chunks, because you're either winning a chunk of hard currency or you lose your whole buy-in. For example, if you play in a $30 buy-in tournament, you may win $150, $90, or $60 for a first, second, or third finish; but you lose all 30 bucks if you don't finish in the money. A losing streak can be fairly dear.

Tournaments are wide and varied. You can play for nothing and win hard currency (in a tournament known as a *free-roll*), or you can play in huge multi-player affairs where a relatively modest sum gives you a shot at thousands of dollars. Depending on what you play, you can win as little as $5 or score a fabulous all-expenses-paid vacation to an exotic destination. For much more about tournaments, have a peek at Chapter 10.

After you register for a tournament, you will play in it, unless you hit the "un-register" button. After the tournament starts, you don't get a chance to un-register. If you're unavailable to play, the site automatically makes your blind bets and folds your hand in turn (known as being *blinded-off*), and you eventually lose all your chips. Most sites inform you of your tournament registration if you try to log off, but if something forces you off a site (a computer crash or a disconnect — see Chapter 5), you should always log back on (even if you don't plan on playing any more) to make sure you didn't forget a tournament entry.

Hold 'Em tournaments tend to be no-limit affairs (although you can find fixed-limit games). Omaha tourneys, in all variations, use pot-limit betting. And Seven-Card Stud tourneys are fixed-limit.

Sitting down for single-table tournaments

On-demand single-table tournaments run rampant in the online world, and in the online world only. You register for the tournament and after enough people register based on the table format, you play. On-demand, single-table tournaments are very common; the players at your table make up the entirety of the tournament.

Full single-table tournaments

If you look at the numbers of people playing full single-table tournaments online on a daily basis, you see why full table is the most popular form in the single-table tournament world. The tournament

---

Turbo tournaments: Playing at breakneck speed

At the request of players, some sites have sped up their game play by reducing the amount of time it gives players to act (say, reducing your action time on any given decision from 15 to 7 seconds) and by having the tournament blinds increase at a faster rate. You see these tables or tournaments listed under headings such as "Turbo."

Although you do see a few multi-table tournaments run in turbo format, the vast majority are on-demand single tables.

The caliber of play is nearly identical to turbo's slower siblings. We've never had any problem playing at these tables, although some people may find the speed difference disconcerting. If you play turbos and you start wigging out, consider dropping back down to regular speed play. The difference in speed isn't worth the difference in mindset.

Turbos are definitely not the place to start your online career, but you may want to try them out after you broaden your online experience. We talk more about the concept of speed in online poker in Chapters 3 and 5.

starts when your table seats fill up (with either 9 or 10 players, depending on the site) and ends with only one player remaining. Payout structures vary slightly, but typically first place gets 50 percent of the prize pool, second gets 30 percent, and third gets 20 percent — you should check your site for the exact payout schedule.

Single-table tournament experience proves valuable, even if your interest lies in larger tournament types, because if your luck and skill bring you to the end of a large tournament, you end up playing a single-table tournament (known as the *final table*).

The recent huge successes of online poker players in the brick-and-mortar tournament world (such as Chris Moneymaker winning the main event at the World Series in 2003 and Greg Raymer in 2004) may be due to the online players' single-table tournament experience. Experience can be the best teacher, and before the Internet, final-table experience was very difficult to obtain without becoming a leather-bottomed casino regular.

If you have any interest in the tournament world, single-table events are a good place to start. The tournaments are relatively short (typically an hour if you make it to the very finish), and you get plenty of poker practice for your buck. Chapters 12 and 13 are dedicated to single-table tournament strategy.

Short-handed tournaments

Short-handed tournaments are a relatively new breed in the single-table world. Here you play at a single table of five or six players (depending on the site), with the top two players getting an unevenly distributed amount of money (two-thirds to first place and one-third to second).

Oddly, we find that these tournaments play radically different from the full-size single-table version. The players you oppose here tend to specialize in this form, making the games extremely difficult to win.

You gain valuable experience by playing short handed at some point in your online poker career, but you should think of short-handed tourneys as one of the very last stones you turn over. Take a look at Chapter 12 to learn more.

Head's-up tournaments

Head's-up tournaments are easily the most brutal and cutthroat form of poker, which may be why you almost exclusively find them in the online world. You find yourself versus just one other player, and the winner takes all. Until you get used to playing head's up, the dynamic can be a little intimidating and disconcerting due to the game speed and the fact that you put your entire focus on one other person. Unless you have the skill to dominate brick-and-mortar tournaments, gaining head's-up experience means playing online.

The advantage of these tournaments is their speed — you usually finish in less than 30 minutes, and because you only face one other player, your winning percentage is higher.

Head's up is definitely worth trying, but not as your first online tournament. But as you gain experience and skill and get serious about online tournaments, you need to master head's-up poker. Good head's-up play literally means the difference between finishing first and finishing second in a tournament — often double the difference in cash. See Chapter 12 for strategies on winning in the head's-up world.

Mixing in multi-table tournaments

Multi-table tournaments take any and all comers, literally attracting thousands of players. Prize pools can grow gigantic, which attracts even more players (which can be a mixed blessing — winning money is tough because you have so many people to beat.) As people get knocked out one-by-one, the site continually re-balances individual table populations to keep them full. For example, say you're playing in a tournament with 100 players. After 10 players bust out, the site chooses a table at random, breaks it up, and sends each of its players to fill the empty seats at other tables.

Be sure you budget enough time to play. You can approximate by checking out how long other tournaments have lasted; just look through the lobby under the tournament tab for completed tournaments of roughly the same size and compare the start time to the end time. To win the tournament, or even to finish high enough to get a taste of the prize money, you have to play until the end.

Multi-table tournaments usually have breaks — something like five minutes of every hour. You stay in the game as long as you have chips, so even if you get disconnected or miss a few hands to talk to your mom on the phone, you still have your seat in the tourney. The site blinds you off and folds your hands in turn until you come back.

Unless you play in a tournament with no entry fee (a *free-roll;* see Chapter 10), you're probably better off playing in a few single-table tournaments before you hook up with one of these multi-table monsters.

The table-balancing act of multi-table tourneys

Multi-table tournaments have an interesting dynamic in that, due to table balancing, you essentially play at a full table for several hands (sometimes hours) on end, with at most one or two empty seats at any time. Toward the end of the tournament, you start playing at tables with a few seats open; and then half the seats empty (when barely two tables remain); and then a single full table that withers down to the eventual winner. See Chapters 10 and 11 for more about mastering multi-table tourneys.

At times it can feel extremely disconcerting to get moved to a new table due to table balancing — roughly approximating what it feels like to travel by transporter beam. After you land at your new table, make sure to take stock of the differences in chip stacks to get a feel for who the strong and the vulnerable players are.

Chapter 8

Building Your Online Poker Skills (Without Going Broke)

In This Chapter

▶ Understanding the value of free chips

▶ Gambling for hard currency

▶ Picking your limits

*T*he stage is truly set when you pick a site, zero in on the sign-up bonus you want, and transfer some of your hard-earned bucks into the ether.

Now's the time to get down to work. In this chapter, we talk about the pros and cons of free chips and show you how to ease your toe into the bigger pool of hard currency. Although you can get in over your head, the water is only as deep as you make it. Stay shallow before you dive into the deep end.

Playing for Free

Getting free chips from your site of choice is simple:

1. **Launch your poker client and sign in with your User ID and password. After you sign in, you go to your site's home page.**

2. **Pick the game you want to play (Hold 'Em, a variation of Omaha, or a variation of Stud).**

3. **Look for games labeled free, fun, or some such title; you can usually find them at the bottom of the list.**

4. **Sit down at any open seat.**

   You either start with the free chips provided by the site or you get the chance to request the chips (request the max amount — use all the free bullets you can).

With free chips, you can count on practicing, playing, and learning without charge. You can squander thousands and never worry about how to explain it to your spouse, and you don't endanger your kid's college fund. But you can also develop bad habits, which can be difficult (not to mention costly) to break when you move to hard currency. You have to be careful; you don't want to end up in the ironic situation where playing with free chips now costs you real money later on.

Reaping the benefits of free chips

Well, your chips are free, for starters, and you can't beat that price. Seriously, though, free chips have several positive aspects.

Adapting to a new site

Every time you try out a new site, you should play with free chips first. No matter how many other sites you've played, and regardless of how high a roller you claim to be, you should play for free to get a feel for the interface of your new home. Most poker sites are different, and the differences show up in the user interaction, speed of play, and general look. Play for free to get used to the new dynamics.

When you practice for hard currency play, be certain to play hands the same way you normally do at a money table (even if no one else at the table acts that way). This way you can be sure to fully exercise all the controls and have everything work the way you like with no surprises.

Learning a new game

If you tire of playing Hold 'Em and want to embrace Omaha, free chips are the perfect way to do it. You get the full game dynamic and the full action with none of the fiscal penalty associated with general game ignorance. We also find it easier to get advice and tips from other players at a free chip table. (Go easy on how much credit you give the advice, however; you may well get what you pay for.)

Adjusting to computer speed

If you haven't played online before, but you're familiar with the game you want to play, the biggest benefit of playing with free chips is getting used to the speed of online play. You play hands about twice as fast online as you do in the brick-and-mortar world, and you definitely want to get used to that level of action before you start playing with hard currency.

Avoiding bad free-chip habits

Free chips share a similar problem with that beloved hall monitor in your elementary school: They have no real authority, because no one takes them seriously. To give you some idea, you should expect a fixed-limit $5/10 hard currency Hold 'Em game to produce an average pot size of about $100. In a free chip, fixed-limit $5/$10 game, the pot size often swells to $450. People stay in, raise, and play more garbage hands. Hey, why not stay in until the river on that inside straight draw against a few other players if it doesn't cost you any actual money?

That type of play sounds dopey, sure, but fake chips tempt you to make those kinds of calls and worse. Just like too much candy eventually rots your teeth, too much free chip play eventually decays your playing skills. Your play gets loose, your judgment gets buggy, and then you wonder why you can't win when you move over to hard currency.

Simply put, if your goal is to play for hard currency, you should use free chips only until you completely understand the game and the site. After you nail down the dynamics, move to small-limit (*micro-limit* — see the section "Playing low-stakes games" later in this chapter) tables to play with hard currency. Moving up only when you get comfortable with the game is absolutely one of the best things you can do for your bank account, especially when you first start out.

Deciding You're Ready for the Real Deal

After you play with free chips on the site of your choice and you feel comfortable with the way the site works, pull out your real money and let it hit the virtual felt (and check out Chapter 4 to get all the money basics).

Prepping for real play

Before you take the hard currency plunge, here are steps you can take to ready yourself:

✓ **Mentally prepare yourself to lose.** Raw statistics assure you that you'll lose fairly regularly. If you play no-limit and you lose an all-in bet to a weaker hand, you have to shrug it off.

Mathematically, you did the best you could do. (For an example of this, see the sidebar "You're going to lose a few" later in this chapter.) In the long run, you win more than you lose by making good, strong plays, and, when playing poker, you need to focus on the long run.

✔ **Bet in accordance to your bankroll.** You need to have enough money to withstand the swings of chance. You should start with 300 big bets in limit play (if you want to play $1/$2, that means $600), 10 full buy-ins in no-limit play ($50 if you plan to play at a table that allows a $5 max buy-in), or 20 tournament buy-ins in tourney play. Every time you lose one quarter of your bankroll, back down to a lower limit. Continue doing so until you start winning regularly.

✔ **Get your poker journal in shape and ready to go.** You can't really be aware of your wins and losses if you don't have a way to track them. See Chapter 5 for more on creating a journal.

✔ **Make your poker nest cozy.** You're going to be spending hours in front of your computer, so make it play-friendly and comfortable. Chapter 2 has more on creating a good domain.

✔ **In ring game play, keep in mind that you can always switch tables.** You have to realize you may not be the best player on the Internet — and you may not even the best player at your table. If the table you're playing at seems too tough, make player notes on the good players you observe (in case you run across them in the future) and move along to an easier game. (Chapter 6 has more note-taking info.)

You're going to lose a few

Assume you're playing pot-limit Omaha, and you hold Ad Qd Ks 10c as your hole cards. The flop comes Kd 2d 9c, and the turn brings the 7d.

You hold the nut flush (you can't be beat by another flush), and you correctly make a pot-sized bet that pushes you all-in.

Although he doesn't know it when he calls, your opponent, holding Kc Kh Jh 10d, only has nine ways to win this hand (the three remaining deuces, the three remaining nines, and the three remaining sevens to make a full house). If 40 cards are left in the deck, he has a little less than a 1-in-4 chance of beating you.

The river is the 2s, so your opponent beats your flush with a full house, kings full of deuces. Even though you took a bad beat here, you made the right play. Three out of four times you win the hand. This just happened to be the other time.

Taking the game seriously

It may sound dumb, we know, but the most important thing about playing for hard currency is to take the game seriously. We talk about adjusting to online money in Chapter 5, but it bears repeating here: Because you only see it as pictures of chips on your computer screen, your money may feel fake, but it doesn't feel that way if you lose it and check out your bank account balance the next day. When you lose, you lose real money — money that you could have put to any other use. If you ever find that you don't care about the outcome of a hand or game (or worse, you want to lose just to clear an account you've set up with a site), stop playing and come back later. Winning online is hard enough without adding a financially apathetic demeanor to the mix.

Choosing where to start

Picking where you should start depends on your previous poker experience and where you want to go in the future.

Starting out with Stud

If Seven-Card Stud sounds appealing, go to your site's home screen and find the lowest game it offers: $0.04/$0.08, for example. Start there.

If you have an extensive amount of brick-and-mortar experience and want to get started on the Net, play your first few hard currency games with one-quarter the limit you normally play.

Heading into Hold 'Em

If you normally play $3/$6 Hold 'Em in the brick-and-mortar world, find yourself a seat at a $1/$2 table on the Net.

You want to become a no-limit Hold 'Em hotdog like the poker glitterati you see on television. Start with fixed-limit free chip play — fixed-limit gives you a better feel for playable hands. Switch over to a $0.02/$0.04 micro-limit game to get a good feel for pure game technique. Watch a $20 buy-in single-table tourney. Find a no-limit free-roll Hold 'Em tournament to play. Watch another $20 buy-in single table. Read Chapters 12 and 13 about single-table tourneys, and then you can sign up for a $5 single-table adventure.

Trying out Omaha

You have always played $2/$4 Hold 'Em, but you want to try Omaha. Have a seat at a $0.25/$0.50 Omaha hard-currency table.

If you have extensive experience playing ring games of a certain form of poker, but you want to try out tournaments, play one free-roll of that tourney variety to get used to the tournament dynamic (see Chapter 10 for free-roll info). You can also watch two medium-limit multi-player tourneys of that type (medium-level players are experienced and provide better watching instruction than low-limit players) before you play one at the lowest level.

Going for Omaha High/Low

You've always been an Omaha High/Low pot-limit player, but you want to try an Omaha High/Low tournament. Play in one Omaha High/Low free-roll (look for the listing on the tournament home screen — your site should filter the listing and look at free-rolls only); watch two $20 Omaha High/Low pot-limit tourneys; and then play in an Omaha High/Low tourney with a $1 to $10 buy-in (depending on what your site offers). Watch for sloppy play at the $1 level; the low cost may make it too recreational to be instructional.

If you don't have much poker experience, but you want to start off as a tournament player, you should start with free chips in ring games of the poker variety you want to play. Switch over to micro-limit tables of the game. Watch a medium buy-in, no-limit or pot-limit tournament to get a feel for the level of play there. Participate in one free-roll tournament. Watch another medium buy-in tourney to see how much you've soaked in, and then get in there and play the lowest level buy-in tourney yourself.

Playing low-stakes games

We know, we know . . . you're good and ready to play with hard currency now. The time has come and the bell has tolled. Get your cash ready; you're about to break into low-stakes games.

In the brick-and-mortar world, *low-limit* typically means anything under $6/$12. Sometimes you can find brick-and-mortar limits as low as $2/$4 for Hold 'Em and Omaha and maybe a $1/$2 Stud game. The Net offers a whole lower spectrum, sometimes starting as low as $0.01/$0.02. (The site's home screen always tells you the available limits — just pick a game type and scroll to the bottom of the list.) We refer to anything lower than $1/$2 as *micro-limit;* we call everything from $1/$2 to $5/$10 low-limit.

Micro-limits

At the micro-limits, the level of play typically isn't very high. These games tend to be relatively easy to beat; a good ego boost for a skilled player. Players at this level are considerably more congenial than their bigger-monied brethren on the higher-limit tables, because, after all, who gets that bent out of shape after losing a dime?

Another good characteristic of micro-limit games is that the house often doesn't take a rake (meaning that the site doesn't take a portion of each pot). Many sites don't take a rake until the pot reaches $1, and if you play fixed-limit games with stakes of $0.02 and $0.04, well, the pot just never gets that big. Rakes usually don't amount to much, but when you first begin and just get good enough to beat your fellow humans, you'll be glad you don't have to out-pace the rake, too. And if a few extra pennies in your online account add to your happiness, how can that be a bad thing?

Don't become blind to the difference between a $0.02/$0.04 game and a $30/$60 game. Winning at the micros doesn't mean you can automatically go sit down with the heavy hitters. Micro-limit games are played much more loosely than their upper-class cousins. The caliber of play rises as you move up in limit on the tables.

Low-limits

If you've played low-limits in the brick-and-mortar environment, the play on the Net should seem very similar to you. The biggest difference is the caliber of player you face. In the brick-and-mortar world, we have run across some very good players at the lowest limits, people who study and practice the game and prey on the ineptitude of other low-limit players.

You don't find these veterans on the Net as much. The caliber of play on low-limit online tables seems to be considerably lower. A fair percentage of these players may be people who want to see action above the micro-limits but don't have skills to match the new limits.

Because of the average online play, low-limit online tables are probably the most lucrative place you can play when you consider the amount of money you can make per hour relative to the limits.

Picking a low-limit game type

As you may expect from the world's biggest poker rooms, you have a broad array of betting formats at your disposal. If you find yourself confused about any game type in the following list, flip back to Chapter 7 for a more detailed explanation of the games.

Fixed-limit tables

In fixed-limit ring games, you can find Hold 'Em, Omaha, and Seven-Card Stud at limits as low as $0.02/$0.04. Hard-currency play is infinitely more expensive than free, mathematically speaking (because any number is infinitely bigger than zero if you multiply), but risking money is also infinitely more valuable to your playing expertise.

No-limit and pot-limit tables

You can find no-limit Hold 'Em ring games for as low as $0.01/$0.02 with a maximum buy-in of $2. You can check out pot-limit Omaha for as little as $0.01/$0.02 with a maximum buy-in of $5. Some sites describe no-limit ring games by the size of the blinds ($0.01/$0.02), and others use the maximum amount they allow you to buy-in for ($2). With the no-limit and pot-limit games, if you're unclear about the buy-in and limits from looking at the home page, go to any table and try to sit in an open seat — the site gives you very explicit details of limits and buy-ins from the chip purchase dialog (and you can always cancel if the requirements are too rich for your blood).

Online no-limit and pot-limit ring games are a bad place to go if you want to eventually play in no-limit and pot-limit tournaments. The general play in these ring games is strikingly different from tournaments, so practicing here can do more damage to your tournament play than it does good. If you lust for no-limit and pot-limit tournaments, go to the fixed-limit versions of your game first and then switch over to the tourney of your choice after you get enough practice and accumulate regular successes. (For more on the differences between fixed-limit and no-limit, see Chapter 7.)

Small buy-in tournaments

The smallest tournament buy-in is a free-roll, where you pay no entry fee but still have a chance to win real money. The good news is that you can truly get something for nothing more than your time, a little hard poker labor, and (undoubtedly) a smidgen of luck. For more information on free-rolls, see Chapter 10.

One step up from free are the $1, $2, and $3 buy-in multi-table tournaments, available in Hold 'Em, Omaha, and Stud flavors. These contests are as heavily populated as the free-rolls, but the level of play is noticeably higher than in the free-rolls. You don't see nearly as many players staying in and trying to outdraw you with only one out.

Small buy-in tournaments take hours to play, but unless they serve as satellite qualifiers for larger tournaments (satellite tournaments take the top finishers and place them into more lucrative, more competitive tournaments), they always finish in one day. The low-limit tournaments typically pay the top 10 percent of the tournament field. (You can find out more about multi-table tourneys in Chapter 10.)

In the single-table tourney world, the cheapest tournaments you can find are $5 entry fee on-demand contests in all limit forms of Hold 'Em, Omaha, and Seven-Card Stud. A little more expensive, yes, but they go quickly, typically finishing in little over an hour, and your odds of winning cash are much better because they typically pay the top three people at the table — a whopping 30 percent of the field. (We have an extensive run-down on single-table tournaments in lucky Chapters 12 and 13.)

Continuing to play, and play, and . . .

After you play a bit for money, keep right on going, with a couple of caveats:

- ✔ Keep an eye on your bankroll. Any time you lose 25 percent of your bankroll, you should back off one level of limits and keep playing.

- ✔ Don't automatically ramp up to the higher limits after you win on the lower limits. You're just as likely to have a string of bad luck as you are to have a lucky streak. Slowly ramp up your play if you start winning. Give yourself at least 30 solid hours of play at any given limit before you advance to the next level (and never skip a level). Yes, it means that you experience plenty of lower-limit play, but you become very aware of where your skill level lies.

- ✔ Keep a poker journal as we describe in Chapter 5. After you log 30 hours of play at a certain limit, check your journal to see if you're winning. If you are, consider moving up a level (don't feel like you have to, however — because hey, you're winning). If you've been losing, back down one limit.

- ✔ If you continue playing at limits so low that it still feels like you're competing against cretins and coneheads after 10 hours of play, move up one level (but make sure you have the bankroll to support it — see the section "Prepping for real play" earlier in this chapter).

And always, always remember: If you're losing, and you keep losing, study along with backing off in the limits. Reading and researching are the single best things you can do for your game.

Chapter 9

Strategies for Short-Handed Ring Games

....

In This Chapter

▶ Coming to grips with short-handed play

▶ Mastering head's-up poker

▶ Preparing for tourneys through ring games

....

*B*ecause online poker rooms can generate an infinite number of poker tables, you have more table-size possibilities than in the brick-and-mortar world. On the Net, you can find short-handed tables, limited to just five or six players, or you can explore the head's-up format, where you alone battle a single faceless opponent. Any table that isn't a filled, normal table (9 or 10 players, depending on the site), we call *unusual-size* (our term, not crazy poker slang).

Unusual-size games are fun for the amount of action if nothing else. Because fewer players participate, you get to bet more often, fold more often, and see more cards per hour; you just *play* more. Like any other specific subset of Internet poker, unusual-size tables can be very profitable if you decide to focus and specialize exclusively in these games.

If you're a regular full-table ring game player, you may want to play some low-limit short-handed tables to get a feel for the poker action. If you want to become a serious tournament player, short-handed practice is required, because all tournaments ultimately end with a dwindling final table (see Chapter 10 for more on tourneys).

Adapting to Short-Handed Ring Games

Short-handed tables earn their designation in a few ways: The site can automatically construct the table to accommodate only five or six players (you can tell by the seating layout — the site's home screen labels these tables with terms like "5 max"); a larger table may lose players faster than it gains them (referred to as *breaking down*); or a new table may have just recently started up and is just beginning to gain players.

If you come from a world of only full-table experience, short-handed play can be a little intimidating and overwhelming at first. Hands begin and end about 40 percent faster than full tables (because you have 6 players rather than 10), and as a result, you see many more hands per hour.

Also, because you face fewer players, the general quality of a winning hand doesn't need to be as high as on a full table, because you have fewer players to beat.

Due to these characteristics, it shouldn't surprise you that short-handed play tends to draw in players hungry for action and speed (along with the occasional lazy straggler who's unwilling to get up from a dwindling table).

Unless you have a fair amount of short-handed experience in the real world, don't start your online poker career here. If you want to experiment with short-handed games, start with full tables first and then work your way on down to the short-handed world. Playing large tables gives you more time to absorb the rhythm, aesthetics, and behavior of the online poker world.

Breaking into the short-handed world

When you feel ready to break into a short-handed ring game, decide first on the stakes you're comfortable playing. Take the limits you normally play in full-table games, pick out a table from your site's home screen that shows a short-handed amount of players on its number of players indicator, and make sure that table's limits are somewhere around one-quarter of your normal limit comfort zone. You want to ease yourself into the game here and not put too much money at stake too fast. If you often play $3/$6 Omaha on full tables, start at the $1/$2 short-handed tables. If you lose as you gain short-handed knowledge at the low limits, you don't lose as much; but if you win, well, you still win.

Before you sit down to play at your table of choice, you should watch the play at the table. Watch as much as you possibly can, take a break, and then watch some more. The differences in play compared to full tables are subtle, but you can definitely find them. Pay special attention to the role of the lead bettors versus the blinds to try to find clues as to why they took the lead.

Meeting short-handed experts

Like with all forms of poker on the Internet, some players special-ize in short-handed games and play them exclusively, and some of these specialists can be very good. If you've been playing on a full table and it starts to break down, but none of the members have changed (no expert has spotted the diminished size of your table and has dropped in to play), you're less likely to be playing against a short-handed specialist than if you sit down at a table that the site limits to short-handed play only and the experts are probably lined up to play.

If you're sitting at a short-handed table with a player who's becom-ing heavily stacked or playing exceptionally well, use your site's *find a player* mechanism (look in menus on the home screen) and see if you can find that player on more than one table. If he is, and the other tables he graces are also short-handed, you know you've spotted a specialist.

As always, if you're playing against someone you think may be better than you, take it easy on your pocketbook and get up and move to another table. But if you're really interested in getting better and learning on the job, you should consider your losses to be tuition fees.

Molding your betting strategies to short-handed play

As you observe and dip your feet into short-handed ring play, you see that raising is much more common — especially on tables with bigger stakes. In fixed-limit games, you commonly see two raises before you see more cards after the flop. The reason for the aggres-sion is that players want to establish who has a hand of strength; essentially, you enact a version of playground boasting. One raise says, "My hand is better." The next one proclaims, "No, my hand is better!"

Channeling aggression on short-handed tables

To illustrate the aggressive betting that you see on short-handed tables, here's a hand from a $3/$6 fixed-limit Hold 'Em ring game we recently observed on a short-handed table.

Six players are seated and playing (not players sitting out). Player 1 is in the small blind and 2 in the big.

Player 3 raises pre-flop. Player 5 calls. Player 1 re-raises. Player 2 on the big blind folds. Player 3 calls the re-raise, as does Player 5.

The flop comes 9s 10s Qd.

Player 1 bets $3. Player 3 raises to $6. Player 5 re-raises to $9. Player 1 folds, abandoning his original $3 bet. Player 3 calls the additional $3.

The turn is the 7h.

Player 3, keeping in mind the re-raise from the previous round, checks. Player 5 bets $6. Player 3 calls.

The river is the 2c.

Player 3 checks. Player 5 bets $6. Player 3 calls. Player 5 shows As Qc for a flopped pair of queens with the top kicker. The site folds Player 3's cards because the runner-up doesn't show.

Our guess is Player 3 almost certainly had a pair of queens on the flop with a high kicker due to his betting pattern throughout. Player 1 may have had A-K, or a large pocket pair, but dropped the hand when the other players clearly showed the board had been paired.

This aggressive betting pattern and style of play is very common on short-handed tables. We only had to observe about four hands (the other three didn't even make it to a flop) before we saw this particular hand.

This jostling for position comes in handy for the raising and re-raising players, both when they win (because the pots are bigger) and when they bluff (because they acted as though they had a big hand pre-flop and may be able to get players to drop mediocre hands later on with continued betting action).

When you start to establish an image (find more in Chapter 6), you'll find it much easier to bully one or two other opponents on a short-handed table than four on a full table. This zealous betting action provides yet another reason you should start on tables with slightly lower limits, because, ironically, the average amount of money you end up putting into a pot tends to be higher on any hand you play in short-handed games compared to full-table play.

As a rule of thumb, especially in fixed-limit Hold 'Em and Omaha, always raise pre-flop if you're the first player to come in after the blinds. During short-handed play, you don't want to let anyone see cards for free, which gives other players the chance to draw good hands.

During a short-handed Seven-Card Stud game, you want to raise any time you have a high pair (especially when compared to your opponents' up cards) or better.

Taking in short-handed play subtleties

Keeping track of a few short-handed nuances can make your new-found short-handed aggression more effective and controlled.

Recognizing the importance of a single player

At a short-handed table, the style of one player can affect the whole game. In ring games, where people are free to come and go, you need to reassess how tight or loose the play becomes (and therefore decide your response) each time a player joins or leaves. The effect of dropping one player and adding another is much larger during short-handed play than it is on a full table, solely because that player represents more of the action (1/10th on a full table compared to 1/6th on a short-handed table — almost twice as much — for example).

Because you have fewer opponents to beat on a short-handed table, you should play a higher percentage of starting hands than on a full table (the quality of starting hands starts to drop as fewer players are dealt in). But, as always, make sure to balance your play against the general play of the table — play tighter against loose players and more aggressive against tight players — to avoid losing big hands to maniacs and to take pots from the timid.

Watching out for the calling stations

Keep an eye out for opponents who always call when their small or big blinds are raised (which happens frequently on lower-limit tables where players can't lose as much money by playing loosely). If this is the case, you should do one of two things:

✔ In no-limit, raise a little more than the last time you brought in the first action. You may be able to find out where this per-petual caller's pain threshold lies — the point where he stops calling you automatically.

> ✔ In fixed-limit, you can't increase the size of your raise (because you can only raise a specific amount), so you may not want to raise pre-flop at all, merely to reduce the damage from bad-beat cards. You don't want to continually invest a large portion of your stack against a player who stays on anything. Let the calling station bust himself out (against others, if necessary).

Players who always call from the blinds affect your game more in short-handed play (again, because they make up a larger total percentage of the table).

Considering lesser hands

In the short-handed world, you should play hands that, roughly speaking, grade one step lower than what you normally play on a full table. For example, if the widest gap you play from a middle position on a full table in a Hold 'Em ring game is A-10, K-9 now becomes a real possibility. If you limit your starting cards for Seven-Card Stud to a pair, three to a straight, or three to a flush, consider also going with three cards eight or greater. When the field drops to three players or you start on a smaller table, give serious consideration to playing yet another step down the quality ladder. With fewer players at the table, you see fewer great hands — so marginal hands begin to have more power. And for head's-up advice, check out the next section.

Making extra money short-handed

If you start to become a short-handed specialist and make good money at it, you can make even more by finding large, dwindling tables and sitting down as they begin to get short-handed. Players who refuse to leave dying tables are almost always easier to beat than short-handed regulars for a couple of reasons.

For one, they've been playing at the table for some time (tables that break up are often "older" tables — one player gets tired and leaves, a couple more follow), so they often deal with fatigue.

And these poor souls are also typically less familiar with short-handed dynamics, giving your experience an edge.

To find tables that may sport breaking possibilities, look on your site's home screen for full-sized tables with several empty seats — especially in the early morning hours, when the number of players tends to drop off. Have a quick look at each player's locations (see Chapter 3 if you're unsure how), and if many of the players are up late for their time zones, you may have a winner.

Playing Mano-a-Mano in a Head's-Up Ring Game

To find a head's-up ring game, you look at the home screen of your site under the particular game type you're interested in (Hold 'Em, Omaha, or Seven-Card Stud) and scan it for statements in the table listings like "head's-up," "1-on-1," or "2 max." Any limits higher than $1/$2 in head's-up ring game play are unusual; micro-limits tend to be the norm.

Surveying your head's-up ring game options

Nearly everything in the head's-up world, in all games types, is fixed-limit. No-limit and pot-limit head's-up ring games are much more rare than their fixed-limit brethren. Although most head's-up ring game action you see is of the $0.02/$0.04 variety, you can find $10/$20 fixed-limit Hold 'Em and Omaha and $8/$16 Stud head's-up play if you really search.

One reason sites don't support many larger limits, nor no-limit versions, of head's-up ring game play is that these games don't get much action; but more importantly, governments where the host sites are based put a great deal of pressure on site owners to not allow money laundering (the passing of funds from one player to another — usually for illicit reasons), so they cap the bet sizes on head's-up ring games to keep big money from changing hands easily.

The big dollars in head's-up action change hands during tourney play, not ring-game play ($5,000 buy-in tournaments on demand are possible). We've heard that people on the site staff watch big-dollar head's-up tourneys extremely closely for money laundering possibilities. See Chapter 10 for more on head's-up tourneys.

Bracing for head's-up play

The first few times you play head's up can be the most nerve-wracking times of your poker career. If not for the low-limit nature of most of the play, the tension would be completely unnerving. Fortunately, having less at stake takes off some of the pressure.

Because you face just one other person, you may find it hard not to take losing personally. But you shouldn't. In fact, the first Zen-like thing you need to grasp about head's-up play is to not take it personally. View this attitude as just another aspect of your basic poker skills.

Head's up, in many ways, is the purest form of poker. Given enough time, head's-up play determines who has the better poker game. It may be hard to swallow if you lose, and you may feel defeated. Shake it off and dig just a tiny bit deeper in yourself and understand that if one person beats you over a long session or beats you repetitively over many sessions, you simply have a crack in your poker game. Find out what that problem is by researching your play, going over your notes, and practicing on the micro-limits. When you find the crack, shore it up, even if you never play that particular person again. Any crack that one player finds can be found by others.

Head's-up ring game play typically falls into two categories: playing for just a few hands before one player leaves (usually because he gets bored, scared, or has other commitments) or battling back and forth for a long time (say, 20 minutes or more — which in head's-up play can be over 60 hands). Not many sessions, from our experience, last for a "medium" amount of time, like 10 minutes.

Comparing head's-up fixed-limit to no-limit

After you get your head's-up feet wet, you notice a huge difference between fixed-limit and no-limit play. Fixed-limit play is a long, slow grind; hand after hand of churning cards and constant raises and folds. Because the betting amount never increases or decreases over the set amounts, assuming one player doesn't get on a hot streak, money changes hands very slowly over time.

No-limit, though it's rare in ring games, is at its cruelest in head's-up play. If you like the sudden slashing nature of no-limit in full-table play, you'll love it head's up. Long sessions often end with a good hand getting beaten by a great hand. Because you see such an overwhelming number of hands in head's-up play (conceivably 200 or more hands per hour versus 60 in an online full table), you see more statistical flukes per hour. Oddities occur more often, like seeing your flopped two pair dropping to a set of flopped trips or watching in stunned silence as a flush bests your flopped straight on the turn.

For this reason, if you find yourself against the same no-limit ring game opponent for an extended period of time with no noticeable changes in stack sizes (an even stack size after a very long session means that your skill level is about even with the other player's), your best move may be to take a break or switch tables. The turn of one bad card could cost you your entire stack, and when you play someone with similar skills, you don't want a long, hard match falling to the whims of chance. Remember, you can always stand up from any ring game table at any time. And, especially at the lower limits ($1/$2 and less), you can always find easier opponents than the one you're playing right now.

Prepping for (and playing) a head's-up ring game

Playing head's up is an art you perfect mostly through experience. Although the basic approach is similar to playing short-handed (meaning you play far more hands and bet more aggressively when you do make a hand), you gain no real advantage by having short-handed experience before you try out the game. Head's up is different enough from every other game form that it qualifies as its own animal.

Watching head's up in action

You do reap great benefits, however, from spending some time watching the game before you play. Get a feel for the play and style. Keep an eye on winning streaks. Take notice, as much as you can, of the cards that the opponents play from starting positions and the way they bet those hands (you don't see very many of the players' cards because most hands end before the showdown). Because only two people are in contention for every pot, you often see strings of five wins or more.

You shouldn't pay as much attention to idiosyncrasies in individual players; what you want to pay attention to is the general tempo and form of the game. Watch the speed of the game. Watch how the betting works, especially check-raising and re-raising when players have a good hand. After you spend several minutes looking at one table, move to another. Head's-up style varies from player to player, so watching several different tables before you dive in gives you an idea of the different playing styles people use and the way they coerce money out of various types of opponents. And although styles may vary, pay attention to the basics: how many more hands the players play and how aggressive the betting becomes.

Diving into play

After your observation, you should be ready to play. Don't wig out, because you can always leave the table at any time if it feels like too much.

When head's-up chat turns ugly

For some reason (probably because only one other person sits at the table and you have nothing else to focus on), we see much more player chat during head's-up play.

Simply judging by the conversations, you can expect to find the nicest and a few of the rudest people in the entirety of the online poker world here. If someone gives you a hard time, turn off the chat mechanism for your site or find another table. You should report abusive players to the site's support crew.

You may or may not pick the individual you play against; either you join a player sitting alone at a table or you sit down at an empty table and wait for an opponent to join you. It really doesn't matter what route you take.

As you start playing, see how quickly you understand how your opponent plays. You may discover that your preferred style works best against certain kinds of opponents and not so well versus others. Because you have control over whom you play (because of the ring-game format), stick with opponents who give you an advantage and ditch people your style doesn't fit with. How quickly you can get a feel for your opponent varies (usually in 5 to 10 minutes), but it should be a feeling that you know in your gut. If you feel comfortable and confident against your opponent, keep playing against him. If you feel overwhelmed, consider going to another table.

Many players lose focus in head's-up play by zeroing-in on which player wins the most hands versus who wins the most money. As you play, especially if sessions drag out, always keep an eye on your chip count. If, after a long period of time, you fall behind, you may not be able to blame it on a bad-luck streak; you may be facing a stronger opponent. If so, don't be afraid to leave the table and cut your losses. Take a break. Cool down a bit. You can always come back against somebody else.

You can't enjoy mental breaks in head's-up play. Every few seconds you need to make a decision, which can be both stimulating and tiring.

If you find yourself unable to give a head's-up game your full attention, you should end your session or switch to a game with more players where you're not involved in every single hand.

Translating Ring-Game Play into Tournament Play

Playing unusual-size ring games can be very good tournament practice. How much you should practice depends on the kind of tournament you're interested in.

Practicing for multi-table tourneys

All multi-table tourneys end with short-handed play. If you want to be prepared for this, you need to first get some practice in short-handed ring-game situations. Multi-table tournaments alone don't offer sufficient opportunities to practice short-handed, however, because you spend the vast majority of the time at full tables.

After you finally make it all the way to the end, and table size starts to shrink, your level of experience becomes critical. Finishing just one position up in the standings can mean as much as double the prize money.

For this reason, if nothing else, we suggest you get plenty of practice with short-handed and head's-up play. When the stakes are high, you become nervous enough without having to think, "Oh great, now I'm head's up. I have no idea what I should be playing, and $5,000 is at stake."

If you endure a long drought out of the prize money in multi-table tourneys, you should consider occasionally refreshing your short-handed experience through ring games (because the drought means you haven't seen a short-handed table in some time).

Gearing up for single-table tourneys

If you want to play single-table on-demand tournaments, you should practice on unusual-size tables first, because these tourneys move from full table to short table quickly. If you play well and have a little luck on your side, you can quickly go from a full table to short-handed to head's up, so you need to make sure you're ready to play at every level. (We walk through this whole process of moving down in table size in Chapter 12.)

After you consistently enjoy success in single-table tourneys, you don't have to come back and keep playing the ring game versions. But if you find yourself continually losing at a specific level in the tournament, even if you're in the prize money, you should sit down in a ring game of the size you're having trouble with and start practicing again. For example, if you're always busting out of no-limit tournaments in second place, play some head's-up ring games.

Part III
Taking Over Tournaments

The 5th Wave   By Rich Tennant

@RICHTENNANT

"Some people just carry a lucky rabbit's foot, but Roger has resorted to the big Gods for his online poker prowess."

In this part . . .

Now we get down to the business of winning money. Here we go into an in-depth analysis of tournaments; we take a serious look at using your chip standings strategically; and we have an extra hard look at that Internet specialty: the single-table tournament.

Chapter 10

Perusing Your Online Tournament Options

In This Chapter

▶ Looking at tourney types

▶ Measuring different tourneys for the proper fit

▶ Picking a tourney that suits you

The busiest online cardrooms have 15 times the number of players you can find in a brick-and-mortar establishment. Due to the sheer volume of players, you can *always* find a thriving tournament scene, regardless of the time of day. Your choices range from head's-up tournaments, where you face down a single player (your entry fee versus hers), all the way to huge multi-table tournaments where you can win armored cars loaded to the gun holes with cash.

In this chapter we slice, dice, and julienne fry the options available to you.

Examining Online Tournament Types

Technically you don't see any tournament *types* online that you can't find in the brick-and-mortar world. However, the fact that they exist in the online world does make them mutate slightly.

Tackling tourney basics

Any given poker site has tournaments on demand that range in size from two-player head's up to short-handed (five or six players, depending on the site) to full single-table tourneys. You also see scheduled tournaments that you can pre-register for and begin on

Tourneys with antes

Some sites also have an unusual wrinkle in their Omaha and Hold 'Em tournaments: After the blinds get large (say 250/500), they add an *ante*, which is typically 10 percent of the small blind (25 percent in this case), that everyone contributes to the pot on every hand. The ante increases as the blinds increase. Sites add the ante to encourage betting action later in a tournament, partially by increasing the pre-flop pot size and partially by putting extra pressure on the short stack.

a certain day and time. Pre-registration tournaments are always large multi-table affairs. To find any of these tournaments, just click on the tournament tab of your site's home screen.

In most cases, you *buy-in* (in free-rolls you register, but don't pay anything) for an entry fee, plus a small registration fee that goes to the house (say $20 + $2 registration fee). In exchange for this money, the site hands you a pre-determined number of tournament chips (something like 1,500) and a seat in the tourney.

Your *tournament lobby* (where you register for your tourney) has a wealth of information, including

- ✔ When the tournament starts
- ✔ The amount of elapsed time (if the tourney has started or already ended)
- ✔ The prize pool and its distribution to the various places
- ✔ The names of everyone playing in the tourney (and how many players are participating)
- ✔ Your chip standing relative to other people in the tournament
- ✔ Rules on re-buys and add-ons
- ✔ The standings of players as they fall

Risking nothing in free-roll tourneys

Free-roll tournaments are the American Dream in the form of a poker tournament. Here you can truly get something for nothing. Hold 'Em, Omaha, and Seven-Card Stud are all offered. You don't have to pay to enter, and the winners receive cash prizes. What could be sweeter than that?

Only in free-roll tournaments

Here's a hand we saw in a recent free-roll no-limit Hold 'Em tournament. The tourney had just begun. With blinds at five and ten, the player in the first betting position *(under the gun)* raised five times the bet. He got two callers.

The flop was Kh 8s 6c. The original bettor pushed all-in. *Both* people on the table called. Now three people were all-in. The turn was the 2h, and the river was the 7s.

When cards were exposed, the original bettor had As Ac. The first caller had 5s 9d. That's right — he called a five times pre-flop bet with 5-9 and then an all-in on a gut-shot straight draw and hit it. The third player had 3c 3d, so she called an all-in bet with pocket 3s.

Only in free-roll tournaments (and possibly comedy shows) do you see this kind of play.

Playing forever (and then some)

Although rare, free-roll tourneys do exist in the brick-and-mortar world. Some are come-ons merely to get people to the poker rooms early. In other tourneys, you qualify by playing a certain number of hands or winning a set amount of other tournaments. One thing you can say for free-rolls in the brick-and-mortar world is that, for the most part, the play is sane and reasonable.

Because free-rolls on the Internet are open to all comers, they get a ton of entrants. You always play them as multi-table affairs — sometimes with a cap of the maximum number of players allowed (like 1,000). Much to the chagrin of the online operators (who offer these games as nothing more than a come-on to play the site), many people only play in free-roll tourneys. The caliber of play you see from your opponents can be so bizarre that you can probably best qualify it as "random."

Psychologists always have a hard time explaining why people behave in a strange fashion (you know, like "Why does Harry walk down the street with a waffle iron on his head?"), but in free-rolls, the crazy behavior is probably some combination of the following:

✔ People not knowing how to play poker. The play is free, so they figure they can do anything.

✔ People not caring what they play and just wanting to see how outrageous they can get.

> ✔ A few people wanting to get big stacks very quickly so they have a real shot at making money; or people just busting out at the very start because they simply don't want to waste time.

And when you *do* win, you haven't necessarily won because you often only get a seat in a larger free-roll tournament later. In order to get a seat in that tourney, you must win an earlier free-roll. By winning the first tourney, you win nothing more than the right to play again.

A free-roll no-limit Hold 'Em tournament strategy

In his book, *Tournament Poker for Advanced Players*, poker strategy demi-god David Sklansky puts forward a no-limit tournament strategy that he calls *The System*. Widely debated in Internet poker circles for questions about its general tournament effectiveness, he originally designed it as a technique for uneducated poker players to compete in professional tournaments against poker professionals — but hey, why not apply it to free-rolls too? After all, it costs nothing to try.

The essence is this:

✔ If you face no raise in front of you, push all-in with any pair, any suited ace, any A-K, and any suited connector higher than 3-4.

✔ If you face a raise in front of you, push all-in with A-A, K-K, or suited A-K.

✔ Fold *all* other hands.

Technically, according to The System, you're supposed to only play A-A in the first four rounds and always push all-in with it, but that's assuming you start with a gigantic chip stack (say, 10,000 tourney chips with the blinds starting at 5 and 10). You don't have that luxury in free-rolls. Depending on the size of the blinds and your initial betting stack, you may or may not want to consider waiting. If your stack is less than 10 times the big blind amount, you definitely don't want to wait for A-A. Because you get pocket aces so rarely, your chip stack starts to dwindle to nothing (due to being lapped repeatedly by the blinds) before you have a chance to play. If The System intrigues you, you should poke around on the Net for it. You can find advanced versions of this strategy, but you quickly get to a point where you're in complex poker theory and no longer playing a straightforward, simple strategy.

Remember, in a free-roll, the number of people who call that would/should otherwise fold is substantially higher than normal because they, literally, have nothing to lose. Calling stations may nullify some of the built-in effectiveness. Still, you may want to try it just for fun. (And if you don't want to test it out in a free-roll tournament right away, you can always head to a money session.)

To give you some idea of how carried away free-rolls can get: One popular site recently had a free-roll *qualifying* event with 8,100 entrants. The top nine finishers landed in a second tournament with 500 others players (who also had finished in the top nine of other multi-thousand player qualifiers) a few days later. The first tournament took six hours to complete, and the second tournament took four and a half hours. After a player managed to fight, laugh, cry, bully, pray, and weep his way through ten and a half hours of play, somehow weaseling past all the other competitors, he received the very top prize: a princely sum of $100. Eighth place got $10 — almost, but not quite, reaping a stunning $1 per hour. Ninth place got a breath of fresh air.

You put forth a big time commitment for a whole lotta play that rewards little cash. But hey, the person who won the example tourney didn't have to lay down a nickel, and he gets bragging rights for life. (Nor was it any burden to the guy who pushed all-in with 7-2 offsuit and was eliminated in the first five seconds of the tourney.)

You should note that not all free-rolls are as bad as the example. The less populated sites don't have these swarms but still have free-rolls — essentially giving you much better odds. You can look at `www.pokerpulse.com` and scroll to the bottom of the list to see which free-roll sites are out there.

Judging the worth of free-rolls

In the pure mathematical sense, free-rolls are the best tournaments going. You can make money without risking so much as a cent. From a mathematical purist's perspective, free-rolls are great.

Many poker purists hate free-rolls, however. The long-playing sessions get very tedious, and the grinding psychology of it all is exacerbated by how little you win. Topping that, the play you run up against is so loose that the game more closely resembles the lottery than it does poker. Playing free-rolls, unless you repeatedly make it far into the tourneys, doesn't improve your general poker-playing prowess and could ultimately be detrimental to your hard currency play. If you only ever play against sloppy and lackluster opponents, and you never risk any of your own money, you don't get the experience necessary to improve your overall play.

The worth of playing free-rolls depends on you. We view playing in free-rolls kind of like watching *Jerry Springer:* Everyone should definitely do it once, for the experience if nothing else. But continuing to do it? Hmm. It does seem a little odd.

Getting one chance with a single-entry tourney

Single-entry tournaments are the most common form of tourney on the Net. You pay a set amount (the *entry fee*), plus a small amount given to the site (a *registration fee* — typically 10 percent of the entry fee), and you play until you either have all the chips or you lose them all. You can find single-entry tournaments in two flavors. *Tournaments on demand* are offered continuously and start as soon as a tournament's worth of people sign up (2 for a head's-up tourney, 10 for a full single table). They usually consist of one table (or sometimes two on sites with more flexibility). *Scheduled tournaments* provide a specific start time and a longer period during which you can sign up. You should expect scheduled tourneys to be larger multi-table affairs. We cover the nuances of these in the following sections in this chapter.

Single-entry tournaments (both scheduled and on demand) come in the following variations:

- ✔ **Hold 'Em:** Fixed-limit and no-limit. Every now and then you can find pot-limit.

- ✔ **Omaha:** Fixed-limit and pot-limit in both Omaha High and Omaha High/Low.

- ✔ **Seven-Card Stud:** Fixed-limit in both Seven-Card Stud High and Seven-Card Stud High/Low.

After you start paying for tournaments, the skill level immediately gets markedly better when compared to the free-rolls. As you should expect, the higher the buy-in, the better the play.

Any tournament theory you know from the brick-and-mortar world applies here, although you need to be aware that players are more likely to bet boldly in no-limit and pot-limit online than they are in person (as we discuss in Chapter 5). We go into extended detail of single-table tournaments on demand in Chapter 12.

Living nine lives with the re-buy tourney

In many tournaments, and in *all* tournaments on demand, after you lose all your chips, you're truly done. The site assigns your finishing position at the very moment you bust out. So if you're playing in a 100-player tournament and 20 people go down in front of you before you bust out, you finish 80th.

Step right up and re-buy

You buy in to a $20 pot-limit Omaha tournament. To play, you pay the $20 entry fee and a $2 registration fee. The site automatically assigns you to a seat with 1,500 in tournament chips. You lose your very first hand and drop to 1,450 in tourney chips. At this point, you *could* click on the chip rack of your poker site, and for another $20 (no registration fee this time), you get 1,500 more in chips for a total of 2,950. (You can't re-buy until your stack gets below 1,500 again.)

Ten unlucky hands later, you're busted to zero. The site automatically prompts you: "Would you like to re-buy 1,500 chips for another $20?" If you answer yes, the site deducts $20 from your balance (again, no extra registration fee) and hands you a stack of 1,500. If you say no (or say nothing and get timed out), the site automatically boots you from your seat and doesn't allow you to return to the tourney. In this particular tourney, the site gives you the option of re-buying only during the first hour.

But not all tourneys are this way. Take the particular critter known as the *re-buy tournament,* for instance, where for a limited period of time (typically the first hour of the tournament), you have a chance to *re-buy* into the tournament if you go below your initial buy-in stack size — all the way down to, and including, bust-out status. For more on what we think of re-buying chips (and its possible evil side effects), head to Chapter 11.

To re-buy, you click on the cashier button for your site. If your site doesn't have a cashier button, click on the chip rack on your table. When you re-buy, you typically don't have to pay another registration fee. After the re-buy time limit expires, you can longer re-buy, and busting out of a tournament eliminates you permanently. The sidebar "Step right up and re-buy" in this chapter illustrates the mechanics.

Tournaments with re-buys are always specially marked on your site's home screen, either with phrasing like "$22 + Re-buys" or "$20 R." The tournament lobby always has all the details on the re-buy rules and stipulations.

Re-buy tourneys are most common in "large betting" games (no-limit and pot-limit) and are very rare in fixed-limit — primarily because one or two cataclysmic hands in a large betting game can wipe you out. The betting ramps so gradually in fixed-limit that you lose your chips far more slowly, and as a result, you don't often see re-buys and add-ons offered.

Adding-on at bargain prices

Re-buy tourneys often give you the choice of an *add-on* — another way to buy more chips no matter how many you have. The add-on typically comes at a mild bargain rate compared to the initial buy-in and is almost always offered at the first break (typically one hour into the tournament).

As an example, in the $22 pot-limit tournament we discuss in the "Step right up and re-buy" sidebar earlier in this chapter, a pal of yours makes it all the way to the first break. By clicking on the chip rack, he receives an offer from the site for a chance, during the break only, to buy an additional 2,000 chips for $20 (his first 1,500 chips were $20, plus a $2 registration fee).

Typically you only find re-buys as a feature of large, scheduled tournaments. Add-ons are *only* offered in tourneys that have re-buys, but not all re-buy tournaments have them.

You should definitely find out whether a tournament allows re-buys and add-ons before you sign up (by looking in the tournament lobby where you register), because the difference can have a big impact on how much it costs to compete effectively. We talk more about making re-buy and add-on decisions in Chapter 11.

Measuring Online Tournament Sizes

Because of the sheer number of players in the online world, you can play any size tournament at almost any time and at any game/limit type (that is, Hold 'Em, Omaha, and Seven-Card Stud in fixed-limit and no-limit/pot-limit varieties). This section lists what you have to choose from.

Playing just one person: The head's-up tournament

You can't find head's-up tourneys in the brick-and-mortar world, because the environment just isn't suited for them. The game would take up too much space and personnel (not to mention the insane amount of card shuffling you'd have to sit through).

The online environment is ideal for head's-up tourneys, however. Shuffling and pot payouts are instantaneous. Sites take care of blinds automatically. You don't have to worry if the guy sitting across from you at the table has taken a shower. You have found a truly perfect poker world.

And pretty much all game versions and limits are available in head's up, although no-limit head's-up play is rare (see Chapter 9). No-limit Hold 'Em tourneys often end in as little as 20 minutes. Fixed-limit Stud battles may take more than an hour.

To see how a tournament ends head's up and to get an idea for the way it all blends together, including the kinds of starting hands you can consider, have a look at Chapter 12.

Diving in head first — at head's-up speed

The action in head's-up tournaments is fast and furious. Playing head's up is like having a newborn child — you just can't believe how much attention it demands. You may well see a dealing rate in excess of 150 or more hands per hour, so if you sign up for one, don't expect to do anything else during that period of time. We don't advise playing multiple tables during any event, but you should *never* play head's up on one table and try to sit in any game on another table at the same time.

Something about the head's-up format brings out both the best and the worst in people. Out of all online poker variations, we've met the friendliest people playing head's up, but the land of one on one is also where we've found the biggest swine.

If you want to become a serious tournament player, get plenty of exposure to head's-up tourneys. If you're both lucky and skillful enough to make it through the field, you should gain confidence: Head's up is where all tournaments end. Play, play, play until you feel comfortable.

Strategically speaking: Going head's-up

We find playing head's-up tournaments, especially at first, to be amazingly disconcerting. The whole world consists of you and another guy. He bets. Now what?

Because head's-up tournaments exist almost exclusively in the online realm, not much has been written about strategy (yet). But we can provide a bit of advice:

- ✔ Don't try to win every hand. We know, it sounds kinda weird, but you may find it real easy in head's-up play to roll your eyes back in your head and drop into kill-kill-kill mode. Remember, the chips you win, not the number of hands, determine the victor. If you try to win every hand, you'll lose too much when you try to press through mediocre cards. It all goes back to the fundamental rule of economics: Maximize your wins and minimize your losses.

✔ Make your winning hands count big and your losing hands count little. Especially when you call bets, always take a look at the amount you have to risk to cover any bet you've already made — if it seems unreasonable, especially for a marginal call, drop the hand and wait for better cards.

✔ Don't reveal your pre-flop hand through your betting. Bet fair hands exactly the same way you bet your strongest hands. You want to keep your opponent guessing as much as reasonably possible. The harder it is for her to figure you out, the tougher it is for her to develop a strategy to beat you. (See Chapter 6 for more on disguising your play.)

✔ Pay special attention to variations in your opponent's betting. If she always raises pre-flop by a single bet and then suddenly raises five times the blind, let the hand go because she probably has something good.

✔ If you win a string of hands in a row, become more and more willing to fold any given hand to your opponent. The psychological strangeness of losing several hands in a row is tough, and players are more likely to bite you harder when they get a hand if they haven't eaten in a long while. To combat this blind aggression, let go of the occasional hand so you can ultimately win more. If you thought your opponent was frustrated when he couldn't get a hand, imagine if you fold right away when he has A-A.

✔ If you run across an opponent who seems to want to push all-in or over bets *every* hand, play super tight. Fold everything until you hold extremely strong starting cards (Hold 'Em: A-8 or better or a pair of 9s or better; Seven-Card Stud: pair of 9s or better or three cards 10 or higher; Omaha: four cards 10 or better or a pair of 10s or better) and then fire back *hard.* You almost guarantee yourself a mathematical edge this way, but you should be prepared for the occasional bad beat.

Playing just one table: Single-table tournaments

Strictly speaking, head's-up tournaments are just a specialized form of single-table tournaments. If you exclude *satellite qualifiers* (situations where winning a single-table tourney automatically gives you a seat in a larger tourney) for larger tournaments in the brick-and-mortar world (as well as some wimpy 'lil cardrooms), you find single-table tourneys almost exclusively online.

Single-table, on-demand tournaments are simple: You sign up for one, and as soon as the tournament table fills, you're off and playing. We have an extended description of single-table tournaments, as well as introductory strategic advice, in Chapters 12 and 13.

Playing just one planet: Multi-table tournaments

Multi-table tournaments are always scheduled tournaments that you sign up for ahead of time during a registration period (anywhere from an hour to several days; the tournament lobby where you sign up on the site always has details). Sometimes they have caps with the maximum number of people and sometimes not.

The number of players determines the number of tables in the tournament. Ten thousand players in a tournament require 1,000 tables. As soon as 10 players bust out of the tourney, the site *breaks down one* table and puts all the players from that table in the holes left by the eliminated players in a process called *re-balancing*. Re-balancing continues until 10 players remain at the final table.

Although multi-table tournaments do exist in the brick-and-mortar world, the size of these tourneys in the online world is unmatched. The most popular sites routinely draw tournaments with more than 5,000 players (especially if the entry fee is $5 or less).

Because of the number of entrants, if great play and good fortune are on your side, you can take a few dollars and win big. To give you some idea, a recent $2 entry no-limit Hold 'Em tournament paid $1,000 to the winner. A more lucrative big brother, a $215 entry-fee affair, paid $90,000 to the top dog. Not bad for a weekend's worth of work.

You can also parlay tournament success in the Internet world into brick-and-mortar tournament entries. The ultimate winners of both the 2003 and 2004 World Series of Poker $10,000 main event in Las Vegas won their WSOP seats from multi-table events in the cyber poker world. The 2003 winner paid $40 for a tournament that granted a $10,000 entry seat in the WSOP. He ended up winning the WSOP and over $2 million in cash. These kinds of parlays exist in the brick-and-mortar world as well, but right now they enjoy the most popularity on the Net.

Choosing an Online Tournament

With all the tournament choices, you may feel like a kid in a too-many-flavors ice cream store. We have a few comments and ideas that may help you decide what's right for you. (And no, you don't have to pick vanilla just because your brother did.)

Picking your game

You need to decide what you want to play and how much money you want to play for.

Finding a good stake

If you've never played tournament poker before, play one free-roll (see the section "Examining Online Tournament Types" earlier in this chapter) just to get a feel for the tournament dynamic. Don't expect to gain any poker prowess in a free-roll. You just want to get a feel for the way tourneys work. After you get comfortable, move to something with a small entry fee (less than $5). The small entry fee eliminates the free-playing riff-raff (free-play games can become glorified versions of bingo because of loose, bad play), and you actually gain some true poker experience.

If you do have tournament poker experience, and you're already comfortable playing online, try playing a tournament with an entry fee at about half of what you normally play in the brick-and-mortar world. That amount puts you in the right general caliber of play, but if something goes horribly wrong, you haven't ditched too large an entry fee.

From an entry fee perspective, you should remember that online tournaments go much more quickly. If you're used to playing $200 brick-and-mortar events where you essentially wile your hours away on a Sunday afternoon with your buddies, you may feel pretty unsatisfied after blowing $200 online in less than an hour. If you want to feel like you get your money's worth, play in large multi-table tourneys or divide the number of dollars you typically spend in a tournament by six and play in different single-table matches. For elapsed time, you can better spend your $200 bankroll among $30 to $35 entry-fee single-table tournaments rather than on a sole $200 tourney.

Be prepared for large swings in your bankroll if all you play are tourneys. You shouldn't play at any stake that you don't have at least 20 entries for. If you lose 25 percent of your initial stake, back down one entry-fee level before you keep playing.

Seeking the right tournament

Picking the right poker tournament is like picking the right pair of jeans — you want to be satisfied with something that suits you best.

If you haven't played in tournaments before, don't assume that the hand value and type that you typically play in ring games are the same as what you play in tournaments — especially in pot-limit Omaha High and no-limit Hold 'Em. If you're familiar with these ring games, play several tourneys at the lowest stakes possible or just observe several games at the stakes you want to play to get a feel for what's actually a "playable" hand. Trust us, doing so saves you dough.

With the exception of head's-up play tourneys, which are relatively new in the poker world (thanks to the Net), tons of books cover tournament poker play in the brick-and-mortar world. All the theory applies just as readily to the online world, and if you're a serious player (or want to be), you should buy some books and study up. (We cover some great book sources and forums where you can read people's opinions about what's best in Chapter 16.)

The single-table pros and cons

Red's favorite tournaments are the single full-table (and on some sites, double-table) tournaments. They always finish in less than 90 minutes (often in less than an hour). The game dynamic changes as players are eliminated from the table, making the action more interesting. Also, if you get caught by a bad beat (as you inevitably will at some point), you haven't poured hours into a single game only to get your money taken away by the turn of a very unfriendly card. And because you only play against one table full of folks, you win money more often.

The downside of single-table tournaments is that you can't win as much as you can in larger tournaments. The top prize, typically, is the amount of your entry fee times five. (We cover single-table tournaments extensively in Chapters 12 and 13.)

The multi-table ins and outs

If you're hunting down the big money, and you don't mind going through long dry spells, multi-table tournaments are the only way to go. A big advantage is that your general table strategy doesn't have to change much, because these tournaments can be so large that it takes hours to see the table sizes diminish — even by as much as one player.

Just as in the brick-and-mortar world, during multi-table tourneys you want to keep an eye on your stack size, both relative to your table and to the tournament at large. One great thing about the online world is that all sites calculate the average stack size in the tournament to give you an easy way to judge how you're doing relative to other players (a *much* better indicator than your stack's standing relative to the current top dog). All this information is available to you in your tournament's lobby (the place where you signed up) as you play.

The head's-up ups and downs

If you plan to play multi-table tournaments, you need to sharpen your head's-up skills. Although you may not need them very often, it makes a huge difference in how you fare when you do (because first place often takes home almost twice as much prize money as second).

Head's-up skills are vitally important for single-table tourneys because, from a raw probability point of view, you have a 1-in-5 chance (2 people of the 10 starters) of playing head's up. Those odds increase, obviously, as your play sharpens.

Finding play where you have the edge

Most tournaments tack on a tournament registration fee to the player of something around 10 percent of the entry fee to enter. (Your poker site takes the registration fee as a rake for the tourney.) This means you typically have to do 10 percent better than average just to break even. Not such great odds.

You can, however, find ways around this to put the odds in your favor. Look for tournaments that have *added* or *guaranteed* funds. These tend to be more common on the lesser-populated sites that want to gain players. For example, you may find a tournament with a $10 entry fee, a $1 registration fee, and $100 the site adds to the prize pool.

If only 20 people play in the tournament, the house essentially puts in $5 extra per person. That means that although you put in a grand total of $11 to play, the amount put in for every player is $15 (your $10 entry fee plus the $5 the site adds for you). You get a great deal because, in a strict math sense, every person on average makes $4 ($15 paid to every player minus the $11 you use to enter). Try to find this great deal, rivaled in pure mathematics only by the free-roll, by seeking out the lesser-populated sites.

Recognizing a good deal

You're interested in a site that has added $1,000 to a tournament prize pool. You see that 323 players have signed up and paid a $20 + $2 registration fee. Is this tourney a good deal (does it have a positive expectation)?

If 323 players put in $646 worth of registration fees, and the site pays back $1,000, or $354 more than those registration fees, you've found a good deal.

To encourage the first players to sign up, tournaments often have guaranteed prize pools, representing the minimum amount that the site spreads out among the successful players. If the number of entry fees doesn't add up to the guarantee, the site adds enough to get there. Of course, the tournament hosts hope to entice more than enough entrants to achieve the prize pool size that they promise.

A situation where the money coming out of a tournament is bigger than the money going in (remembering to add in the registration fees) is called *positive expectation* by math-heads.

To assure that you're in a positive expectation situation, make sure the total prize pool is bigger than all entry and registration fees combined, and then enter the tournament very close to the cut-off time. You don't want a sudden surge of players at the end to eliminate your possible profits.

Positive expectation tourneys tend to happen most frequently in Omaha and Stud. Because of their inherent edge, these tourneys are definitely worth your time and effort to seek out.

To find a lesser-populated site, go to www.pokerpulse.com and scroll down to the bottoms of the lists. Hit some of these sites and see if they advertise adding any money to tournaments.

Chapter 11

Clueing in to Tournament Chip Standings

In This Chapter

▶ Keeping track of your chip standing

▶ Working your chip standing into your game

▶ Continuing play with re-buys and add-ons

▶ Hanging on as the money point approaches

*T*he main characteristic that makes tournaments stand apart from ring game play is your chip stack. In ring games, as long as you have the ability to put more money down on the table, you can keep on playin'. Lose all your money at the table? No problem, just bring in some more. (Check out Chapter 9 for more ring game info.) In the tournament world, you get a set number of chips and no more. When your chips are gone, you're *out.* Usually.

The situation isn't always cut and dried. You may encounter a specific mutated little critter known as a *re-buy* tournament: a certain type of multi-table affair where if you get busted out, you can buy more chips, come back from the grave, and keep playing. And some of these re-buy tourneys have a sick and twisted variation known as an *add-on,* where you can add the amount of your buy-in to your stack one time at a discounted rate. (See Chapter 10 for more about re-buys and add-ons.)

One fascinating characteristic of tournament play is that your chip standing can (and should) affect your poker play. Your standing changes the types of hands you play, the amount you bet, and the calling decisions you make.

In this chapter, we help you make sense of it all. We give you some advice on how to get the most value for your chip dollar. We toss out some tips for improving your small stack and how to maneuver through a re-buy tournament. And we also give you some tips on how to hang in there until you make it to the money. After all, they say the worst place to finish in a tourney is one out of the money (and if you have, you know what we mean.)

Making Sense of Your Chip Standing

Your *chip standing* is your money position relative to everyone else in a tournament. If you're familiar with brick-and-mortar tournaments, one of the tasks that can drive you slowly insane is trying to understand how many chips you have relative to everyone else in the tournament. In theory, players are always supposed to keep their tournament chips in plain view, but players have found a million ways to obscure their chips: physical obstacles like drinks and arms/hands on the table; massive chip stacks (which hide yet more chips); and sloppy chip mounds without definitive valuation. Even if you can see your opponents' chips, you have to be able to count and evaluate them relative to yours. If you're playing in a tournament with more than just a couple of tables, knowing your exact standing is almost impossible, unless you have the math and observational skills of Rain Man.

Ah, but the beauty of the Net! You get your chip standing instantaneously online. All you have to do is look in your tournament lobby window to see the full run-down on your standing relative to everyone else, as well as an exact chip count for the entire tournament. Broadly speaking, you should pay attention to four things:

- ✔ Your chip standing relative to the average stack throughout the tournament. This gives you an idea of how well you're doing in the tournament as a whole. Your standing doesn't matter so much early in a tournament, but it becomes important when you approach the money line and as the tournament starts to wear down. If possible, you want to be no lower than 10 percent below the average stack. After you drop below this level, you need to tighten up a little and make sure you maximize your winning hands.

- ✔ Your chip standing relative to the opponents at your table. Your table position is hugely important — determining what role you take on the table and what image you project — as we show in the next section.

- ✔ Your chip standing in the tournament (7th place out of 135 players, for example). In small tournaments, including single-table tournaments on demand, your rank is especially important because it gives you an idea of your standing relative to the rest of the field (if one player gets an early good hand and knocks out two players, it skews the average — but not your standing). Where you stand isn't as important early on in big multi-table tournaments (although you get a special rush by winning a quick first hand in a huge multi-table and then seeing your ranking as 1 of 5,000), but it does become critical later on — your standing determines if you're in or out of the money.

✔ Your chip standing relative to the blinds (or blinds + antes in later tournament rounds on some sites). If you have fewer than 10 big blinds left, you need to drop into short-stack kung fu mode, which we describe in the following section.

Using Your Chip Standing to Your Advantage

If everyone at your table has about the same number of tournament chips, and the tourney isn't close to the money line, you should play in your usual merry way. But when the stacks get out of balance (and they *will* get out of balance), the balance of power shifts, and odd things begin to happen.

Bullying with a bigger stack

If you're fortunate enough to build a large chip stack at your table — anywhere from 30 percent over your closest opponent — you get some luxuries not afforded to lesser mortals.

In Hold 'Em and Omaha, you should consider raising any pot you go into that another player hasn't already raised. The reasons for this strategy are two-fold:

✔ You don't want to let the blinds see any cards for free.

For the time being at least, you run the show; therefore, when you play, everyone plays at slightly higher stakes.

✔ Poker, possibly more than any other game combining skill and luck, is a game of momentum.

When you've got momentum, you can feel it, and you seem like an unstoppable force. And when you feel it, players at the table feel it, too, and they become more likely to give you leeway. This strategy holds true as much in the online world as it does in the brick-and-mortar world.

Big stacks in Seven-Card Stud

In Stud, a bigger stack doesn't serve you quite as effectively, but it still has some force. You should never let more than one single round check all the way around the table. In other words, make sure you place a bet in every round, unless you have strong reason to believe someone has a hand better than yours, or you have the mortal nuts and want to extract as many bets as possible out of the opposition. In theory, it takes a better hand to call than it does to bet; so if you make the bet, hands of roughly the same caliber should fold. Over time you start creeping ahead of the competition by being aggressive.

By getting aggressive, you get a bigger investment from other players when you do hit your hand on the flop, and you play against people who are far less likely to bet into your hand when you don't get the cards. You also have a better chance of clearing out other players with marginal hands early on, thereby averting any freakish draws that could wipe you out. This strategy is especially important for both Hold 'Em and Omaha, where the betting is usually no-limit or pot-limit.

We're not saying that you should bluff more often with a heavy stack, because as you win, you bring out the bad will of the table — and you make those people want to come after you when they have a hand. We're just saying that when you sport a big stack, you have considerably more big blinds you can play (no matter what the current blind is) than your competitors. Use your stack to your advantage.

You need to be careful around short-stacked opponents, however — especially in no-limit play. People with stacks less than five times the size of the big blind are more prone to push all-in on you — so if one of those people still has to call behind you, and you don't have a dominant hand, you should strongly consider calling the big blind without raising. You don't want to donate your chips to a desperate, needy cause. However, if you have a very strong hand, the raise is merited, because you may provoke an all-in when you're a heavy favorite.

Clawing back in short-stack kung fu

When playing any tournament size or type in both no-limit Hold 'Em and pot-limit Omaha, if you're unfortunate enough to find yourself in a smaller-stacked position (say, 30 percent less than the nearest competitor at your table), the number one thing to do is *don't panic.* The most common error people commit in this position is to lose hope too quickly and bet hands they would never normally bet during more lucrative times (such as pushing all-in with low suited-connectors in Hold 'Em, for example). Remain calm. Yes, the odds are against you. Yes, the chips are truly down. But wigging out doesn't make the situation better, and you often have sufficient time to recover as the world crumbles around you.

Because your chip-heavy opponents expect you to freak out, they call you and your mousy little stack more often. For this reason, you should tighten your play a bit and wait. Play only hands of quality and *never* try to steal a blind (unless you know you're up against a confrontationally shy opponent).

This doesn't mean that you should become timid. No, no. Think of this tighten-and-wait time as your chrysalis stage. You went into your cocoon as a somewhat wounded short-stacked caterpillar; when you emerge, you want to be a feisty chip-spewing monster. (Think of the Japanese film creature, "Mothra," with its above-average intelligence and telepathic abilities.)

When you do receive a good hand, bet it a little harder than usual. You have ground to make up and you want the people acting after you to respect your authority and fold or call so you add their chips to your heap when you win the hand.

Short-stack kung pao (when you don't have enough chips for kung fu)

The short-stack kung fu works well in games where you're short-stacked and can place no-limit or pot-limit bets. But in fixed-limit Hold 'Em, Omaha, and Seven-Card Stud, the situation is different — you probably don't have enough to threaten another person's stack significantly. Even at your fiercest, all you can do is lay a series of set bets.

What you need to do is find a decent hand and bet it to the end. If you pair the flop in Hold 'Em, and the cards don't suggest a large board threat (for example, if you hold 9-9, you don't want the flop to be A K Q), start betting and keep going. You need to rack up those fixed-limit tourney chips.

In Omaha, if you have the nut flush draw, the nut straight draw, any trips, or two pair, start betting and don't stop 'til the river. In Stud, bet any starting large pair and call with any medium-sized pair. Kung pao certainly isn't as threatening as kung fu, but when you have to gobble up some spicy tourney chips, it's the only way to go.

But keep an eye on the size of your stack. You need to have enough ammunition to shoot at your opponent to be scary. If you wait too long to make some of your moves, you get callers you don't want simply because you don't pose any immediate threat to their stacks — no matter what you bet.

A poker truism rings loudest for the short-stacked: When you have a winning hand, you want to maximize the amount your opponents will give you. If you think they'll call an all-in, bet it. If you think they may call just a single, scrawny bet, go that route.

If you make a bet because you want an opponent to fold (for example, you have a good hand that can be beaten by a drawing hand, such as a small pair against two overcards), your bet needs to be big enough to threaten your opponents' stacks. Consider the stack sizes of other players in the hand and think about how large a bet you need to make to put a dent in their stacks.

Re-Buying and Adding-On Chips

Some large multi-table tournaments give you the option of *re-buying* chips. After your stack falls below the initial buy-in amount, you have the option of paying another entry fee to receive another stack of chips. (For re-buy and add-on basics, see Chapter 10.) We should tell you right now that we're not fans of re-buy tournaments. They often become nothing more than a challenge to see who has the largest bank account, because some folks re-buy, re-buy, and then re-buy again.

The ability to re-buy encourages loose play: "Hey man, I figure if I lose this hand, I can always re-buy." Which means that *your* bad beats start to increase. Remember Red's Law: Any numbskull with a sufficiently deep pocket will eventually knock out any single-entry player in a re-buy tournament. (Being a numbskull, however, doesn't increase your chances of winning the tournament as a whole.)

Understanding re-buying basics

In a re-buy tournament, you can make your re-buy any time your stack falls below the original amount the site allotted you (although a few tourneys allow you to re-buy at any time). The stack you get when you re-buy is usually identical to the stack you received at the start; so if you got 1,500 chips for a $5 entry, expect 1,500 more when you fork over another $5.

Re-buy evil at work

To give you some idea of the evil forces at work here, a recent $5 tourney on a large site had 600 entries, 950 re-buys, and 300 add-ons. This type of tourney is *very* typical.

Good news for the tournament purse; bad news for any single-entry player trying to slog through the tourney, because the tourney had twice as many re-buys and add-ons combined than plain entries. This essentially makes the playing field three times as large as it appears and gives every player two chances to knock out any given opponent.

You can usually request re-buys by clicking on the chip tray (or the action button for buying chips — see Chapter 3 for more about control buttons). If you bust out, your site automatically offers you a dialog to ask if you want to re-buy before summarily kicking you out of your seat.

The re-buy debate is largely a matter of choice. When the time comes to make the actual decision, consider the situation at the table. If you're sitting at a table with a generally sub-standard level of play, and the average chip stack isn't out of sight, you typically get good value for your money if you re-buy, because you have a legitimate chance at growing your stack and snagging some of those old chips back.

If, however, play seems tough or your re-buy still leaves you uncomfortably under-stacked (often due to plenty of wild play followed by many re-buys at the table), you should quit and try another day.

Here are two schools of thought on when to re-buy:

- ✔ **Re-buy when your stack is about 30 percent of the largest on your table.** The underlying thought is that when you *do* get a good hand, you need to have firepower in the form of chips to back it up. This strategy has merit, particularly in no-limit games, because when you have a good hand, you want absolutely as much return as you can get on your hand. No-limit allows you to bet large, increasing your return.

- ✔ **Wait until you lose your entire stack before you re-buy.** You may get on a hot streak and not need to re-buy. For another, great power comes with being all-in. After you put the rest of your money in the pot, you can't be bluffed out and you get to see the remaining cards for free. And if people fight with each other while you patiently wait to the end, all the better — the hand that could beat you may get bet out by another player.

Knowing when to add-on

At the first multi-table re-buy tournament break (typically one hour in), your site may ask you if you want to add-on to your chip stack. The add-on typically costs the same amount as your entry fee, but it gives you *more* chips. Add-ons are a one-time-only deal that expires at the end of the break. If a $5 buy-in gives you 1,500 tourney chips to start, a $5 add-on may give you 2,000 more. From a pure economic perspective, add-ons are a good deal because the amount you spend per chip is less.

On the surface, it looks like you're often forced to add-on in order to stay competitive with other people in the tourney. (And it has the nasty side effect of actually doubling the cost of your tournament — your $5 tourney now becomes $10, not including re-buys.) But that doesn't necessarily mean you should take add-ons.

You should follow one very simple but very powerful rule of thumb with add-ons: Take them if and only if you expect to be below average after the add-on process and the add-on pulls you to within 10 percent of the average; otherwise, you should pass.

The vast majority of players add-on during re-buy tourneys. If you have an average stack before the add-on period starts, expect to be below average (possibly significantly) at the end of the break. If everyone else adds-on and you don't, all your opponents more than double their original chip stacks while you sat waiting.

Having a stack over-and-above the average really doesn't matter because after the tournament has progressed, adding chips probably won't raise your stack significantly enough to make a quantifiable difference in your standing — especially in no-limit/pot-limit games.

When you mentally calculate the cost of a tournament, you should initially assume that you *will* pay for the add-on when the time comes — because you can figure that everyone else will add-on.

Tip-Toeing on the Bubble: Finishing in the Money

You may have heard the expression "on the bubble" used by analysts during the conclusion of the college basketball season. Certain teams are on the bubble when it comes to making it to the tournament of the final 64 — on the bubble meaning they teeter on the edge of being in or out. Poker tournaments aren't much different (only here, making the "64" means you get money). The *bubble* is the point in any tournament of any kind or size where the finishing positions start to pay money. For example, if 10 players are left in a tournament that pays 9 spots, the next player out bursts the bubble and goes home empty handed.

Your chip standing ultimately determines where you finish in the tournament. When your tourney chip balance hits zero, the site determines your finishing position. You clearly want to end up inside the bubble where all that tasty cash floats around rather than outside the bubble in that nasty day-old dishwater. Your chip standing is key to determining the kind of plays you should make on the bubble.

On quality sites (see Chapter 2), when you get close to the bubble in a multi-table tournament, you begin to notice occasional pauses as play goes into *hand-for-hand* mode. You get a message from the site that lets you know when hand-for-hand play starts. At this point, every table in the tournament must finish a hand, across the complete tournament, before the site deals the next hand. Playing one hand at a time keeps low-stacked players from playing slowly in hopes that someone else at another table will bust out first.

You should try to ignore the bubble and play your best poker game — because other people don't. People often play *extremely* tight as the bubble approaches, and you may have the opportunity to pick up a few blinds because of it. Consider raising with any hand you normally play pre-flop in Hold 'Em and Omaha, especially if the blinds are short-stacked (if they have poor cards, they may just let the hand go rather than fight you and potentially end up just out of the money).

You ignore the bubble because your goal is to win the tournament, not just a little prize money. Yes, everyone enjoys winning money. And yes, winning money is *always* better than not winning money. Weak, awkward, or timid play around the bubble, however, damages your chances of winning the Big Prize. You should make it a goal to finish in the money; just don't make it your ultimate goal.

If all players at the table are evenly stacked, and they all focus on the bubble — but you keep your eyes on the bigger picture — extra blinds easier to pick up. This doesn't mean you should get too crazy and overly aggressive. An opponent with an extremely good hand should never drop it. But you should definitely up your aggression a notch — especially if you can see that the rest of the table starts to sit back and wait.

A case study in chip stack ignorance

Perhaps no other story more clearly indicates the importance of chip standing, and a person's awareness of the rank and file, than a tale about the World Series Qualifier Red was playing in. After six hours of no-limit Hold 'Em against a field of thousands, Red made it to the final table with just two other players left. The top two finishers received a trip to Las Vegas and a "free" $10,000 entry into the main event of the World Series of Poker. Red had 225,000 in chips, his burly opponent Action Monkey had 235,000 chips, and the anemic Tiny Tim had a measly 10,000.

Red was on the button, Tiny Tim had the small blind of 2,000, and Action Monkey (a bully throughout the tournament) was the big blind with 4,000. Red was dealt A-A. What could be better? He raised to three times the big blind to make a bet of 12,000. Tiny Tim folded. Action Monkey paused and then pushed all-in.

Red squealed, as he is prone to do when excited, and called. What could be better than taking away this brutal simian's half-dozen hours of play? The cards were exposed to show the Monkey holding A-K off-suit, automatically making Red a 93 percent favorite to win (only kings, a miracle straight, or flush could save the monkey now). Favorite, that is, until the flop came K K 7, reducing Red to a less than 5 percent chance of winning. The turn and the river were no help, and Red was eliminated. Tiny Tim got to go Vegas. Was this a bad beat? No doubt.

But the bigger problem here (like always, it seems) was Red's mental faculty. In just a couple orbits of the dealer button, Tiny Tim would have been forced all-in. And whenever Tim did make his move, he could be of no possible danger to either player. Red could easily call with any hand against the small stack, and do so *repeatedly*, waiting for whatever sweet final moment that Tim would play no more.

The right move here, even with pocket rockets, was for Red to fold to the raise and watch Tim sweat it out. No matter what hand Red was playing against, he had about a 7 percent chance of losing by calling; his odds of losing if he folded on the spot were easily much less than that. (For info on how to find a poker odds calculator, check out Chapter 16.)

The exception to this is when you play in games where all the top qualifiers get the same prize. For example, if you're in a tournament where the top 10 players win identical poker cruises, you shouldn't care if you finish first or finish last; your goal is to finish in the top 10. Pay attention to players getting pushed all-in. If they go out, you come closer to the prize. (After you reach the final 10, you can gain good final-table tournament experience without the pressure of losing.)

Stay away from any fighting between larger-stacked opponents when you're trying to cross the bubble. If two large stacks start going toe-to-toe against each other, they do more damage to you if you get caught in the middle because your chips are more valuable. You have fewer to lose before you're out.

Chapter 12

Winning Single-Table Tournaments

- -

In This Chapter

▶ Gunning for single-table pay-outs

▶ Hunkering down at the full table

▶ Slipping into short-handed play

▶ Heading into head's-up play

- -

*Y*ou want pressure? Play in a single-table tournament. You want fun? Play in a single-table tournament. You want to win? Read this chapter . . . and then play in a single-table tournament.

A winning player is the person who can master all the dynamics at work in the wonderful world of online single-table tournaments. With a little study, practice, and a well-worn copy of this book by your side, you can be the champ left standing. We promise.

In this chapter (and in Chapter 13), we cover the single-table battleground that you can often only find in the online world, and we talk about the aspects of poker that you normally don't have to think about during ring games or until the final table of multi-table tournaments. We're talking about stuff like quickly diminishing table sizes, wildly swinging chip stacks, and those pressure-filled moments when you need to go all-in.

 As a reflection of what you find on the Net, we show a heavy bias toward no-limit Hold 'Em in this chapter. Well over 90 percent of all tournament play online is no-limit Hold 'Em — the remaining fraction is split almost evenly between Seven-Card Stud (which is always fixed-limit), Omaha (both fixed and pot-limit), and fixed-limit Hold 'Em.

Entering the Land of Single-Table Tournaments

Single-table tournaments in the online world go something like this: You and up to nine other players pay a set entry fee. After the table fills up to the pre-determined amount (which normally only takes a couple minutes), you get a pre-set amount of tournament chips. For example, you pay a $5 entry fee and you get 1,500 in tourney chips. You gamble these chips through the normal poker process (if you don't know this process yet, you're reading the wrong book — check out Wiley's *Poker For Dummies*), and players bust out one-by-one until only one person remains. That last person is the champ, and we want that person to be you.

Recognizing single-table idiosyncrasies

You need to pay attention to characteristics specific to tournaments. Unlike ring game play, where even the most clueless player can dip into his bank account endlessly and keep right on playin' (see Chapters 10 and 11 for info on re-buys), the field in a single-table tournament dwindles over time because players can't continue to refill the chips they lose. When you run out of chips, you're done.

As the crowd thins, the caliber of play at the table typically increases (the bad and unlucky players get knocked out). Matters get further complicated because the stack sizes between players become massively uneven. The big, meaty chip stacks start to intimidate players with thin and under-chipped stacks.

You need to recognize that blinds have a much greater effect on you here than in ring games (where the blinds stay the same). The blind level increases over a set period of time (you can see the tournament lobby for how often they increase — typically every orbit of the dealer marker or every 10 minutes). Because the blinds continually escalate, they can eventually grow to a crippling level if you don't build up your chip stack.

Looking at single-table pay-outs

You can always find the pay structure of a single-table tournament in the tournament lobby. With little exception, the payouts look like this:

> ✔ Full-table tourneys (9 or 10 players):
>
> - 50 percent of entry fees to first place
> - 30 percent to second place
> - 20 percent to third place
>
> ✔ Short-handed tourneys (5 or 6 players):
>
> - 65 percent of entry fees to first place
> - 35 percent to second place
>
> ✔ Head's-up tourneys (2 players):
>
> - 100 percent of entry fees to first place
> - Don't you feel like a middle child coming in second place?

Developing Table-Size-Specific Strategies

Single-table tournaments are unique in the tournament world, in that you have to deal with decreasing tournament size immediately. The decreasing playing field isn't a slow process, and the changes in game dynamics aren't subtle. You have to stay focused and react quickly, often, and with purpose.

In the following sections, we divide table sizes into three categories: full, short-handed, and head's up. As your table size changes, you need to know how to adapt your play to each stage.

Searching for fortune at the full table

Your site of choice starts the full single-table tournament when your table has 6 to 10 players, depending on the pre-determined limit. Your strategy should vary, depending on whether you play limit or no-limit.

Playing in a fixed-limit tournament

When your table is still relatively full, your game strategy in a fixed-limit tournament is essentially no different than your ring game strategy. Your starting hand selection and general hand play should be basically identical. In the early stages, all you want to do is get a feel for the various players at your table and take down the occasional pot when you have a good hand. As the limits escalate, the hands increase in importance because the bet sizes get larger — mistakes early on aren't nearly as fatal as mistakes later. If you want to find out what kind of strategy you should use in general, check out *Poker For Dummies* (Wiley). We talk a bit more about fixed-limit ring game play in Chapter 7.

Taking on a no-limit tournament

In no-limit single-table tournaments, you need to be a little more cautious with your play for two reasons:

✔ One big mistake can cost you your entire stack. (Remember that in single-table tournaments, you only get a set amount of chips, and after you lose them, you lose them forever — at least for this tourney.)

✔ You don't want to come out swinging until you get the hang of the general playing styles of your opponents. The more information you collect, the more intelligent your decisions will be. (See Chapter 6 for more about both note-taking and figuring out your opponents.)

You should be especially cautious if you've never played a no-limit tournament before. Before you even play a no-limit tourney, you should watch a couple of tournaments played in their entirety, which — we swear — is much better prep work than playing in no-limit ring games or tourneys with free chips. Free chip play is much looser than money play, and the differences in strategy between ring game no-limit and tourney no-limit can be substantial. (Check out Chapter 9 for some short-handed ring game info.)

Use the time at the start of a no-limit single-table tournament to establish a *table image* that helps determine the way the other players perceive you and your playing style. Initially, you want to make your opponents think you're the most solid, tight player at the table, only betting when you have a great hand. You can take advantage of this image later when you steal some pots by bluffing with less-than-ideal (otherwise known as *complete garbage*) hands. (Chapter 6 has more on how you define your table image in the online world.)

Surviving the early, full-table stage of the tournament puts you in position to go into chip accumulation mode as the table becomes short-handed.

Avoiding an early exit

You're playing in a $5 no-limit Hold 'Em tournament. Three hands into the tourney, you're dealt A-2 in the big blind. Five players stay in the hand with no raises, and you check.

The flop comes A Q 10, giving you a pair of aces. The small blind pushes all-in. What should you do?

Yes, you have the top pair, but you also have an easily beatable kicker (your deuce). The board shows a freak straight possibility if the small blind has K-J, and any ace with a bigger kicker currently beats you, as does two pair or any trips. Worse, you have three people who still have to act behind you, any one of which may be able to beat you. The best thing to do here is fold and wait for the next hand — all it costs you is a big blind, which isn't worth fighting over if you stand to lose all your chips.

Shrinking to short-handed play

Short-handed play consists of tables with three to five players left. You have to react quickly to the changes that take place at this stage. Because full single-table tournaments typically pay three places, the tournaments reach a magical changing point when you only have five players left. Players typically start playing more conservatively, because they get their first glimpse of prize-light glittering from the end of the tournament tunnel. And when the light hits them, they start to believe they really can win money, so many times (especially in lower entry-fee tourneys) they back off on the aggressiveness of their play in an effort to score a little cash.

Your job here is to make that glittering light your opponents see be coming from the front of your highly tuned poker express train. Take over the aggressor role and run them down.

Shifting your play

With five players remaining, you should shift from playing a little tight to being a little more aggressive, *especially* if the rest of the table starts to tighten up.

Be sure to balance your aggression with the attitude of the rest of the table. You want your play to be on the other side of the spectrum — aggressive when they become passive, tight when they become aggressive. As best you can, always categorize and identify the style of your opponents before you make your moves. As a tournament field winnows, play in a manner that best beats the player(s) you're up against.

Taking more risks

You need to take more risks if the escalating blinds start to threaten you in a tourney (a much different feeling than you get during a ring game, where the blinds don't escalate). You need to put more pressure on the stacks smaller than yours, and be more cautious against the stacks larger than yours. Check out Chapter 13 for more on these ideas.

Getting raw experience

We could type until our fingers bleed, but the truth is nothing beats raw experience when it comes to mastering short-handed dynamics.

Practice on short-handed tables. Although the dynamic isn't *exactly* the same because of slight differences in starting hands, the way betting changes in ring games when you essentially have access to an infinitely deep stack of chips, the blind structure, and payout tension, short-handed tables *still* have the ability to make you much more comfortable when the playing field shrinks in a single-table tourney. (For advice on playing in ring games of this size, have a look at Chapter 9.)

Playing Short-Handed Stud, Hold 'Em, and Omaha

So you have to shift your play, take more risks, react to how your opponents are playing, and play in the opposite manner. Now what? For the low-down on short-handed play in the big three games — Seven-Card Stud, Hold 'Em, and Omaha — step this way.

Looking at Seven-Card Stud

Seven-Card Stud isn't nearly as complicated as Hold 'Em or Omaha, because the cards trickle out in a steady one-by-one fashion. To win during short-handed play, we suggest you consider playing more hands of slightly lesser quality than you normally play at a full table.

If you usually start only with a pair at a full table, a hand like A-K-10 may be reasonable now, because the decreased playing field makes for fewer dominant starting hands. Make sure that you always raise the bring-in hand in any pot you enter. You don't want anyone seeing any potentially damaging cards for free. Any time you think you have a better hand than the table, make sure to get a bet down — even if it becomes obvious that you have a nut or near-nut hand.

Knowing when the odds are against you

You're playing Seven-Card Stud with the fixed limits at 15/30. Only two players are vying for the pot, you and Mr. Trips, and you're evenly stacked.

Mr. Trips shows 8c 8h 10d Kc.

You have As 3s in the hole with 7s 9s Qd 10h showing. A flush possibility. From Mr. Trips' betting pattern and style of play, you put him on two pair or trips.

The pot sits at 30. Mr. Trips has just bet 30 on his sixth street card, and you have to call to see the river. The odds of you catching the final spade to fill your flush are 9 in 42, or about 4 to 1 against. If you call here, four times out of five you lose your $30, and one time out of five you win the $60 in the pot. Mathematically, over five hands, the loss of $120 compared to the gain of $60 means that calling here is a bad decision. (If you're unfamiliar with pot odds, see a basic poker text like Wiley's *Poker For Dummies*.)

You need the bets on the table because you need to win chips at every possible opportunity. You don't play no-limit in Stud — only fixed limit; so when you have a winning hand, you don't have an opportunity to sit back. You have to maximize the hand's value.

On short-handed tables, you get correct pot odds for your drawing hands less often. Flushes and straights, therefore, lose much of their value.

Taking on Hold 'Em and Omaha

We group Hold 'Em and Omaha together because the game dynamic is basically the same: You get hole cards and you bet; the flop comes, and you bet; the turn is revealed, and you bet; and finally, the river card drops, and you bet. Because you play Hold 'Em and Omaha in no-limit/pot-limit variations, you see a considerable difference in the play compared to Seven-Card Stud — one bad bet or call and you could be out of the tourney (and the money).

Acting before the flop

Before the flop, in a tournament of five players or less (and assuming all chip stacks are roughly even), keep the following advice in mind:

> ✔ Consider playing less-dominant starting hands than what you normally play on a full table. Because the number of players has decreased, you have fewer chances to hold a very strong

hand; and you don't need as much strength in your hand, on average, to win.

If the highest ranked five-card gap you play from a middle position on a full table is A-10, K-9 now becomes a real possibility. When the field drops to three players, consider yet another step down, such as Q-8.

✔ Assuming you're not short-stacked against the rest of the table, always raise the big blind if you're the first player to bring in action on the hand. You never want to give the big blind a free look at the flop. Especially in lower buy-in single-table tourneys, you can snap up many blinds this way.

✔ If people merely call in front of you, you should:

- In Hold 'Em: Raise if you hold an ace (with any other card) in your hand or pairs from Q-Q to A-A. In Omaha: Raise if you have a pair of queens or better, four cards jack or better, or a suited ace with a different suited king (for example, Ah 7h Kd 10d). In both cases here, what you want to do is display to the table the dominance of your hand and get a feel for what other people around the table may be playing.

- Call if you have a hand you normally play in that same relative table position at a full table. (J-Q in middle position in Hold 'Em or A-J-10-10 in Omaha, for example.)

✔ If another player raises the blind in front of you, you should call only if you have a hand you normally consider playing on a full table with few players in the pot, and even then only if you have at least an average chip stack. At this point in a tournament, don't be afraid to drop a marginal hand, especially if you see unusual pre-flop action in front of you. It may be hard to remember in the heat of battle, but the idea is to try to get into the money and eventually win the tourney, not win every hand. Focus on winning larger pots, not every pot.

✔ Fold in all other cases. You don't want to try too hard and press marginal hands into play; you want to take good hands, maximize the money you can win, and minimize any losses you may be unable to avoid.

When you're playing no-limit Hold 'Em (or pot-limit Omaha when the pot size is large enough) and the table is short-handed, re-raising a player pre-flop is roughly equivalent to saying, "Please push me all-in right now." You can derive your own rules of thumb, but we suggest re-raising pre-flop only if you have Q-Q, K-K, A-A, or A-K.

If your opponent does re-raise you all-in, you should call with any of these pocket pairs. Flip a coin to make a decision if you have A-K (and pull out your rosary if you call), after you take into account that player's previous betting behavior (check your player notes — see Chapter 6), because you may well be in a classic coin-flip situation: a pair versus two overcards. If, based on previous betting behavior, you have reason to believe that player has K-K or A-A, click that fold button double-quick. And, as always, if you believe you are a better player than the raiser, don't risk all your chips on a coin-flip. Grind him out of the tourney.

Dealing with blinds

When the tournament gets to short-handed play, you start becoming more aware of your blinds. Because fewer players are in, the dealer marker orbits quickly, and your blinds per minute begin to increase.

If the chip levels are fairly even, don't try to over-protect a blind from a player you perceive as trying to steal, especially if you have a hand you don't consider playing in a normal situation. You'd be surprised at the number of times your opponent is actually betting a strong hand (remember, the other players don't want you to see a free card from the blind position either). And you really want to avoid being surprised in a no-limit tournament.

Keep an eye on anyone you perceive as a habitual blind-stealer; if you see someone continually snatching from any of the later betting positions, fire back hard with a raise when you get a quality hand. (Any time you do run across a chronic blind stealer, make sure to make a note of it in the player notes — that keeps you from guessing the next time you run across this person. See Chapter 6 for more on taking notes.)

The reverse is also true of your play in later table positions. If the chip levels are even, you usually shouldn't try to steal blinds from the dealer position. Many people want to defend their blind bet and, unless you match the board, you're at the mercy of whatever diabolical betting strategy they aim at you. Just wait for the next hand. Your cards will get better.

If stealing *is* your game, you may have more luck from one position before the dealer spot. You have to make one more player fold a hand to successfully steal, but it makes other players think you have a stronger hand. Just don't overdo it. People eventually start to suspect you're stealing and decide to come after you.

When you're the small blind

If you're playing on a short-handed table from the small blind, and everyone folds to you, you should:

✔ Call if you have any two connectors (6-7) or two suited cards in Hold 'Em. In Omaha, call with anything (your drawing possibilities are magnified and your opponent numbers decreased).

✔ In Hold 'Em, raise if you have

- Any pocket pair

- Any two cards 8 or better

- Any two suited connectors (3d 4d). Know that raising in this situation is essentially a *semi-bluff* (you don't have a great hand, but you have great possibilities). If raising feels too aggressive for you, or your chip situation, merely call.

- Seriously consider folding all other hands. Playing marginal hands isn't a good idea anyway, and folding gives you more respect from the player to your left when you do play a hand, because he knows that you aren't too stubborn to lay some hands down.

✔ In Omaha, raise if you have

- Four cards 8 or better

- A pair 10s or better

- Any suited ace

- A double-suited hand (10c 6c Ks 2s)

- Call with anything else. Omaha has enough variance that any hand is potentially good after the flop, and the half-bet is worth seeing what chance has to offer.

When you're the big blind

If you're the big blind and you face a raise (no more than three times the big blind), call if you have a hand you normally play from the middle of the field on a full table (possibly Q-J in Hold 'Em or Ah 10h Js 9s in Omaha). If the raise comes from the small blind, call if you have any of the hands we list for the small blind in the previous section. Be ready to quickly let go of any hand that doesn't pair the flop in Hold 'Em or have tremendous potential in Omaha (flush or straight possibilities).

If you're the big blind and the other players simply call the blind, don't raise unless you have an extremely good starting hand or you have reason to believe another player wants to limp in to have a cheap look at a flop. In both cases, the underlying theory is that you need to punish weaker hands for trying to play.

Hitting the Home Stretch: Head's-Up Play

Head's-up play occurs when only two players are left battling for the prize. Head's-up play can drag on, sometimes for a considerable length of time. This back-and-forth battling happens for a couple of reasons. One is that players want to figure each other out and find a weak spot. Another is that the hands tend to be weaker (because only two people get cards), and judging how strong any given hand is becomes difficult, so players don't often bet heavily. Even when you get a monster hand, you shouldn't bet too strong, because you want to maximize the hand's value by not scaring away the other player with a large bet. Much of the theory you find here we cover from a slightly different angle in the head's-up portion of Chapter 9.

In the head's-up world, you always have a blind of some size in front of you. Typically, the dealer marker (and first action) rests with the small blind, and the big blind (and second action) sits with the non-dealer.

The following sections outline hands from the two possible positions.

Assuming you're the small blind, pre-flop

If your chip stack is roughly equal with your opponent's and you're on the small blind, you want to make a modest raise (because you don't want to indicate the strength of your hand) in the situations we outline in the following list (the situations translate to Seven-Card Stud as well). The reason you raise with these hands is you have a better than average chance of winning from the get-go (exactly how big your chances are depend on your individual starting cards and what your opponent has).

In Hold 'Em, raise if you have

- ✔ Two cards 8 or better
- ✔ Two suited connectors

- ✔ Any pocket pair
- ✔ An ace

In Omaha, raise if you have

- ✔ Four cards 7 or better
- ✔ A pair of 8s or better
- ✔ Any suited ace

Fold all other hands. Yes, really. In this battle, you want to save your bullets for hands of value. The half-bet-size call isn't even worth it when you have junk.

At this point you may be asking yourself, "Let me get this right. If I'm playing Hold 'Em and raise with 2d 3d, I should make a similar raise with A-A? Are you insane?" The answers are: "yes" to the first question and "no" to the second.

You want your head's-up opponent to be befuddled and confused. Leave him guessing as to what you may have. If you push all-in every time you have high pocket pairs and merely call when you have 9-10, you may as well just show your foe your cards. (For more on camouflaging your hand online, see Chapter 6.)

Considering when you're the big blind, pre-flop

If your opponent merely calls your blind, you should raise back at twice the blind if you have any of the small blind pre-flop action hands we list in the previous section, because your opponent may be trying to limp in and see a flop for a half-bet. If you follow our advice and rarely limp into a hand to see the flop, you shouldn't allow your opponent to either. A hand of value needs to be paid, especially when you're playing head's up. Don't give opponents a chance to draw and beat your stronger starting hand without paying for the opportunity to do so.

If your opponent raises your big blind by nothing more than three times, you should call if you have any of the pre-flop small blind action hands we list in the previous section (give serious consideration to dropping hands like 8-9 off-suit and the tiny suited connectors) and fold everything else. You only want to play hands of quality against strong bets.

Playing the pair-of-deuces blues

To show you the kind of trouble playing minimal hands can get you into, imagine you're playing Hold 'Em with 2-5 off-suit in the small blind. You call the big blind. (To be clear: We *don't* recommend this play; we recommend you fold.) The big blind decides not to raise, and the flop comes 2 10 Q.

You now have a pair of deuces. You make a minimal bet, and your opponent raises with half his stack. Now what do you do? You really only have two choices: re-raise all-in or fold. (A call only gets you pushed all-in on the turn.) Do you really want to call all-in on a pair of deuces? Didn't think so. If you didn't play this hand in the first place, you wouldn't be having this problem.

If the raise to you is significantly larger than your big blind (such as an all-in), consider calling only if you have A-Q, A-K, or any pair jacks or better; all other calls are probably too risky (depending largely on what you can glean about your opponent, as well as the current chip standing and his possible desperation). Against the very biggest of bets you only want to play the very best of hands. Give yourself the best chance of winning. You often see, especially in small buy-in tourneys, players push all-in with any ace and a low suited kicker. If someone does, and you call with the suggested cards here, your overall odds of winning are very high.

As time elapses, keep a close eye on your opponent and his general betting style. If he seems to always call or always raise you a set amount pre-flop, and then he suddenly bets much more on a single hand, be ready to let your hand go quickly.

Be very suspicious of any player who merely calls after a long series of raises in any specific hand — this tactic is a common trap set by people playing high pocket pairs. Although you're a poker animal, you don't want to get trapped and show up as a trophy on someone else's mantle.

Playing head's up, post-flop

After the flop, the road opens up a bit. Make sure you put bets on the table any time you have a pair in Hold 'Em and with anything better than one pair or with a high flush draw in Omaha.

Pocket deuces versus A-K

In Texas Hold 'Em pre-flop, 2-2 versus A-K is a 50/50 proposition. (The true odds vary from 50.3 percent versus 49.7 percent in favor of the pocket deuces to 53.2 percent versus 46.8 percent for the deuces, depending on the suits involved — you can play with the percentages for this hand, or any hand, on www.cardplayer.com/poker_odds if you're curious.) In the brick-and-mortar world, you usually don't see people push all-in with 2-2 — and a 2-2 call is even rarer — but on the Internet such plays are much more prevalent, possibly because you encounter so many newbie players.

And these newbie players are thinking: If I have 2-2, and somehow I put my opponent on A-K, given that I'm a slight statistical favorite, why not just push all-in as the aggressor during head's-up play (or even at a more populated table)?

Well, you certainly can do that, but the newbie isn't looking at the problem the right way. The real question you need to ask yourself is: Do I really want to reduce my table match to a 50/50 coin flip?

If you have reason to believe you're a better player than your opponent, you don't want to give him the opportunity to beat you based solely on chance — especially when the odds eliminate all the advantage your skill holds. If you really are a better poker player, the longer you fight, the more the statistical edge grinds in your favor, and the more likely you are to ultimately put your opponent down.

Calling an all-in with 2-2 seems foolhardy and possibly suicidal. For all practical purposes, any pocket pair beats you outright (you're a 4-to-1 underdog with a lower pair), and any two overcards are essentially an even bet.

We can think of a few situations where calling an all-in with 2-2 may conceivably make sense: you're falling asleep at the keyboard, your house is on fire, you're about to give birth, or your boss is starting to walk around your desk to see what you've been doing for the last hour. You probably shouldn't be playing during these times anyway, so yeah, go ahead and make the call.

Place small raises any time you have a high board pair in Hold 'Em (two pair or better for Omaha), outside straight draws or flush draws, and get slightly more aggressive if you have combinations of these hands that present good opportunities. Any time you believe you have a winning hand, or something likely to be a winner (say the top two pair in Hold 'Em or trips or better in Omaha), get fairly stiff bets down but not so large that you can't induce a call.

The whole idea when you get to head's up in the single-table tourney is to winnow your opponent's chip stack, and carving it up slowly is just fine. If you rush at him quickly and aggressively, over and over, he may hunker down until he has a hand that he knows can beat you, at which point he proceeds to make a serious effort at taking you out. By slowly bringing your rival down, he often won't be as aware of his impending doom. By the time reality takes hold, you have a firm upper hand because his chip stack has become small relative to yours; and now you're the heavy favorite. Now you can put on the death grip and go for the kill.

In both Hold 'Em and Omaha, if you get a strong reaction to a fairly large bet, especially from an otherwise docile opponent, read the board closely. Look for possible big five-card hands (straights and flushes) and be leery of board pairs that could potentially bear trips or a full house for your enemy.

If you suddenly get pushed all-in by someone who has otherwise been Captain Happy, never call with anything less than top pair, and even then you should be like Aretha Franklin and Think! hard. Show some respect. Be willing to call a bet you believe screams out single-card flush or straight draw, but, as Elmer Fudd says, be vewy vewy careful with everything else.

Making an all-in bet is a much bigger weapon than the all-in call. When you place an all-in bet, you go on the offensive; the all-in call is defensive. Be sure to consider this bit of advice anytime, but especially as you near the end of head's-up play.

Remember, you can always forget about playing a single hand. Fold and play another. (But you may never forget the hand if you make a fatal all-in call.)

Chapter 13

When Your Chips Are Flying: Single-Table Strategies

. . . .

In This Chapter

▶ Keeping an eye on your chips

▶ Picking your spot to make a move

▶ Pushing your chips all-in

. . . .

*I*n a single-table tournament, your *chip standing* (how much money you have compared to the other players at any given point) relative to your opponents is the most important aspect of your game. After all, the standings determine which players get paid at the end of the game based on the order in which they lose their chips.

In this chapter, we discuss managing your wildly swinging stack of chips and knowing that gut-churning moment when you need to bite the bullet and make your big betting move to win that single-table tournament. After all, your chip standing bears a significant impact on the hands you consider playing and the way you bet these hands after you jump into the pot.

Analyzing Where You Stand — Chips-Wise

You chip standing matters. It makes the difference between what you bet on and what you don't. So you always need to keep a watchful eye on what you have and compare it to what your opponents hold.

As you progress through a tournament, two players often acquire larger stacks than the rest of the table. Watch any growing monsters closely. If they seem to want to bully people a bit, try not to get in the middle of any hand where they battle head-to-head. You should always choose to watch *Godzilla vs. Mothra* from a distance . . . you don't want to be one of the citizens of Tokyo getting trampled underfoot.

Finding your chip standing

To find the up-to-date standings for your tournament, head to the tournament lobby (see Figure 13-1). (The lobby is usually the place where you originally registered for the tournament.)

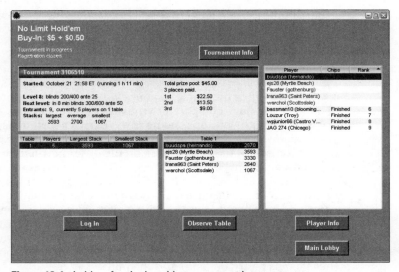

Figure 13-1: Lobby of a single-table tournament in progress.

As you can see from Figure 13-1, the information is straightforward. You can see the players registered for the tournament, as well as the start time, the blind sizes (during play at any time), and the stack size of every player. Although the information itself is easy to comprehend, the way it affects the game is a bit more subtle.

Making sense of your position

To make complete sense of your chip standing, you need to consider several factors:

✔ Any large discrepancies between the stacks

✔ The blind sizes relative to your chip stack and any small stacks

✔ Your standing relative to the other stacks

Pay attention to players with big chip leads or those falling rapidly behind; both have a mild tendency to over-bet hands (the leader because of bullying instincts and the trailer out of desperation). If you have a high-quality hand, don't be afraid to go up against these desperados; in fact, you should raise when you get the opportunity to show you're serious about the hand.

Always have a rough idea of how many current-level big blinds your stack is equal to. Anytime you have fewer than 10 big blinds worth of chips, be ready to swing into the "5-to-10" rule, which dictates that you conserve chips and then get aggressive when you have a hand (see the section "Making your '5-to-10' move" later in this chapter).

Leading a single-table tournament in the early stages doesn't do much for you, aside from the mental comfort that comes with knowing you're not losing.

If you find yourself down after an early knock or two — especially if an opponent catches you bluffing — tighten your play considerably and wait for hands of high quality. Don't guard blinds when you have marginal hands. Again, you want to be conserving your chips to use them only when they can get you more chips back in return.

Using Your Chips to Your Advantage

You can use your stack size to your advantage whether you lead or trail in a tournament. Read on to find out how.

Playing with a lead

If you put yourself in a position where you lead a tournament significantly (say, two times your closest opponent), especially after the table becomes short-handed, raise every pot you come into pre-flop in Hold 'Em and Omaha that another player hasn't already elevated. In this position, you play the troll of the table: No one gets to see a card without paying the price for crossing your bridge first. You don't want to let people see free cards. A lucky draw can be deadly to your stack, so you need to try to force people to drop junky hands.

In Seven-Card Stud, if you take the lead, always raise any time you bring in the action. Again, you want players to pay to see cards. Because you always play Stud as a limit game, you need to get a bet down on the table every time you appear to be winning the hand, and *especially* when you're chip leader.

Don't try to steal any more blinds than you normally do. In fact, you may want to consider stealing fewer. People are expecting you to steal anyway, and like the tiny Lilliputians they are, if people think you're overly aggressive, you may get multiple table members trying to take you down. After all, the more people who call, the more likely you are to lose.

Playing from behind

Don't sweat trailing so much early on, but be careful after your stack size is half the size of any of your opponents' — especially when playing no-limit. The natural tendency of a player hovering well above you is to think, "Well, if I call this all-in bet and lose, I still have half my stack." And if this loose cannon wins, of course, his frivolous all-in bet wipes you out.

Having said that, if you're down, but you still have a chip stack that can put a sizable ding in the other player's battleship (say one-quarter of his stack size in no-limit), don't be afraid to push all-in with strong hands (such as pocket 8s or better). Two situations can unfold: Your opponent passes, and you win the hand automatically, or an opponent may call with a losing hand and double your stack. You're even more likely to be successful with this strategy during short-handed play because you have fewer players to beat or bully out.

Making your "5-to-10" move

Not all battles go exactly the way you plan. Just ask Napoleon. You can think, strategize, and employ clever tactics; but a cold run of cards, a called-out bluff, a superior play by someone else, or an especially unfriendly card in no-limit can leave you schooling with the bottom feeders in Lake Poker. Face it: Only one person wins a tournament.

The danger of being low stacked

We witnessed an interesting event involving a short-stacked player in a recent single-table tournament.

At the table in question, in a middle position with no previous callers, the shortest-stacked player pushed all-in quickly on his turn. Everyone folded to the table gorilla, who had three times the nearest stack size of the next player, sitting in the big blind. She paused for a moment and then called.

As is customary with all-ins, both players exposed their cards. Mr. Tiny had A-A, and Ms. Big had 3-5 off-suit.

The community cards rolled:

As 2d 7d 4c 6h

Mr. Tiny's trip aces got crushed, first by a *wheel* (an ace through five straight) and then by a larger straight (while Tiny hoped the board would pair for a full house).

At this point, Mr. Tiny went something close to insane. It was hard to tell exactly what Tiny said, because the site's profanity filter sucked down the majority of it and replaced it with symbols, but you can safely assume Tiny wasn't happy.

In fact, Mr. Tiny was so unhappy that he continued to moan as an observer for another five hands or so, getting all the more infuriated by the fact that Ms. Big refused to respond to his taunting in any way.

"How could you POSSIBLY call with that hand?" Mr. Tiny (or at this point, Mr. Whiney, really) asked.

Here's how, Mr. Tiny: You were the significant table weakling, and she was the big table boss. The amount it cost her to call was negligible, and after you bust out, you never return to the table. Was Ms. Big's call wrong? We don't think so. Any given hand isn't *that* much of an underdog to any other hand, and the amount she risked bordered on the insignificant. She based her call purely on single-table tournament stack size, not on hand value, because the amount that she could lose just wasn't that big.

The more short-stacked you are, the more vulnerable your hands become, regardless of quality. It sounds bratty, but that doesn't make the statement any less true: The best way to protect a short stack is to not let yourself get there in the first place.

When your stack gets low, your play needs to be sharp and deliberate, and your focus needs to be on. The beauty of playing online is you can mumble to yourself, scream at your dog, or make faces like our favorite silent film actor, Buster Keaton, but all that comes out over an Internet table is the purity of your play. So you should make your plays good.

When your chip stack gets to between 5 and 10 times the big blind, you should apply the *5-to-10 rule* (our name for it, not a common piece of poker slang). The 5-to-10 rule means this: Always keep track of your stack size relative to the blinds. When you have only 5-to-10 big blinds left, you need to start thinking about when to make your move.

Making your move is the point where you decide to make a few well-placed bets on the virtual table. If you win these bets, you stay in the tournament to fight on, probably even growing a bit as you go. If you lose these bets, you end up watching from the sidelines and twiddling your mouse.

You base the timing and the severity of your move on the impression other players have of you at this point. If you've given the other players at the table the perception that you're a tight player, you need to start playing a bit more loosely and get aggressive with your betting. Come in for a few more hands and see a few more flops. Play a tad more positionally (meaning you should be willing to come in from the final betting spot a bit more). But don't forget that you're running out of bullets here. If you do foresee doing battle over hands where you don't have much or hands where you could obviously be outmatched, let your cards go before the battle begins.

If you've given your tablemates a reason to think of you as a loose player, your task becomes more difficult, but not impossible. Play only quality hands, and don't play positionally. When you do get a hand of quality, play it fairly hard, and if everyone drops, make sure to expose your cards to show that you indeed had a hand. You want to try and change your table's opinion about your loose play and show that you've learned your lesson and now play only the good stuff.

Conserving your chips for a better hand

You're dealt 9-9 pre-flop in a Hold 'Em tourney, with a stack equal to eight blind sizes. From late position, with no previous callers, you raise three times the big blind and get a call from the small blind only.

The flop comes A K Q.

The small blind bets two big blinds worth, which is half your stack. Time to fold, move on, and wait for your next move. 9-9 is a good starting hand, but the small blind had something worthy enough to call you with at the start, and now three overcards have hit the board. The flop is unfortunate, but you should let it go and live to fight another day.

Looking at real-life situations

What's an example of a situation where you should make your move? We thought you'd never ask.

Say you're playing no-limit Hold 'Em. You have 1,000 in chips left, and the blinds are 50 and 100. The pot is at 350. You have Jc Qd with one caller behind you who has 2,000 in chips.

The flop comes Kh 10h 9h.

The good news is that you currently have the nut straight; the bad news is that any heart in your opponent's hand gives him a flush draw, and you have to be aware of the small chance he's made the flush already.

You should push all-in, right now. Depending on your opponent's exact hole cards, and assuming he holds a single heart, you're at least a 60 to 40 (at most about 65 to 35) percent favorite to win the hand. You simply can't afford to let him outdraw you.

 In all cases, when you're within the 5-to-10 range and you have the nut hand, you want to maximize the amount of money you can take from the table. You need this money badly to keep from being crushed by the treads of the ever-increasing blind tank.

Flopping the high flush, pushing all-in, and getting no callers does you no good. You make more money if you check to the river and then place the minimum bet on the end, picking up that single bet. If you check through a hand, your challenger may get some cards he perceives as worthy, and then all you have to do is make a bet that your opponent will call and let the site automatically show your cards during the showdown to prove his inferiority.

Of course, you shouldn't get carried away with hands that have built-in vulnerability. If you get too cute and try to bleed money out of your opponent, he may outdraw you and bust you out. Only slowplay like this if you know you have a probable nut hand.

If you do have the nut hand, and you're short chipped in both Omaha and Hold 'Em, don't ever check the river. Make the minimum bet (or if you think you can get away with it, the maximum your opponent will call). If you act first on the river and you check, especially if you've seen action earlier in the hand, your opponent(s) may well check through and cost you a bet.

Many players interpret these end bets as an attempt to steal the pot and will raise you back. If you do get raised, re-raise them the minimum amount. We say it again: You want to maximize the amount you can take from this hand. You need the bullets, so try to win as much as you possibly can. The more chips you win, the longer you play and the better your chances of coming back and taking the whole tourney.

In Seven-Card Stud, if all players have checked up until the sixth card comes, make a bet. If you get called (but not raised), follow with a bet on seventh street. Especially in lower buy-in tourneys, a shocking number of people let hands go even against a mediocre hand if they don't hit their draws. After you have some success with this type of betting, lay back and don't try it again for several hands. You want the technique to pay as much and as often as possible.

Playing hands of desperation

Nine out of ten players bust out of a single-table tournament. The vast majority of these folks (including you at some point) are forced to play hands of desperation. And although you see hands of desperation in all tournament types, they happen much more frequently in single-table tournaments, because the distance from start to finish isn't very far.

Desperation is the point where you have a very small chip stack — so small that you may not be able to live through the next set of blinds (the small blind and the large blind add up to more than you have). You've now entered that dreaded area below the glorious 5-to-10 rule, the crawl space of the beautiful edifice that is the single-table tournament, where vermin, darkness, despair, and '80s acid wash jeans live.

Say you have about two large blinds' worth of stack left. You need to look at hands very carefully, remembering that almost any hand you call will get action from others at the table who want to see you go down (as we describe in "The danger of being low stacked" sidebar earlier in this chapter). At this point, the cruel reality is that you're not a threat to others at the table; you're only a threat to yourself. The key, therefore, is to treat yourself the best you can.

Hold 'Em

If you get A-K; A-Q; a suited A-J; or a suited K-Q, A-A, K-K, or Q-Q in Hold 'Em push all-in (or raise in limit), no matter what the action is in front of you, from any position. What you want to do here is win with an extremely good hand in a last-ditch effort.

From a middle position, add 10-10 and J-J to the list above. Consider any K-Q, depending on the playing style of the person in front of you. Again, these cards may be your best chance to win and double up; from middle position, your cards don't have to be as good.

We think playing Q-J all-in here is a sucker's move. Too many anemic overcard hands (like K-2 off-suit) can sit with players who may be tempted to call. More often than not, you lose to these hands because you already have lower starting cards, meaning you have to pair the board to avoid elimination, and when you're short-stacked more people are prone to call.

If you're the last to act, with no action in front of you, push all-in (or raise in limit) with any pocket pair, any two cards 10 or better, or any ace. You want people to fold and let you win automatically, or you want a fighting chance with a fairly good hand if someone does call.

If you're in a desperate position in the large blind, and the small blind raises you, you should call with any pocket pair and any suited connectors. We strongly advise calling with any two cards 8 or greater because the small blind may simply be trying to force you out, and the amount required for you to call is one-third the size of the pot — and nearly any two cards in Hold 'Em have a 1-in-3 chance of beating any other two cards.

About the only time you don't want to risk all your chips is if you're right on the money bubble and it seems possible that someone may go out before the big blind gets back to you, giving you a real shot at winning cash. (See Chapter 11 for more on bubble play.)

If you're in the small blind, with no previous callers, and you're not on the money bubble, push all-in with any two cards 8 or better. Merely call with low suited connectors, and if the big blind raises you all-in, call that bet. You already have a little money out on the table; if you merely fold, you give away a huge percentage of your table life. You can't just hand that over, especially not when you're desperate.

If you find yourself with a tiny chip stack after seeing the flop, and you pair any part of your hand, push all-in or call any bet in front of you, both in Omaha and Hold 'Em. Again, you're desperate, and the board has been friendly. Your opponent may fold, in which case you win automatically, and even if he doesn't, you may have him beat at the moment. You need to maximize your return to have a chance at making the money or taking the tourney.

Omaha

In Omaha, push all-in (or raise if you can't get your entire stack in the pot in pot-limit) with any pair jacks or better, four cards 10 or better, or a large double-suited hand (say, Ah 2h Kd 9d). You want the other players to fold and make you an automatic winner, or you want a caller with a weaker starting hand. Desperation makes you the most aggressive of all when your hand is "good enough."

From middle position, add any pair 10s or better and any four cards with straight possibilities. You need to maximize the return on your hand. Your back is against the wall, and when you have a fairly good hand, you want to lock, load, and come out guns a blazin'.

A sample short-stack exercise

Here's some short-stack analysis from a limit game to give you a general feel as to how basic poker theory applies to a real problem.

Assume that you have 2-5 off-suit on the button at a five-handed limit Hold 'Em table, and your chip stack equals two times the large blind. The first player to act single raises, and the next person (the player in front of you) calls. Now you have to do something. Should you play or fold this hand?

The short answer is you should almost certainly fold. Take a look in more detail.

If you call and win, you're guaranteed to get at least five-and-a-half bets for your two large blinds by pushing all-in. If either the small or large blind call (psychologically more likely because you're the wimpy little person in the pot), your odds become even better.

And if either of the blinds get frisky and raise yet again, you're now *protected* because you're all-in, meaning you can't bet or lose any more money. The other callers have to decide whether to stay in, but you already made your decision by putting all your chips in. Anyone who folds at this point just improves your odds of winning, because you're all-in and guaranteed to see all community cards. (Any amounts over and above the bets you were involved with get split only among the other players.)

The big problem here, however, is that your 2-5 is probably an underdog to every other hand on the table right now. You need to do *something,* and you haven't got much time. Almost any hand you go in on is sure to get callers. If you fold now, you know you have three more chances (including when you get the big blind) to catch a better starting hand than this one. Like always, wait for better cards. In this case, your cards will definitely get better — after all, you won't catch many hands worse than a 2-5. Even if you're ultimately forced to go all-in by playing the big blind, you're almost assured of pulling a better hand than this one.

Keep your eyes on the odds you get with your money — you figure the odds by comparing the amount of money you bet versus the amount of money you can potentially win if a favorable set of community cards matches your hand. Always be sure to balance your possible return against the other hands you potentially have left in your ever-dwindling chip lifespan. In general, when short-stacked, the more return you can get on your money, the more you want to be in the hand, but always try to balance this with your overall winning potential.

Firing Up for the Final Stages

After you start the single-table tourney and make it past a few opponents, you can start concentrating on winning some bucks.

Vying for the money

We know it sounds obvious, but the whole point of playing a single-table tournament is to win money. Always, always keep your eyes on the prize. Know how much money you can win and how far you have to travel to snag it. If your stack situation becomes desperate, but you're close to the money bubble, hang on as hard as you can to limp into the prize ring. If you're the chip leader, push around people who lie considerably beneath you in the standings to make them nervous enough to start making poor plays.

Watching personality and play changes

As the game goes through its natural stages, keep tabs on the psyche of the table as a whole, as well as the individual personalities of your opponents. Know who plays more aggressive and more timid. Watch for sudden changes in behavior. Take notes on each player for future use (see Chapter 6), but don't let your note-taking get in the way of thinking about, and playing, the tourney.

Many players tighten up when the table becomes short-handed and the money bubble approaches (see Chapter 11 for more about the bubble). If you see your table tightening — especially if your stack size is above average — step in and play a bit harder. You can pick up some spare chips this way.

Folding for dollars (and pizza)

Red once played in a single-table tournament resulting in an interesting theoretical poker question . . .

Four players were left in a tournament that paid three places. Although cards early in the tournament had been favorable for our hero, they had gone cold for several rounds. Aggressive players kept him from playing marginal hands, and the blinds grinded him slowly into what the rock band Screaming Trees would refer to as "Sweet Oblivion." As a result, Red trailed badly with a measly 50 in chips against an average stack of 3,400.

Under the gun, he found himself with A-K off-suit. The best drawing hand in poker would normally be a welcome relief here, except for one small problem: The blinds were at 100/200. This meant that even if Red pushed all-in, *and* everyone called, *and* he managed to win the hand, he would still only win 200 (exactly the size of the big blind), and he'd have to win the next hand to stay in the tourney anyway. Worse, he would have to win next hand no matter how many callers he had here. So, in the grand scheme of things, all Big Slick (A-K) offered was an earlier chance to lose but no greater chance to win.

Red took his full time allotment, and contrary to the way his grandma taught him, dropped the hand. But not everyone else followed suit.

In fact, the two most aggressive players at the table took this moment to slash fiercely at each other. Both ultimately pushed all-in pre-flop. By the time the smoke cleared, pocket 7s had fallen to pocket 10s, knocking one player out of the tournament and assuring Red snack money for the night.

The 200 big blind rolled on top of Red's 50 "stack" like a sumo wrestler on a cupcake, and predictably, both callers beat his 8-6 off-suit.

Think this is a bad ending for Red, the guy who won money in the tourney by folding A-K? Perhaps that's a good question for his pizza driver.

If you're at least at the average stack size, on any hand in which you bring in the action you should always raise at least three times the big blind size (or single raise in limit). You're not trying to steal blinds; you just want to set a bar for people to start playing. If everyone folds, you win those tournament chips 100 percent of the time. You may be surprised by how frequently this happens on lower buy-in tables.

Going for gold after you burst the bubble

When three players remain in a single-table tournament that pays three places, the bubble has passed, and you're guaranteed a prize. From here, you play to determine who gets the top prize money. Players now begin to play more liberally — they feel like, "Okay, great, I've won money, and now I can play again." If you see this happening, tighten up a bit (remembering also that short-handed play allows you to play many more hands) and play on. (Head back to the short-handed section in Chapter 12 for more on winning strategy.)

As with playing short-stacked, your intention should again be to maximize every pot you win. You want to whittle your foes down, pushing yourself into a better position. If you get a nut hand here, or something that may as well be (such as flopping the high two pair), bet the highest amount you think your opponent will call. Don't over-bet and lose money or under-bet and stifle your winnings. Your entire goal now is to finish as high as you possibly can. Maximize the amount you take down with every hand.

When you inevitably go all-in, make sure you have a hand of decent quality if you're not the lowest stack. You should avoid flat-out bluffing if you're in a higher chip position because the desperate may call you, even if they don't think you're bluffing.

Reflecting on the Tournament

Okay, win or lose, after your single-table tourney is over, you should sit a minute and breathe. Before you go and compulsively click on the next tourney to get even with the idiot who beat you on that two-out river draw, you must reflect.

Post-tourney is the best time to sit beside the stream in your mind and reflect on the tournament:

- ✔ What did you do wrong?
- ✔ What hands could you have played better?

✔ Did you ever over-play or under-play a hand? What did it cost you?

✔ Did you miss or ignore a nuance or a subtlety of the game? Or do you know of a nuance you don't fully understand?

✔ What worked for you and why?

We're not talking about a new-age religious ritual involving years of silence and riding a yak; we just suggest that you provide yourself with a moment to bring the whole experience together. Yeah, sometimes your opponents get lucky, and sometimes you don't, but you can find trends in your play.

And right now, while your memory of the events is fresh, record what happened in your poker journal. (What? You don't have one? Better turn to Chapter 5 to set one up.)

Spot the trends in your play, and you can get better; if your opponents spot them, you never will.

Part IV
The Part of Tens

The 5th Wave   By Rich Tennant

"Now remember. If your parents ask what you do when Mrs. Smith yells 'Head's up' after nap-time, it has nothing to do with Internet Poker."

In this part . . .

*E*veryone's favorite Dummies part, the Part of Tens. Here you find 10 superb poker resources, 10 ways to keep your head (instead of losing it), 10 things people often do to screw up their Internet poker game, and 10 things to watch for when you take your Internet poker prowess to the dreaded brick-and-mortar world.

Enjoy!

Chapter 14

Ten Common Internet Poker Mistakes

The online poker world features many differences when compared to the casino world, and along with a new form of poker come many new ways to screw your play up. In order to achieve online success, you need to steer clear of the potholes created by your online poker inexperience. This chapter highlights the most common mistakes we have seen.

Playing Too High of a Limit

At a full table in the online world you see roughly three times as many hands per hour as you see in a brick-and-mortar environment. If you play losing poker, it means you stand to lose three times as much as you normally would.

If you begin to consistently lose, backing down a step or two in the limits you play eventually puts you up against opponents you can beat. (And if that doesn't work, back down more until you start winning.) See Chapter 8 for information on how to determine a good limit size and Chapter 5 to discover micro-limits.

Playing Too Low of a Limit

The online world gives you exposure to micro-limits — games like $0.01/$0.02 Hold 'Em and $0.05/$0.10 Stud. Playing limits that allow you to not care about winning or losing can cause you to hand money (albeit small amounts of money) to people who *do* care. The micro-limits can also instill bad habits in you for when you hit the bigger tables. You should always play for fun (stop when it becomes anything but fun), but you should definitely play games where the money matters to you. The moment the money stops mattering, you need to stop playing. (See Chapter 5 for more on micro-limits.)

Playing Poorly Because You're Anonymous

Sounds weird, we know, but anonymity actually provides an excuse for some people to play a poor game. In the brick-and-mortar world, you can only dip into your wallet so many times before the peer pressure of others watching finally gets to you — well, either the peer pressure or the fact that you start feeling stupid after awhile because you've lost so much money. In the online world some people can't find anything to be ashamed of, so to speak. They simply go to the cashier and get *just a little* of that money left in the account.

Don't do it. If you're losing, take a break. If you're continually losing, read a few strategy books and study some poker forums. Drop down a level or two to lower limits until your bankroll improves, or maybe consider another hobby. We know it's harsh advice, but we're thinking of you — and your wallet.

Playing Too Quickly

Future action buttons — combined with all the beeps, buzzers, bonks, and bells (not to mention the occasional whiney opponent) — prodding you to play make it easy to act too quickly. You don't need to rush. Take the appropriate amount of time to make every necessary decision on every hand.

You have all the way until the timer reaches zero; use that time if you need it. Make your time management decisions out of strategy, not out of haste. Check out Chapter 6 for more info on using the clock to your advantage.

Playing When You're Distracted

Playing online can be the equivalent of watching a drive-in movie from the inside of a stereo store while a letter carrier drops mail in your lap and the paper boy throws a copy of the daily paper in your face. (And that's assuming your phone doesn't ring.)

Or you can make it a focused experience with you, your computer, and all your attention directed in one spot.

Think about these two worlds and pick the world where you have the best shot at winning . . . we'll wait. Our guess is you picked the latter. (And make sure not to stray from your focus.)

Playing Without the Necessary Know-How

Reading this poker book is a great way to sharpen your online poker skills and improve your overall gamesmanship. You're already developing good habits. Now keep going and study more.

Even if you see a popular poker book out there that you already know you don't agree with (because of some theory or playing strategy you don't agree with), read it anyway. Your opponents may be reading the same book (especially those focused on the higher-limit games), and you should always strive to know how they think.

A stunning percentage of online players have done nothing more than watch poker on television, and they now consider themselves to be poker experts. In the old brick-and-mortar world, people read books between sessions, mostly to relieve their poker jonesing. With the online world so close and easy, however, many people think, "Why bother reading about it when I can just do it?"

If you don't beat these beginners, someone else who studies poker will, so it may as well be you. You can start by picking up a copy of *Poker For Dummies* (Wiley).

Playing at the Wrong Table

The Internet is the most gigantic poker parlor in the world. If you sit at a table where you just lose, lose, lose, you should just leave, leave, leave. You can always find a game running at another table (or site). Never forget: No matter how good you get, the world has several players who are better than you. And you may be sitting at a table with some of them.

One of the biggest advantages of playing online is that you can go somewhere else without having to leave your chair, let alone drive down the road. Take advantage of it. Sharpening your poker skills as you win is better than improving your poker prowess as you lose. Always. Give yourself the best odds of winning and move up through the limit ladders slowly.

Falling into Common No-limit Pits

Playing no-limit is similar to jumping out of a plane without a parachute: The lack of safety doesn't make the tricks any harder; it just makes the penalty for mistakes more severe. Making a mistake in no-limit can cost you dearly; especially in ring games, because a session's worth of play can be wiped out on a single hand.

Playing no-limit with no experience

A great way to lose your shirt in no-limit is to assume the game dynamic is the same as fixed-limit. Bad idea. If you're new to no-limit, read up on the game and watch others play before you try it. (And go back and read and re-read Chapter 8 of this book.)

Learning no-limit by playing with free chips

You shouldn't try to get in no-limit by playing with free chips. Free chip no-limit play couldn't be further from a realistic depiction of the competition and essence of the game because of the sloppy way people play. You're far better off starting with small buy-in tournaments or micro-limit ring games in hard currency, where real money is at stake and the play is as real as it gets.

Another possibility for learning no-limit is to try pot-limit first. One round of betting is slightly less cataclysmic in that game. Jump out of a plane with a parachute, if you will.

Assuming no-limit ring games and tournaments are the same

Don't make the mistake of thinking you play no-limit tournaments the same way you play no-limit ring games. They two are different dragons requiring two different swords. The starting hands you play are different, and you get a set number of chips. On the ring-game side, you can re-buy to your heart's content. See Chapter 8 for more on the differences.

Playing Without the Perks

Think about it. If you were playing in one cardroom in the brick-and-mortar world, and you knew that if you simply walked across the street to play at another place you could get extra money as a bonus, what would you do?

For some reason, people often pick one poker site on the Net and then just stay there (as if they have to get out of their chair to go somewhere else). Don't hang on to one site if it means you can pick up more cash as a bonus elsewhere.

You'll most likely use a third-party holding company as your money transfer agent, so you don't face extra risk to your bank account information by going to multiple sites. (In fact, facing less risk is one argument in favor of employing a third-party holding company — see Chapter 4 for more on the subject of you and your hard-earned cash.)

Sign-on and special promotions bonuses are a nice inoculation against the potentially debilitating disease of *house rake* (the money that the site keeps for itself), and you can keep up on who's offering special promotions by signing up for newsletters and updates from every site you haunt. (Chapter 2 talks about how to choose sites of quality and possible bonuses.)

Playing Without Taking Notes

Notes serve two very valuable purposes. The obvious one is that the more you can keep track of the behavior and style of a player, the more likely you are to beat him.

But you need to realize the hidden advantage: Taking notes keeps you focused on the game. If you pick one player and really try to figure him out, and you keep track by jotting the occasional note throughout the game, you play at a much higher level.

In fact, note-taking is a good litmus test. If you sit at a table and think, "You know, I'm just too tired to take notes right now," you need to ask yourself why the heck you sat down in the first place. See Chapter 6 for more on note-taking.

Chapter 15

Ten Things to Keep in Mind in the Heat of Battle

*I*mmediately before a shark attacks, it rolls its eyes back in its head for protection. This mechanism helps make it a ruthless killing machine, but it also means your favorite vicious fishy ends up devouring a wayward license plate or tricycle along the way because it can't pay attention to what lies ahead while indulging its primal urges.

When you play poker (especially in the online world, where you don't have to even pretend that you can act), your adrenaline flows and your impulses fire heavily in the "hunter" (versus "gatherer") part of your brain. We provide some tips here that, we hope, can keep those annoying license plates out of your gums.

Don't Bluff Lesser Opponents

If you run up against an opponent who plays worse than you — *especially* if he has a tendency to call most bets — don't try to bluff him. Your dunderheaded opponent may think you have the hand you try to feign and call anyway because he thinks he can get lucky. As a result, you end up losing because of his loose play. And that's not good.

Don't Make a 50/50 Bet Against an Inferior Player

Sure, pushing all-in in a no-limit Hold 'Em tournament with a 2-2 is a mild favorite against an A-K suited, but why reduce your skill level to a mere coin flip against a player you can beat in the long run?

Conversely, don't be afraid to push all-in against a superior player in a tournament. You want to have the odds on your side, no matter how slim, for one go rather than to sit and battle it out for hours on end with a player who holds an edge against you.

Don't Insist on Winning Every Hand in Head's-Up Play

Something about the super-competitive nature of head's-up play really brings out the beast in people. We've seen an endless number of players who insist on trying to win every single hand, as well as their more mild cousins who push all-in every time they have a dominating hand.

When you play head's up, the whole point is erosion of your opponent. You don't have to move your opponent's chip stack to your side of the table in one svelte move. Slowly but surely also does the trick.

You don't have to win the majority of hands either — just the important ones. When Chris plays head's up and finishes first, he often finds that he only won about one out of three hands in the tournament.

When you get an unbeatable hand, try to place a bet small enough to stay within calling range of your foe and large enough to get the maximum amount of money out of your cards.

Drop Marginal Hands

It gets frustrating if you keep seeing marginal holdings hand after hand. The temptation to play them becomes nearly overwhelming. Don't.

The only time you should feel pressured to even *consider* playing marginal hands is when you begin to get short-stacked in a tournament. Any other time, especially in ring games, keep clicking your hand straight to the trash heap.

Chant it like a religious hymn in the key of "A" (because it is): My cards will get better.

Take Your Time

The speed of Internet play can whip you into a frenzy. Take your time to make the right decisions, and ignore the incessant beeps, buzzers, and bells of your poker site. You can make the correct play in the allotted time. Take your time and don't worry about it.

Don't Give Up Prematurely

Players who throw in the towel before being eliminated commit probably the most common error we see in tournament play. Many players see their chips dwindle down to 20 times the big blind and seem to go mildly insane and start making extra-large bets or calling with long-shot draws. Although a 20 times stack may seem small in relation to the number of chips you started with, especially if you catch two bad beats in a row, you still have plenty of chips (if there can be such a thing). The game is far from over. Hunker down and play the good cards. Let weaker mortals panic and run. The time to get a little more frenzied is when you get down to 10 times the big blind size and start thinking about the "5-to-10 rule," which we describe in Chapter 13.

Play When You're at Your Best

The beauty of Internet poker is that you can always find a game. But this doesn't mean you *have* to play. If you don't feel well, you just had a fight with your significant other, you seem overly tired, or even if you just find your attention wandering, wait and play later. You can always find opponents; make sure to be on top of your world when they find you.

Pay Extra Attention to Unusual Behavior

If your opponent has acted the same way for most of the game, and then he suddenly shifts to something different, stop and think hard before you react. This behavior often signals a trap. Examples include betting the minimum after raising aggressively all night, an unusually long pause before calling (or especially raising) a big bet, or a push all-in from a seat that played extremely timid all night.

If the situation doesn't feel quite right, it probably isn't. Fold and play another hand. Better to take a detour and find another path through the jungle than to charge along on a path that may have a pit.

Shake Up Your Play

Due to the speed of online poker, you can easily exhibit a betting pattern in just a few minutes. If you have a tight style and often check and fold when the board misses your hand, you should be aware of how obvious your behavior is to your opponents. If they saw you do that in seven of the previous ten hands, they may start to take advantage of your predictability. Occasionally change your behavior with little strategies, like alternating between flat calling and variable raising a big blind pre-flop in Hold 'Em or varying your betting style on third and fourth street in Seven-Card Stud.

You want to keep your opponents guessing as much as you possibly can, but don't get carried away. Make opponents pay to see drawing cards if they have a chance to beat you. Don't play hands that may easily be out-matched.

Reflect

Win, lose, or draw, always take some time to consider your recent session. What did you do that worked? What could you have done better? What was your worst mistake? Did you see a play by an opponent at the table that you thought was spectacular? Answering these questions and refining your play as a result are probably the best things you can do for your game.

Record the results of your reflection in your poker journal — see Chapter 5 for a refresher.

Chapter 16

Ten Great Internet Poker Resources

. . . .

In This Chapter

▶ Reading online publications

▶ Keeping track of your play

▶ Surfing the Web for poker play

. . . .

*Y*ou have a computer (we hope), and it must be good for some-thing more than just playing poker . . . like, maybe, enjoying poker more? In this chapter, we give you a list of resources that can help you improve your game, find out more about poker, and just have plain old fun.

And we're big fans of free stuff. Every resource we list in this chap-ter doesn't cost so much as a nickel to use or look at. So take the money you save and the information you discover from the follow-ing resources and hit the tables!

Card Player Magazine Online

You can find an online version of the popular brick-and-mortar magazine *Card Player* at www.cardplayer.com that carries every-thing the print version has. The site includes superb poker writing by many of the top authorities on the game for both brick-and-mortar and online players, a poker forum, a daily poker quiz, an odds calculator, and much more. It provides you with an excellent way to keep an eye on the poker world that lies just beyond your computer screen.

Card Player also has special online promotions and free-roll tour-neys where you can have a one-in-a-zillion chance to win huge prizes. (If you prefer getting ink on your hands with a hard copy, you can subscribe to the magazine for $39.95 for one year (just go online or call ☎ 1-866-LVPOKER).

The World's Largest Poker Newsgroup

In the old, old computer days before Web browsers (say, 10 years ago), you could use a resource called *Usenet;* it was essentially a super bulletin board filled with newsgroups of every topic imaginable (along with a few you don't even want to imagine). One of the biggest newsgroups was *recreation,* and burrowed deep in its spleen were the poker mavens. The group's moniker was rec.gambling. poker, and users came to the board to chime in about all things poker (usually with a geek slant).

Rec.gambling.poker went through the mildest upgrade when it starting using a Web-based front-end, reachable through the site www.recpoker.com. But don't let the fancy new paint job fool you (and actually, the site isn't even that fancy); underneath the new facade, the bulletin is still the brooding mass of poker nuts putting their two cents in.

The flavor and quality of the stuff you can find on here varies, but the site is searchable, and pretty much any information you want is here. You can find all the info on brick-and-mortar tourneys, good online promotions, rising stars of poker, and so on here under one online roof.

Be certain to search the site and read several postings before you post an item of your own. You want to get a feel for the culture and style of recpoker before asking a question, and especially before adding an opinion of your own. Recpoker welcomes new users, but the site residents frown on input from the uninformed and unacquainted.

Pokercharts

Pokercharts.com is a free service that lets you "easily record, chart, and analyze your poker-session playing" in your home game, brick-and-mortar, and online play. Pokercharts focuses exclusively on the money aspect of your game — essentially like having a super-accountant hovering over all your banking transactions. The service is free and easy to understand, and you don't have to be an Excel wizard to use it.

Book Stores

Your online poker goals will fall short if you don't have the proper poker knowledge to back them up, and one of the best ways outside of experience to build knowledge is by reading poker texts.

Gambler's Book Shop

Red loves Gambler's Book Shop, physically located in Las Vegas. (Where else?) Gambler's Book Shop has been doing business for 40 years, and it rightfully boasts "the largest selection of gambling books, videotapes, and software in the world." Don't be put off by the plain-Jane nature of the Web site (www.gamblersbook.com). It has many books that you can't find anywhere else. Looking for that copy of Konstantin Othmer's *Seven Card Stud Poker?* You can get it here, along with everything else.

You can sign up for automatic notification of new arrivals on a monthly basis. And ordering online means that you don't have to hike through the 110-degree Nevada heat to get your poker print fix. The only downside of the online version of Gambler's Book Shop is that you can't treat yourself to a 99-cent shrimp cocktail after you browse through the online version of the store.

If you're unsure on how studying can help you, see Chapter 14 for more.

ConJelCo

Chris digs ConJelCo (www.conjelco.com). It also has everything on the planet relative to poker (yes, yes, including Mr. Othmer's *Seven Card Stud Poker*), and the site has a great Google search engine embedded in it. Check out the historical listing of the World Series of Pokers from 1995–2000.

But wait, you get more!

It also has the *Gambler's Corner,* where you can find information about casinos, cruises, and gambling publications. Have 15 minutes to burn before your next tourney? Go here.

The World Series of Poker Online

Binion's Horseshoe (now owned by Harrah's) has been home to the World Series of Poker (WSOP, www.harrahs.com/wsop/index.html) in the brick-and-mortar world for over 30 years. (In 2005, for the first time, the early stages of the tournament will be held on the strip at the Rio; the final two days of the tournament will be held at Binion's.) The winner of the $10,000 buy-in no-limit Hold 'Em event is considered the Poker Ruler of the Universe (our term, not theirs) for the year. Binion's online presence (www.binions.com) has stepped up each year; in 2004, the site included some live Net-casting from the series events.

Dreamers, as well as the deadly serious, should check here for qualifying information and anything else that has to do with the World Series of Poker after the event begins. (From time to time, you can find the best available room rates at the Horseshoe here — always worth checking if you're headed to the Home of All Things Poker.)

Poker Odds Calculator

Two Dimes' poker odds calculator (www.twodimes.net/poker) shows you the chances of any set of cards you specify winning or losing on any given pot. You can use the tool to go back and analyze hands after-the-fact with "what-if?" scenarios.

When knowing the odds helps

You're playing $3/$6 fixed-limit Texas Hold 'Em and holding Ah 2h. Only one other player is still in the pot, and the board comes out 5h 7d Qh Kd.

From your opponent's betting pattern and style, you put her on at least one pair. In order to win this hand, you need another heart to hit the board (or maybe an ace) to give you the ace-high flush.

$36 makes up the pot, including the $6 bet by the player in front of you. Should you call?

According to the poker odds calculator, your chances of drawing a heart are 19.6 percent (9 hearts left out of 46 remaining cards). You risk $6 to win $42 ($36 pot + your $6 bet), which is the same as 1/7th of the pot (14.3 percent). Because the amount you risk is less than your odds of making the draw, you should call. If you're unfamiliar with pot odds, see any basic poker text, such as *Poker For Dummies* (Wiley), for details.

Knowing odds is good in fixed-limit games where you can get an idea of *pot-odds* (how much you bet compared to how much you can win). In no-limit, the poker calculator is good for seeing just *how bad* the beat was that you took.

The bad news is that the poker odds calculator on this site is stripped down to the barest of bones and is a little clunky to use. The good news is that it has deadly accuracy — useful for analyzing Hold 'Em, Stud, Omaha, and even Draw. And the coolest of the super-cool is that the site has a mini version of the calculator that works on your cell phone.

Be sure to look at the sample hands on the Two Dimes' Web site to get a feel for what kind of information the poker calculator expects from you to run properly.

Poker Analyzer

The somewhat hideous-looking software you get from www.poker tracker.com does an absolutely beautiful job of recording, tracking, and analyzing your Hold 'Em play — even across multiple sites.

The tracker lets you

- Track your starting hands to see how many times you
  - See the flop
  - Raise
  - Win with those cards
- Track your play by position
- Track your hand results (straight, flush, and so on) and how much money you made with them
- Track your best and worst opponents — those you win the most from and those you lose the most to
- Track the betting actions of every player who has ever played against you
- Replay hands, sessions, or tournaments

With the poker analyzer, you can track your first 1,000 hands for free; after that, it costs a one-time fee of $55 (at press-time).

Information Blood Hound

Don't forget the power of a great search engine to find anything and everything you want to know about any sub-species of the poker animal kingdom. We like Google (www.google.com) because of the speed, relevance, and the high-powered tools it has built-in (like the ability to search for certain images and the ability to translate foreign poker Web pages from five different languages to English).

To see what Google can do for you, explore the links immediately above the Google logo. Not only does Google search for certain keywords on the Web, but it can also find images and groups that match your requests.

Poker Potpourri

Without so much as even the slightest nod to David Letterman, the Poker Top 10 (www.pokertop10.com) is a truly fun site where you can find almost anything: Top 10 Online Poker Rooms, Top 10 Bad Beats (and believe me, the beats you see are *much* more costly than anything you've ever experienced), and Top 10 Bizarre Poker Terms. And those are just the appetizers.

If you can't find anything interesting or amusing on this site, you should check your pulse. You may be dead.

Online Discussion

Red and Chris man a discussion board about this book at poker book.gamesgrid.com. Drop in to read further discussions, questions, or comments about the topics in this book.

Chapter 17

Ten Mistakes to Avoid during Live Action

In This Chapter

▶ Understanding how to play with real chips

▶ Figuring out how to handle your cards

▶ Knowing how to interact with other players and the dealer

*W*e focus this entire book on differences between live action and Internet poker play, and we hope we've covered every little idiosyncrasy that the online world dishes out.

In this chapter, we turn the tables and look at common mistakes Internet players make when they switch over to the brick-and-mortar world. Every player should watch for these mistakes, but you should pay special attention if your path has led you from the home game world, to the Net, and finally to brick-and-mortar play.

One or two infractions typically result in a mere scolding from a dealer or floor person, and a few of the people at your table may get their feathers ruffled. But multiple violations can get you removed from a game altogether.

Playing Out of Turn

In the online world, future action buttons can really spoil you. You can make a snap decision (folding before you turn, for example), and your computer remembers your choice, acting on your request when your turn arrives.

But in the brick-and-mortar world, you must play in a clockwise fashion, strictly in order. Keep an eye on the game and don't ever act until the person to your right has acted. If the person you're watching has a tendency to jump the gun, keep an eye on the next player over.

Betting an Incorrect Amount

Many players in the online world cut their teeth on no-limit games, but they decide to play fixed-limit when they sit down in the brick-and-mortar world for the first time. They think that no-limit play is either too expensive or initially too intimidating.

When you play fixed-limit, you can only bet set amounts, determined by the name of the game ($3/$6 Hold 'Em, for example). The dealer may politely tell you the first couple of times you try to bet too much, but he may not keep up the cordial attitude for long.

Causing a "Chip Tell"

As you already know, poker is a game where people try to find out anything that may give them an edge during play. They often try to get an edge by watching you to see if you give signs as to your betting intentions. If players can sense by the way you handle your chips or cards that you're likely to bet or fold, they may modify their actions.

One way to help thwart tells, in all games, is to not take your first look at your hole cards until the action comes to you. Be careful, however, because all eyes are on you when you peek at your cards. If you have noticeable tells as you look, the whole table knows.

Exposing Your Hole Cards

Looking at your hole cards without letting anyone else see them is something you don't have to worry about online. But in the brick-and-mortar world, you need to be aware of how you peek at your cards, because your nearest opponent may be just inches away. You want to shield your cards with your hands as you look at them so your neighbor can't take a gander.

How to bet in fixed-limit games

If you play $2/$4 Omaha, you can bet $2 or raise another player's $2 bet (assuming your table hasn't reached the maximum number of raises for the betting round — ask the dealer if you're not sure) before and after the flop. After the turn and river, you can bet or raise $4. No other betting options are possible.

Sshh! Don't tell

You're playing Hold 'Em and you have the dealer position with A-A pre-flop. You begin counting out money for a raise while other players fold in front of you before you can act. A player in front of you with a somewhat meager hand thought about calling the big blind, but after seeing your eagerness, she folds before you even get a chance to raise. Your anxious behavior just cost you at least one bet.

Nearly all brick-and-mortar poker rooms use all-plastic cards now (as opposed to the wax coated cardboard ones you probably grew up with). You can bend them fairly severely without putting a permanent warp on the cards. Feel free to bend them if it helps to give you more concealment of your hand.

Remember, if you expose your cards inadvertently, the other players at the table aren't likely to clue you in.

Showing Your Cards During the Hand

You may be used to the option of showing or mucking your hand when you get beat online during a showdown. What some players don't remember is that you can *only* show cards at the showdown, not while the hand is still in play, in the brick-and-mortar world. You don't even have the option online. Any time you decide to fold and other players still have to decide, you should pass your hold cards to the dealer face down and not allow other players to see them.

This concept is doubly important if you don't want to fold. In some cardrooms, especially during tournaments, showing your cards during a hand is illegal. If you show them, your hand may be declared dead, even if you have the winner.

Mucking a Winning Hand

In the online world, if you have the best hand at the showdown, you always win your share of the pot. Your poker site is all-knowing and never lets you throw away a winning hand.

Mourning a dead hand

You're playing Seven-Card Stud and suspect that the player opposite you, showing four clubs, has missed his flush. You call his river bet with your straight and ask, "Did you hit it?"

"Yep," he says. You toss your hole cards to the center of the table, thereby mucking your straight. He continues, "I hit two pair," and he exposes a pair of aces and a pair of eights. He wins by default because your hand is officially dead.

The brick-and-mortar world doesn't afford you this luxury. As soon as you muck your hand, consider it dead and gone.

Never take the word of other players as to the value of their hands unless you see their cards yourself or hear the dealer call the hand out. Always rely on the dealer to call out the winning hand.

Making a String Raise

A *string raise* occurs any time a player first puts out enough chips to call the current bet and then goes on to say "raise." String raises are illegal, and the dealer declares the raise portion void and returned, making the action a call instead.

Any time you want to make a raise, you should say "raise" first. If you're too afraid your voice may somehow give you away when declaring your intentions, put all your chips together and place them all forward as a call and bet, simultaneously.

Leaving Your Hand Unprotected

When you play Hold 'Em or Omaha in the brick-and-mortar world, you're expected to *protect* your hand — typically by placing chips on top of your cards (still face down, of course). The reason you protect your cards is to keep mucked cards from being confused with your hole cards, which could void your hand. (Cards thrown down in anger by other players tend to be the ones that can cause you the most problems and foul you.) Protecting your hand also lets the dealer know that you haven't folded and that she shouldn't take your cards.

Stud players don't have to protect their hands — mainly because the players' up cards automatically protect their hole cards.

Giving Advice to Another Player on a Hand

"Only one player to a hand" is a common phrase you hear in the brick-and-mortar environment. Even if you're no longer in a hand, you may have knowledge of cards or something else relative to the current cards in play that can give an unfair advantage to another player.

If another player ever asks for your opinion on how to play a live hand in a brick-and-mortar game, simply say, "We can talk about it when the hand is over." That keeps you from having any sort of ongoing dialogue and politely indicates to your advice-seeking pal that you don't want to break the rules.

Forgetting About Your Dealer

Dealers are the people to go to for any question you have while playing in a brick-and-mortar establishment. How much you should bet, where you should sit, and the level of the blinds are bits of info a dealer is happy to share with you. After you ask anything of the dealer, ignore any other comment from other players at the table. The dealer is the authority, no matter how knowledgeable the other players may think they are.

If you want to leave the table for a moment or move seats, it pays to ask the dealer about the effects of such a move, especially if you expect to be gone during your next turn. Sometimes you're required to post the amount of the blinds or wait until the big blind when you sit back down.

Dealers are commonly tipped a buck anytime you win a pot — two if what you win is substantial.

Appendix

Glossary

· ·

all-in: Any bet that puts every one of a player's chips into the pot.

bad beat: A poker hand where you start out as the statistical favorite to win the pot, but you lose because of a lucky draw by your opponent.

brick-and-mortar: The phrase we use to describe real, physical card rooms where you sit across a table from live human beings. It doesn't necessarily have to mean casinos; in most cases, you can just as easily think about any home game you play in.

chip stack: All the chips a person has at any given moment. We typically use this phrase in relation to tournaments.

client: The name we use for the program that you download from your poker site to play cards. Chapter 2 has more on poker clients.

dealer marker: On a poker table, it indicates the last player to act in the betting round. The marker rotates clock-wise around the table one position at the end of every hand. Because of this token's shape in a real card room, brick-and-mortar players sometimes refer to this as the *button*. Chapter 3 has pictorial examples.

fixed-limit: A form of poker betting where the amount you can bet must bet a set amount at any given moment. You can play Hold 'Em and Omaha as fixed-limit games. You always play Seven-Card Stud as a fixed-limit game online. Chapter 7 discusses these games and Chapter 8 has more on limits.

free chips: Play money that sites give you to practice with. Chapter 10 talks about free chips in depth.

hard currency: When we use this phrase, we mean the money that you have on deposit with a poker site — the actual money that you gamble with. When you place a $1 bet online, you put hard currency on the line. We use this phrase to minimize confusion with money as a general concept. Chapter 4 is where we talk about transferring your money online.

high/low: A variation of poker where the high hand splits half the pot with the low hand (A 2 3 4 5 is lowest possible hand — straights and flushes don't count against the low, but they can serve as the high). The low hand can have no cards higher than an 8 (aces can be low or high), with no pairs. If no low hand is possible, the high hand takes the entire pot. Chapter 7 has more about this game variation.

Hold 'Em: A poker game where all players are dealt two hole cards with five community cards coming face up on the table. Players make the best five-card hand from a combination of their two hole cards and the five community cards. Easily the most popular game on the Net today. You can find more discussion on Hold 'Em in Chapter 7.

no-limit: A form of poker betting where you can bet a variable amount, from a prescribed lower limit all the way up to your entire chip stack. You can normally only find Hold 'Em in the no-limit form for cash on the Internet. Chapters 7 and 8 dig deeper into limits.

Omaha: A poker game where all players receive four hole cards with five community cards laid face up on the table. Players make the best five-card hand, using exactly two of their hole cards and exactly three community cards. Look for more discussion on Omaha in Chapter 7.

pot-limit: A form of poker betting where you can bet a variable

amount, from a prescribed minimum limit all the way up to the size of the pot at its current state. Many games feature pot-limit betting. Chapters 7 and 8 have more on this game form.

ring game: A single poker table, with anywhere from 2 to 10 players, where everyone competes for hard currency. You can come and go as you please in these games. Some brick-and-mortar players call this game form *money play*. Chapter 9 has more on ring games.

Seven-Card Stud: A poker game where players receive two hole cards, four up cards, and another hole card to make the best five-card poker hand. Chapter 7 has more on this game form.

tournament: A special form of poker where you pay a set entry fee, plus a smaller registration fee, to receive a set amount of tournament chips. Players compete, busting out one by one, until only one person remains. Part III is where we get down with tourneys.

Index

Notes

BUSINESS, CAREERS & PERSONAL FINANCE

0-7645-5307-0   0-7645-5331-3 *†

Also available:

✔Accounting For Dummies †
0-7645-5314-3
✔Business Plans Kit For Dummies †
0-7645-5365-8
✔Cover Letters For Dummies
0-7645-5224-4
✔Frugal Living For Dummies
0-7645-5403-4
✔Leadership For Dummies
0-7645-5176-0
✔Managing For Dummies
0-7645-1771-6

✔Marketing For Dummies
0-7645-5600-2
✔Personal Finance For Dummies *
0-7645-2590-5
✔Project Management
For Dummies
0-7645-5283-X
✔Resumes For Dummies †
0-7645-5471-9
✔Selling For Dummies
0-7645-5363-1
✔Small Business Kit For Dummies *†
0-7645-5093-4

HOME & BUSINESS COMPUTER BASICS

0-7645-4074-2   0-7645-3758-X

Also available:

✔ACT! 6 For Dummies
0-7645-2645-6
✔iLife '04 All-in-One Desk Reference
For Dummies
0-7645-7347-0
✔iPAQ For Dummies
0-7645-6769-1
✔Mac OS X Panther Timesaving
Techniques For Dummies
0-7645-5812-9
✔Macs For Dummies
0-7645-5656-8
✔Microsoft Money 2004 For Dummies
0-7645-4195-1

✔Office 2003 All-in-One Desk
Reference For Dummies
0-7645-3883-7
✔Outlook 2003 For Dummies
0-7645-3759-8
✔PCs For Dummies
0-7645-4074-2
✔TiVo For Dummies
0-7645-6923-6
✔Upgrading and Fixing PCs
For Dummies
0-7645-1665-5
✔Windows XP Timesaving
Techniques For Dummies
0-7645-3748-2

FOOD, HOME, GARDEN, HOBBIES, MUSIC & PETS

0-7645-5295-3   0-7645-5232-5

Also available:

✔Bass Guitar For Dummies
0-7645-2487-9
✔Diabetes Cookbook For Dummies
0-7645-5230-9
✔Gardening For Dummies *
0-7645-5130-2
✔Guitar For Dummies
0-7645-5106-X
✔Holiday Decorating For Dummies
0-7645-2570-0
✔Home Improvement All-in-One
For Dummies
0-7645-5680-0

✔Knitting For Dummies
0-7645-5395-X
✔Piano For Dummies
0-7645-5105-1
✔Puppies For Dummies
0-7645-5255-4
✔Scrapbooking For Dummies
0-7645-7208-3
✔Senior Dogs For Dummies
0-7645-5818-8
✔Singing For Dummies
0-7645-2475-5
✔30-Minute Meals For Dummies
0-7645-2589-1

INTERNET & DIGITAL MEDIA

0-7645-1664-7   0-7645-6924-4

Also available:

✔2005 Online Shopping Directory
For Dummies
0-7645-7495-7
✔CD & DVD Recording For Dummies
0-7645-5956-7
✔eBay For Dummies
0-7645-5654-1
✔Fighting Spam For Dummies
0-7645-5965-6
✔Genealogy Online For Dummies
0-7645-5964-8
✔Google For Dummies
0-7645-4420-9

✔Home Recording For Musicians
For Dummies
0-7645-1634-5
✔The Internet For Dummies
0-7645-4173-0
✔iPod & iTunes For Dummies
0-7645-7772-7
✔Preventing Identity Theft
For Dummies
0-7645-7336-5
✔Pro Tools All-in-One Desk
Reference For Dummies
0-7645-5714-9
✔Roxio Easy Media Creator
For Dummies
0-7645-7131-1

SPORTS, FITNESS, PARENTING, RELIGION & SPIRITUALITY

0-7645-5146-9

0-7645-5418-2

Also available:

- Adoption For Dummies
  0-7645-5488-3
- Basketball For Dummies
  0-7645-5248-1
- The Bible For Dummies
  0-7645-5296-1
- Buddhism For Dummies
  0-7645-5359-3
- Catholicism For Dummies
  0-7645-5391-7
- Hockey For Dummies
  0-7645-5228-7

- Judaism For Dummies
  0-7645-5299-6
- Martial Arts For Dummies
  0-7645-5358-5
- Pilates For Dummies
  0-7645-5397-6
- Religion For Dummies
  0-7645-5264-3
- Teaching Kids to Read
  For Dummies
  0-7645-4043-2
- Weight Training For Dummies
  0-7645-5168-X
- Yoga For Dummies
  0-7645-5117-5

TRAVEL

0-7645-5438-7

0-7645-5453-0

Also available:

- Alaska For Dummies
  0-7645-1761-9
- Arizona For Dummies
  0-7645-6938-4
- Cancún and the Yucatán
  For Dummies
  0-7645-2437-2
- Cruise Vacations For Dummies
  0-7645-6941-4
- Europe For Dummies
  0-7645-5456-5
- Ireland For Dummies
  0-7645-5455-7

- Las Vegas For Dummies
  0-7645-5448-4
- London For Dummies
  0-7645-4277-X
- New York City For Dummies
  0-7645-6945-7
- Paris For Dummies
  0-7645-5494-8
- RV Vacations For Dummies
  0-7645-5443-3
- Walt Disney World & Orlando
  For Dummies
  0-7645-6943-0

GRAPHICS, DESIGN & WEB DEVELOPMENT

0-7645-4345-8

0-7645-5589-8

Also available:

- Adobe Acrobat 6 PDF
  For Dummies
  0-7645-3760-1
- Building a Web Site For Dummies
  0-7645-7144-3
- Dreamweaver MX 2004
  For Dummies
  0-7645-4342-3
- FrontPage 2003 For Dummies
  0-7645-3882-9
- HTML 4 For Dummies
  0-7645-1995-6
- Illustrator CS For Dummies
  0-7645-4084-X

- Macromedia Flash MX 2004
  For Dummies
  0-7645-4358-X
- Photoshop 7 All-in-One Desk
  Reference For Dummies
  0-7645-1667-1
- Photoshop CS Timesaving
  Techniques For Dummies
  0-7645-6782-9
- PHP 5 For Dummies
  0-7645-4166-8
- PowerPoint 2003 For Dummies
  0-7645-3908-6
- QuarkXPress 6 For Dummies
  0-7645-2593-X

NETWORKING, SECURITY, PROGRAMMING & DATABASES

0-7645-6852-3

0-7645-5784-X

Also available:

- A+ Certification For Dummies
  0-7645-4187-0
- Access 2003 All-in-One Desk
  Reference For Dummies
  0-7645-3988-4
- Beginning Programming
  For Dummies
  0-7645-4997-9
- C For Dummies
  0-7645-7068-4
- Firewalls For Dummies
  0-7645-4048-3
- Home Networking For Dummies
  0-7645-42796

- Network Security For Dummies
  0-7645-1679-5
- Networking For Dummies
  0-7645-1677-9
- TCP/IP For Dummies
  0-7645-1760-0
- VBA For Dummies
  0-7645-3989-2
- Wireless All In-One Desk Reference
  For Dummies
  0-7645-7496-5
- Wireless Home Networking
  For Dummies
  0-7645-3910-8

HEALTH & SELF-HELP

0-7645-6820-5 *†   0-7645-2566-2

Also available:
- Alzheimer's For Dummies
  0-7645-3899-3
- Asthma For Dummies
  0-7645-4233-8
- Controlling Cholesterol For
  Dummies
  0-7645-5440-9
- Depression For Dummies
  0-7645-3900-0
- Dieting For Dummies
  0-7645-4149-8
- Fertility For Dummies
  0-7645-2549-2

- Fibromyalgia For Dummies
  0-7645-5441-7
- Improving Your Memory
  For Dummies
  0-7645-5435-2
- Pregnancy For Dummies †
  0-7645-4483-7
- Quitting Smoking For Dummies
  0-7645-2629-4
- Relationships For Dummies
  0-7645-5384-4
- Thyroid For Dummies
  0-7645-5385-2

EDUCATION, HISTORY, REFERENCE & TEST PREPARATION

0-7645-5194-9   0-7645-4186-2

Also available:
- Algebra For Dummies
  0-7645-5325-9
- British History For Dummies
  0-7645-7021-8
- Calculus For Dummies
  0-7645-2498-4
- English Grammar For Dummies
  0-7645-5322-4
- Forensics For Dummies
  0-7645-5580-4
- The GMAT For Dummies
  0-7645-5251-1
- Inglés Para Dummies
  0-7645-5427-1

- Italian For Dummies
  0-7645-5196-5
- Latin For Dummies
  0-7645-5431-X
- Lewis & Clark For Dummies
  0-7645-2545-X
- Research Papers For Dummies
  0-7645-5426-3
- The SAT I For Dummies
  0-7645-7193-1
- Science Fair Projects For Dummies
  0-7645-5460-3
- U.S. History For Dummies
  0-7645-5249-X

Get smart @ dummies.com®

- **Find a full list of Dummies titles**
- **Look into loads of FREE on-site articles**
- **Sign up for FREE eTips e-mailed to you weekly**
- **See what other products carry the Dummies name**
- **Shop directly from the Dummies bookstore**
- **Enter to win new prizes every month!**

* Separate Canadian edition also available
† Separate U.K. edition also available

Available wherever books are sold. For more information or to order direct: U.S. customers visit www.dummies.com or call 1-877-762-2974.
U.K. customers visit www.wileyeurope.com or call 0800 243407. Canadian customers visit www.wiley.ca or call 1-800-567-4797.